Looking Back
A Marines experiences in Vietnam

Ever since my return from Vietnam in October of 1968, the ghosts and day long memories of my time there have been a part of each living day. There have been times when these thoughts have been of confidence and self-approval of my actions there, but mostly they have been haunting thoughts of guilt, failure and loss that I will have to live with forever.

Countless years ago, I tried to put my thoughts together in a way that at some time, I could share with both my daughter, Michelle, and son, David, to provide them some insight into who their dad was, what I did during the war and its impact on my life. During my 13 months there, for the most part my unit spent every day in harm's way; in that number of months, we participated in 22 major offensive operations. My unit operated in what was called the I Corp area of Vietnam; for those who were not there, we operated in and around the DMZ; not a very friendly place during 1967 and 1968.

Most people have fond memories of their childhood, their youth, high school, and perhaps even more significant, their lives during college. For me and many others like me, college was not a choice and we all needed to make adult decisions at a very young age. I joined the Marines in March of 1966, doing my boot camp at Parris Island. After a brief period of being in a safe place, I eventually volunteered for Vietnam, a decision that would change my life forever.

I went to Vietnam with the thought that I would never be lucky enough to make it home. It is hard for me to sit here today allowing you to know that I not only survived a very difficult time, but I am here today to share what I can of my experiences.

It is hard to glean from my story, but very few of my unit that I went to Vietnam with came home in one piece. For those of us that did, we struggle daily asking ourselves why we were allowed to survive. Thoughts of my time there are with me every single day, many of which force me into times of exclusion and I feel a need to be alone with my thought

I look back at my time there and continue to ask a million questions. Is it really possible that these events really took place or is it an incredibly ridiculous dream? There are times that I wish these thoughts were merely a fantasy but I know deep in my heart that they really took place and I alone have to live with what I did.

Over all these many years I wondered if my thoughts were just what I was stuck with or if others were impacted the same way. After many years of working with combat Veterans I realized that most of us have been affected the same way. We each try to live with our actions of many years ago with an attempt to find peace in our current lives.

For a long time, what I was trying to convey to others were merely rambling thoughts I could not piece together; eventually I realized I needed to put them to paper. Fortunately with the advent of technology, primarily word processing, I began this journey in attempt to put my thoughts into a story.

Over the past 25 years or so, I have had the privilege of finding some of the men that I served with and had also survived Vietnam. I have asked each of them to read this story and each confirmed the actions, as well as content describing our actions during our time together in Vietnam.

I hope that you gain something from my writing. I realize that my style is very different but it is the only way I know of putting my thoughts to paper.

Sgt Robert Janicki AKA (Leech)
Squad Leader
2nd Squad
Alpha Company
1st Battalion 3rd Marines
Sept 1967 – Oct 1968

The Marines I have seen around the world have the cleanest bodies, the filthiest minds, the highest morale, and the lowest morals of any group of animals I have ever seen.

Thank God for the United States Marine Corps!

Eleanor Roosevelt, First Lady of the United States, 1945

Special thanks to my editor Amanda Buttram who painstakingly worked through my drafts converting my ramblings to the story you are about to rea

Many thanks Amanda

The Journey

Looking Back

Wright   Martinez   Smitty   Janicki
Gia Liem(Palace Guard)
March 9th, 1968

I look at this picture every now and then, most often not snagged by the images on display. There are times though when I do take the time to look a little closer and feel them looking back, wanting me to come back, come back to what was at one time, the scariest and most challenging times of our lives. To me, their gaze is magnetic and hard to pull away from. For a fleeting second, I can remember the very instant when the picture was taken and why.

The picture is of four American Marines and one very young Vietnamese boy sitting on the ground in the village of Gia Liem on March 9th, 1968. Why does all this flow so easily, why is it so easy to remember some of these days, the hours, the seconds?

It doesn't always flow so easily- at times these images look back at me and yell, "you left me behind, where are you, why haven't you found me?" There are millions of unanswered questions, emotions and feelings which arise from this simple image.

The four young Marines were very simple people that came from a very broad balance of American life; all were minorities but one, me. I was that one white person that almost didn't fit, but none of us would let that happen. Our existence relied on our closeness, our need to keep each other alive, regardless of what the stereotypes in America told us. We were better than that. We were one, regardless of color, ethnic background or any other category that would make any other American uncomfortable.

This picture, one of the few I have, is the most significant and treasured to me. It was taken in March1968, six months after I got to Vietnam. I shouldn't say I, it should be we, because all but one of us got there at the same time. We went through staging together at Camp Pendleton, California and found our way to the 1st Battalion 3rd Marines, Alpha Company through the attrition of our predecessors. Here we were, halfway through our tour and in a picture together. Unknown to anyone that looks at this not-so-gruesome picture, everyone in the picture was recently wounded.

The looks on their faces are not of pain; there is a look of distance, of what they call the 1,000 yard stare; a scary reality for such young men. I was the oldest in the picture and I was 20 years old- what changed me, what gave me along with the others that deep sense of distance?

The stare is not something contrived; it's unfortunately something that is acquired. Six months of patrols, firefights, listening posts, and major battles takes a toll on an individual. You don't ask for this to happen, you actually have no control of what takes place. When in a daily struggle for life, you take on a different outlook on your life and life in general.

Watching platoon and squad members disappear through injuries and death builds a psychological barrier blocking what you would normally consider real life, as most people understand it.

2

Based on your own personal, emotional and psychological needs, you inherit the ability to remove yourself from the day- to-day and moment-to-moment emotions, or at least you think you do. As this distance is created and refined, the distance in your eyes becomes deeper and deeper. Eventually you are not there emotionally, at least not to a certain degree. You may still be scared to death with the actions going on around you, but you are numb to the emotions of deep personal loss.

What were we like in the beginning, were we already callous and numb to emotions? We all thought we were but that was only young spirits talking. Deep down we were scared to death and still virgins to the horrible, deep emotions of close personal loss which war can bring

Most of our unit went through staging training at Camp Pendleton, California and then jungle warfare training in Okinawa, Japan. We thought this was tough stuff; hot, humid conditions which pushed us to our limits, but later we realized we didn't even deserve to spell the word "limits" yet. We thought we were seasoned, ready- after all, we were Marines and we just completed some very serious training exercises.

Little did we know, Vietnam was something you could not prepare for. Not only did you have the intense heat, the thousands of mosquitoes, bugs, snakes, and the horrible weights to carry on your backs, you also had a very tenacious enemy that was intent on killing each and every one of you. It took getting into a situation where you finally realize how vulnerable you are to really understand how short your life could be.

Staging, the Marines way of trying to get ready for War

The training in California was more physical conditioning, patrol tactics (Vietnam style), searching villages, dealing with anti-personnel mines (better known as booby traps), and survival. The Marine troops that assembled there were from all over the country. Initially, you knew very few people if anyone at all. Daily we would climb, or hump as we called it, the rolling mountains that surrounded the base. Although our packs didn't contain anywhere near the gear we would be carrying in Vietnam, we still thought we had it tough. All the patrolling and village searches were lead by Marines that had already been to Vietnam and they were trying their hardest to prepare us for a difficult task at best.

One of the final stages of our California training was a multi- day operation in the hills of Camp Pendleton. The unit that was going through staging we were "the good guys" and Marines from the main Camp Pendleton base acted as the aggressors. Each day we would move out on patrol much like we would once in Vietnam. At night, we would dig in and protect a perimeter- again, much like Vietnam. We all did what we were supposed to do, but to me it never carried much weight; there was never anything of significance at risk. One thing the night operations did was get you closer to the men that you were training with, similar to what would happen in a few months.

However, there were some interesting moments. One quiet, warm night, another Marine and I were standing hole watch. As I was finishingmy watch, I woke up my hole mate to begin his two hour watch. I tried to lay on the ground but I couldn't get comfortable and eventually, I chose to sleep sitting up in the foxhole, leaning back into a corner. I had fallen asleep but was woken a short time later by something crawling on my exposed neck.

I sat there dripping with sweat as whatever it was began a very slow climb from my uniform collar up the back of my neck, towards the top of my head. Eventually I couldn't take it any longer and I jumped up swatting at my neck where my night visitor had been climbing. Obviously I scared my hole mate half to death, and I was pretty scared myself. It turned out that my night visitor was a huge tarantula, which was very common on the base.

Getting through these days was difficult at best. I was slowly getting to know this new herd of Marines and I knew that Vietnam was only a number of days away. We did get some liberty, and we would venture into Oceanside the closest California town. Known as a Marine hangout, Oceanside was an easy target for the anti-war protestors and we usually got bombarded with verbal attacks as soon as we got off the military bus that brought us to town. This was late August, 1967, and the protestors didn't really have their act together yet- but give them a few months and they would be at a fever level.

The music was another thing that we needed to contend with. We had some wonderful tunes back then but some of the new hits that came out really rocked us. The one I remember most vividly was "The Letter" by The Box Tops. That song came out while we were at Camp Pendleton with only a few weeks left before shipping out. That song caused more men to go absent without leave, or AWOL. Every one of them were trying to get back to their girlfriend, regardless of where she lived.

One Friday afternoon, my friend Tom and I went into town to drop off some laundry that we needed done. The main bus stop was directly in front of a Hires Root Beer restaurant, with the laundry almost directly across the street. After we had dropped off our laundry, we went across the street for a hamburger and some soda. We had picked up our food and moved to a table to discuss our plans for the weekend. We were sitting there eating and talking, and I heard this funny laugh coming from somewhere behind me.

5

Whoever it was, he was definitely having a good time. He had a really deep guffawing laugh, but to me it seemed all too familiar. As he was laughing, I kneeled on the bench seat of the booth that we were in and I peered over to the top to see who was on the other side. Low and behold, I saw Bobby Panaroni, a close friend from my hometown of Branford, Connecticut sitting there. I made my presence known and he jumped up with surprise.

Bob was also in the Marines and was assigned to an Amtrak unit on the coastal part of Camp Pendleton. He would eventually be going to Vietnam, but hadn't received his orders yet-Camp Pendleton was his normal duty station. We chatted for a while and I introduced him to Tomie. He and his friends were just getting ready to go back to his barracks area and asked if we wanted to join them, which we did.

Once in his area we went to the enlisted men's club and started drinking. I don't remember leaving the club, but I do remember waking up in a rack in Bob's barracks; boy what hangovers we had that morning. I told him when I would be leaving for Vietnam and we promised to try to find each other once he got there.

On our way, Jungle Warfare Training

Eventually our orders came down. We were driven to Marine Corps Air Station El Toro and boarded civilian 727s and headed out to Okinawa. We landed at the airport at Camp Hanson and were immediately shuffled onto trucks for the journey to Camp Schwab, which was in a more secluded part of the island. In the Marines, you learned quickly that all the names of the camps, regardless of where you were in the world, were named after famous Marines who earned prestige in previous wars. Camps Hanson and Schwab are just two of the many camps around the world.

We were at Camp Schwab for 3 weeks of jungle warfare training, to better acclimate us to the heat and humidity that would be waiting in Vietnam. This training wasn't as physical as the past phases at Camp Pendleton. Here we concentrated on patrol tactics in the same climate as where we were going. The jungles were what made the biggest difference. In the rolling hills of Camp Pendleton, it was difficult for an enemy force to surprise your patrol. In the jungles around Camp Schwab, it was very easy for the enemy to catch you unprepared, even when you thought you were doing everything perfectly. Like at Camp Pendleton, these days seemed to go very fast; that nasty clock was ticking louder and louder each day.

Along with the change in climate, you also needed to try adjusting to a new culture. The Asian culture is beautiful, but some of what they did didn't fit with how we all grew up.
There was a small Japanese village right outside the gate called Hanoko, which was the only place we could go for non- military activity. Some of the villagers came into the camp during the day, looking to see if anyone wanted their wash done. They did a beautiful job and it was very inexpensive, so many of us had the mamasans do our wash.

One afternoon after coming back from a patrol up in the jungle, many of us were in the shower attempting to get the sweat and jungle grime off of our bodies. Without notice, a very attractive mamasan came walking through the shower, asking if anyone needed their laundry done.

For us naive Americans, this was something unheard of! Many men headed at a safe run back to their bunks with a vanity towel. For the Japanese this was nothing, they were raised to appreciate the body, regardless of sex- something many in our group had a hard time adjusting to.

On days when we didn't have any training exercises, we were sent out on varied work details. The first time , Tom, myself and a couple of others were sent down to this small beach area that was the local beach for the Marines from Camp Schwab. There was a small building off to the side of the beach that we reported to and we met a Sergeant and a Corporal that were in charge of the beach. The beach wasn't that big but it was beautiful- nice sand and that beautiful light blue water. There was quite a bit of equipment for the Marines to use when we had some down time: scuba gear, snorkel equipment, canoes, and a variety of other water-related sports gear.

They sent us out with rakes to scrape the seaweed that had gathered overnight and had us walk the beach area to pick up trash, which there was very little of. Within a couple of hours, we were done and we met back at the shack for our next assignment. Both the Sergeant and the Corporal had been to Vietnam and had both been wounded enough to get them out of being "in-country." They were finishing up their WESTPAC assignment at Camp Schwab and they had a great attitude. They figured in a few days we would be in a very nasty place, so they decided to just let us veg.

There were no more work assignments for the remainder of the morning and we could do whatever we wanted, as long as we stayed within the beach area. Some of us swam or just sat back and it was a very nice treat. When lunchtime came, we got ready to march back up to the company area to head in for chow, knowing we would be given another work assignment after lunch. The two of them knew this as well and wrote a note saying that we were needed back after lunch to finish up our responsibilities down at the beach. When we came back, we were more prepared- some of us had our bathing suits tucked inside our fatigues so we could enjoy the water more. You didn't catch breaks like this very often and you quickly learned to enjoy every second of them when you did.

There were a handful of Marines there who had already been to Vietnam and were going back for their second tour. With no exception, these men were all different, their minds were definitely someplace else. They had no sense of humor and none of us talked to them about Vietnam. We just kept our distance.

They would play a sick game that would send signals to us to steer clear of them. Two of them would sit on footlockers facing each other, with about 4 to 5-foot spans between the end of the footlockers. They would use a single edge razor blade as a dart and try to hit the other Marine's arm. The opponent would hold his forearm down in front of the footlocker, with the back of his hand against the box- his exposed wrist was the target for the propelled razor. When it missed, it stuck into the end of the footlocker; when it found its target, blood would spurt. They would stick one edge of the razor into the cuticle of the thumb and somehow hold the other end of it with their index finger. Then in a sweeping move, they would throw their hand forward releasing the razor, and it would fly forward hitting either flesh or wood.

None of this seemed to bother them at all, and if we watched, it was from a distance because we never wanted them to know we were watching. Most of us who hadn't been to Vietnam couldn't relate to where they were in their minds or maybe it had nothing to do with their prior Vietnam experience, maybe they were just nuts to begin with. We just never knew- possibly if we survived, we would have some idea of why they were the way they were

I never went back for a second tour but I now know how I would have felt if I had- there is nothing good to look forward to, just another year of extreme physical and emotional sacrifices. Dealing with the thought of pending death is a heavy burden on one's mind. Being in the Marine infantry made your chances of survival questionable and these weren't just passing thoughts. You lived day by day, hour by hour in a very high-risk environment. That dark feeling of death was always somewhere near.

For a number of years back in the states there was a very popular TV series that aired weekly called The Fugitive. Dr Richard Kimble was accused of murdering his wife and he was arrested initially. He was adamant that a one-armed man was to blame, but no one would believe him. Somewhere early on, he manages to escape and the series follows him while he tries to find the real murderer as the police try to close in on him. As we were approaching our final days on Okinawa, the final episode of this program was aired and there were actually two versions of the ending. One was Kimble tracking down the real killer, and the other was of him getting captured just prior to getting his man. Back then this was our big entertainment, and here it was, coming to an end while we were getting our gear ready for our final destination.

After our formal training in Okinawa, we all thought we would go together to Vietnam. One day, orders came down announcing one group would be going in a couple of days; the remaining group didn't know when they would be going. I had some close friends in the first group and everyone was somewhat upset that we were not going together.

The night before the first group left, we all walked up to the enlisted club on the top of the hill of Camp Schwab and started our farewell drinking. Happy hour had started and the drinks were 45 cents each regardless of what you ordered, though you were limited to 3 drinks each at any one time. It didn't take long before all of us were completely shot. I can't remember when I left the club for our barracks at the bottom of the hill, all I know is I crawled all the way back.

In Okinawa, as with most islands in the area, the roads were constructed to handle the torrential downpours of the rainy season. In most areas there were very large culverts on either side of the road. These culverts were no less than 10 feet from side-to-side and 3 to 4 feet deep, mostly constructed of poured concrete. When I came out of the enlisted men's club, I attempted to walk on the road, but that definitely wasn't going to work.

Eventually I made my way into the culvert on the club side of the road and began my crawling journey down the hill. Each time I tried to get on my feet, something told me that I was better off closer to the ground. It was a long crawl but I made it to the bottom and then to my barracks directly across the road.

When I got into the barracks, I made every attempt to sober up, and the best way I knew was to take a shower. I stripped down and made my way into the shower area, which was a large tiled room with about 30 showerheads. I turned about 6 of them on and directed the spouts into one general area where I sat. The water wasn't too hot or too cold and it felt
wonderful. The shower didn't do any miracles but I definitely felt better by the time I crawled into the rack. The next morning at formation wasn't a pretty site; everyone was in very bad shape, some helping others stay standing until we were all released.

The first group left that day and much to our surprise, the rest of us were shipped out two days later. We had no idea where we were going or if we would ever see the men that left two days before.

Welcome to Vietnam - September 1967

We flew into Vietnam from Okinawa on C-130 cargo transports, which was not the most comfortable way to travel. I think all of us, as apprehensive as we were, still complained about the plane ride. The seats were not the comfortable ones you think of on a traditional airplane- these were sling seats along the outboard walls of the plane. The noise inside was deafening- the roar of the prop engines outside and the wind blowing by the back ramp was extremely loud

We landed in Da Nang, which was the main Marine transport area. Although the plane ride was uncomfortable, it did not prepare us for our arrival in Vietnam. We thought Okinawa was hot and humid; Vietnam took all of this to a new level. When you came off the plane, you could hear Vietnam sucking the air out of your lungs, and the heat was unbearable. As the back ramp of the plane was slowly lowered, we were all trying to get our first glimpse of this world of terror. The scenes outside were something surreal to us all. There were some troops on the ground, but not as many as I had expected. You could visibly see the waves of heat rising off the runway which made things in the distance look wavy and distorted, like you were looking through a water bottle.

We landed in Da Nang, which was the main Marine transport area. Although the plane ride was uncomfortable, it did not prepare us for our arrival in Vietnam. We thought Okinawa was hot and humid; Vietnam took all of this to a new level. When you came off the plane, you could hear Vietnam sucking the air out of your lungs, and the heat was unbearable. As the back ramp of the plane was slowly lowered, we were all trying to get our first glimpse of this world of terror. The scenes outside were something surreal to us all. There were some troops on the ground, but not as many as I had expected. You could visibly see the waves of heat rising off the runway which made things in the distance look wavy and distorted, like you were looking through a water bottle.

I thought Okinawa was hot and humid, but it was nowhere near the extremes of Vietnam. Still in state side utilities made of heavy cotton, not the lighter jungle fatigues that everyone around us wore, we were immediately drenched in sweat. All we had on were the utilities- no fighting gear, no weapons- yet we were soaked. The smells were very pungent but instead of a nice smell, it smelled like everything and anything was rotting from the constant heat and humidity.

At this point we had no idea who we would be assigned to- I didn't think it would have made a major difference to any of us, as we had no idea which unit did what. Most of us were eventually assigned to 1st Battalion 3rd Marines, a rifle Battalion. This Marine battalion was comprised of four companies: Alpha or A Company, Bravo or B Company, Charlie or C Company, and Delta or D Company.

We were the grunts we heard about from all the previous wars, even though we hadn't seen anything yet. Grunts in Vietnam, what did that mean? On top of that, our unit was currently on Special Landing Forces or SLF status, requiring us to be on board troop ships. At first we thought this was cool, but eventually we learned that it was not. We were basically an emergency reaction team for any unit "in trouble," and in this case, "in trouble" meant under heavy attack from the enemy.

There was a need to keep us in Da Nang a day or two but none of us knew this. Most of us mulled around the transit area, not knowing where to go or what to stay away from. The group we were with was our only comfort, they were the only faces we knew, and no one wanted to wander too far.

Before going to Vietnam, I was stationed at the Charleston, South Carolina Naval shipyard as an MP. I knew some friends from Charleston came to Vietnam and were MP's in Da Nang, and I wanted to try to look up at least one of them. I asked around and learned that the MP area was further up the hill from where we were, near a place called Freedom Hill. I asked some friends to cover for me and I began my journey to the MP base, which was less than a mile away.

I followed some signs and eventually came into a courtyard with hardbacks for offices, a mess hall and sleeping quarters. Hardbacks are long rectangular buildings built off the ground with 4-foot high plywood for walls, then mosquito screening covered with either canvas roofing or corrugated metal. These were not fancy but practical for the varied weather elements and numerous insects of Vietnam. There was a circular courtyard in the center of the buildings with large fist-sized rocks painted white for delineation between road and yard dirt.

As I entered this area, there was a Marine walking along the backside of the circle who looked somewhat familiar. He wasn't my friend Doug from Charleston, but it was definitely someone I knew from somewhere. It wasn't just me; eventually, he saw me and slowed down, letting me know that he recognized me, too. I made my way to where he was; it was obvious he was not going to move in my direction. As it turned out, he was someone I went through boot camp with. At least 99% of my platoon, and probably the whole company, received orders for Vietnam right out of boot camp- only a few escaped going immediately.

The conversation was awkward at best. I had to pry answers out of him and I couldn't understand why. In some ways he looked much different than I remembered him, there was something else besides the Vietnam dirt and sweat. I asked
questions about other men from boot camp but getting answers was a struggle, sometimes simply indicated by a tip of his head or a shrug of his shoulders. Later in my tour all this made perfect sense, but at this point, I was completely at a loss.

What I learned was that quite a few of the men I went through training with went home either badly wounded or dead. Even this information didn't sink in the way it should have, as I was still very distant from my own experiences with this which were still to come. He was at the end of his tour and was sent to Da Nang to await his transport back to Okinawa then to the States. I thought it strange that he didn't show any excitement about going home- it almost seemed as if he didn't want to talk about it at all.

The conversation ended and I began my search for Doug. At this point I was still wearing my stateside utilities, heavy olive green blouse and trousers and the regular black boots, not jungle utilities like everyone around me. Anyone wearing this garb stood out like a sore thumb and I was receiving many an inquisitive stare from the other Marines walking by.

I eventually found the guard shack and asked someone if they knew Doug, which they did. They said that he was currently out on perimeter watch, and I wasn't really sure what that meant. At one point, someone from across the room asked if I would like to go visit him- there was a guard relief truck coming by that could take me. Not knowing any better, I said "sure." To this day, I don't know if I was being set up or not.

The guard truck pulled up and I climbed in with the Marines going out as replacements. The perimeter is a large circle that goes around the entire Da Nang base with observation towers manned by these Marines. Eventually, the truck pulled up in front of one tower and the driver told me this was Doug's position. I climbed out and went up to the structure that was made out of four telephone poles with two platforms, one higher than the other. The upper platform had plywood sides with heavily sandbagged floor and walls.

There were Marines sitting around, probably wondering what the heck someone with stateside utilities was doing out where they were. My rank was obvious, so to them I was truly a non-issue, but none-the-less a strange sight. I got someone's attention and asked him where Doug was. He said Doug walked over to the Air Force area to sneak a decent evening meal. I sat off to the side and answered some questions
regarding how I knew Doug and where I was from in "The World," meaning back home.

They thought the fact that I was there was pretty cool, and we had some good conversations. Eventually one of them said he could see Doug coming and suggested I climb to the upper observation area and they would send him up, so I did. I could hear Doug below and after some subtle conversation, they
asked him to go up and take the first watch. He didn't have a
clue I was there and it was a wonderful surprise.

We talked and talked as it got darker and darker. Occasionally, I would see flashing in the distance. I asked Doug what it was and he said it was most likely some Marine ground troops tangling up with an NVA unit. I was still hours and days away from my first encounter with the NVA or any enemy elements, so this distant action had no meaning to me.

Eventually I told him I needed to be getting back to the transit area and asked when the next relief truck would be coming by. He gave a little chuckle and told me I came out on the last relief truck of the day. The next one would be well after sunrise the next morning, somewhere around 7. I didn't think this was humorous at all. Although I didn't know how to fear Vietnam the way I would in the near future, I was still very afraid. I really needed to get back, men were covering for me during roll calls and my absence would be obvious soon.

By now it was pitch dark. I asked Doug what I needed to do to get out of there and he gave me some directions. He described the dirt relief road that the truck followed when I came out, directly in front of the tower. I needed to follow the dirt road until I saw black pavement to my left. He assured me that if I walked slowly, I would definitely see the black pavement to the left, though I wasn't so sure. Here, I needed to turn left and follow that blacktop to another paved road, which was the perimeter road that went all around the Da Nang airstrip, slightly inside the perimeter Doug was manning. If I took a left on this road and followed it all the way around to the MP area where I started from, I would know how to get back to my transit area.

Believe it or not, I actually set out on this journey. I'm still curious if they ever wondered whether or not I actually made it to my destination, as I never had an opportunity to talk to Doug after that night. I'm sure bets were made all night that I wouldn't make it.

Off I went into the dark in my stateside uniform with my only weapon being a deer knife strapped to my waist; no M-16, no nothing. Scared to death and drenched with sweat, I followed the dirt road until my eyes picked up the black pavement on the left. I followed that road to the main road and took a left like Doug had told me to do.

Off in the distance, I could see the Marine F-4 Phantoms landing and taking off on the main airstrip, coming and going to help support the Marines in the field. I was terrified; I was walking very slow trying to see my way around, which was very difficult. I had no clue as to what the hell I was doing and was pissed at myself for getting myself into such a deadly jam.

All of a sudden, I heard the sounds of bolts going home on M- 16s and someone yelling "halt, who goes there?" from somewhere directly in front of me. I froze in my tracks and said as clearly as I could that I was Lance Corporal Janicki.
They asked me the password, which I tried to jokingly answer; were they really serious?

Obviously I was in deep shit. They told me to put my hands up over my head and to walk forward slowly, which I did. Someone said "halt," and I stopped again quickly. I could barely make out that I was in front of a roadside bunker, manned by 3 or 4 Army soldiers. They asked me what the hell I was up to and did I realize how close I came from all of them unloading their M-16s into me? I told them my crazy story, and I'm sure that they were all thinking that they had never met a more stupid Marine. I wasn't embarrassed- I was beyond ridiculous feelings like that. They said the best they could do would be to let me curl up in the corner of their bunker and they would wake me up in the morning when a transport could get me to the other side. The gap between their bunker and the other side, near the MP area, was a known area for enemy infiltration.

As luck would have it, while we were standing there talking, an Army jeep pulled up with an officer and a driver who were inspecting the lines. The sentries told the officer the story and he wasn't very happy with me either. To my surprise, he offered to take me to the MP area on the other side. I climbed aboard the jeep and it took off. We immediately sped up and didn't slow down until we were within the other perimeter, safe from the enemy area.

During night travel, the headlamps on vehicles were tiny slits that barely allowed the driver to see what was in front of the vehicle in the pitch dark. How he knew where the road was, is beyond me. I couldn't see a thing. We got there quickly and they let me out and I made my way back down the hill to my own area, hoping that my unit had not moved out during all the hours that I was gone. Fortunately, there were only a few roll calls and my absence was not identified.

Joining our unit - Mid September 1967

The next morning, we were ferried out to the troop ships on Mike Boats during a tremendous downpour- it was the beginning of Monsoon season. Before that, we were transported on what we called "6-bys," the typical military cargo truck with a canvas awning and a flat metal bottom, lined with a layer of sandbags. It was a lengthy, very slow, trip and we hoped we had armed escorts because we still had no weapons of our own. We eventually made it to a coastal beach and unloaded our sea bags and gear from the trucks. We had another roll call and then we just lay back, resting on our sea bags while we waited for the boats to come.

Before getting on the Mike Boats, I was watching Vietnamese women walk up and down the beach, picking up dead fish.
From the smell, these fish had been laying there for a while and ever since I have wondered if they were going to eat them for dinner. I assumed they did, and my childhood taste for fish quickly went by the wayside.

Eventually, the Mike Boats neared the beach and lowered the boarding ramps for us to climb aboard with our sea bags.
When we left the beach, I wondered where we were going, as I couldn't see any big naval vessels in sight. In areas like these, the bigger ships stay well off shore, out of the way of enemy artillery.

After many hours, we arrived where our ships were positioned. By this time, it was evening and it had been raining for an hour or two. Without our in-country issue of equipment, all we had was our stateside uniforms and canvas sea bags, not one poncho to be found. Mike Boats are open vessels and all we could do was sit there in the rain, talk about getting wet as we waited to board. We got a good sense of how important we were when other boats full of lumber and other materials were offloaded before letting us come anywhere near the troop ships.

21

We didn't know what to do when we first came on board the ships, as the unit we were assigned to was currently on their way back from a major operation. For the most part, we spent a few hours sleeping on decks and passageways waiting for them to return. Ship life was new to us, especially on naval ships this size. The ships were slowly under way, apparently waiting for the ground troops to be ferried out. It was still very hot even out on open water with the slight breeze from the ship being under way. We all tried to find places out of the rain to sit and if possible, fall asleep.

Finally the ground troops came aboard and what a surprise it was for us new guys. They all came aboard on Mike Boats deep in the hold of the troop ship, finally coming up ladders (the naval term for stairs) to our area. I for one almost fell over. I had never seen a field Marine coming back from a major operation and here they were, coming up the ladders to our area.

The first impression I had was that they smelled so bad it almost made me want to throw up, they were disgusting. There was no humor among them, they had just come back from a very bad operation and they had lost many friends.

Us new guys just stood or sat around in complete awe, we didn't know what to say or do. I was shocked to see another Marine who I was very close to in Charleston coming up the ladder with a M-60 machine gun over his shoulder and his usual cigar stub stuck in his mouth.

I found some courage and called out his name softly, and even though I knew he was happy or shocked to see me, there was no enlightenment in his expression, it was an expression I will never forget. Days later, I had other opportunities to talk with John and there were better conversations where I brought him up-to-date with the most current activities in Charleston- his home.

We met our new platoon and squad leaders and were told where our quarters were-they were no place comfortable, believe me. They were on one of the lower decks on the port, or left, side all the way to the rear of the ship, known as the fantail area. The ship we were on was called a Landing Ship Dock or LSD in Navy terms. It was primarily a Marine transport with multiple vehicles to get the Marines ashore when needed. In the hold, there were the mike boats we came out on as well as Amtrak's. Amtrak's were large transport track vehicles, which you entered via a ramp, and were airtight when closed.

On the back deck of the ship was a helipad which allowed for helicopters to come in and pick up Marines. At night when it was quiet, you could hear the screws, or propellers, churning under the vessel as it was underway. I'm not sure if everyone could hear them, but our compartment was just above the props and I found the sound of their churn relaxing.

All of us new troops attempted to merge with these seasoned veterans, but it wasn't all that easy, they were hard to penetrate. The squad leaders were great, they made you feel fairly at home as quickly as possible, but what did that mean when you had no idea what they had been through? Little by little, they introduced us to the old team and told us what our responsibilities were. I was placed in 2nd squad of 2nd platoon of Alpha Company as an ammo humper. I was part of a fire team, a rifleman, but also responsible for carrying 200 rounds of machine gun ammo- what an intro. My squad leader's name was Bruce Norwood, nicknamed Woody. He was a big black man with a soothing personality who really knew his stuff and never got excited when things got difficult because he knew all us new guys were on edge. He was one of the few I met who took some time to teach you the ins and outs of surviving Vietnam.

At the time, us new guys never really got the scoop on what happened to them during their last operation, they were all quite silent about the details. Way after the fact, we learned the name of the operation was Shelbyville, and 2nd Platoon, and possibly others, were hit real hard. A normal platoon in Vietnam held 40 to 50 men-they came out of this battle with nine.

What hurt even worse was the last casualty. The battle was over and they had begun their move out of the village area and somewhere nearby, a grenade went off. One of the men was walking along and just fell over with no apparent signs of being hit. One small piece of shrapnel went through the tiny opening of his flak jacket and pierced his heart. This was one of the most well-liked men in the unit and I think he had a very short time left in country. This last casualty hit them all very hard and they were numbed by it for days.

Over time, we learned through our own experiences that this was the way it went. When there were casualties, everyone absorbed their individual emotions over it, regardless of how close they were to the Marine who had been killed or wounded. Although this was what you needed to do to survive that hour, that day, that month, many years later, this would come back to you ten times worse than the actual loss.

We'd been on board for a couple of days when we were taken ashore to China Beach for a beer blast. There were small thatched shelters scattered along the beach, each one with its own 55-gallon barrel full of beer and ice. During the course of the day, everyone got loaded and eventually wound up in the water.

Some of the men took advantage of the activities going on at the beach and slipped away to a small area just outside of Da Nang called "Dog Patch." This was an area full of bars and whorehouses, but also a place where they could let off a little steam in a relatively secure area. Later in the day, they straggled back and rejoined us at the beach, most of them carrying hidden bottles of either scotch or whisky. Alcohol was not permitted aboard ship and these bottles were enjoyed by everyone later that night and the next.

So far things weren't too bad, on board ship for two days, good chow, hot showers- not too shabby. A beach party on China Beach with plenty of beer and steaks to eat. Maybe this wasn't going to be as bad as we all thought.

Eventually we got back to the ships and spent another couple of days getting acclimated to the heat and humidity while trying to get to know the squad a little better. Our Platoon Commander, 2nd Lt Debruler, had been with 2nd Platoon for a number of months. Although we were on board ships, he didn't lose sight of the fact that we still needed physical training, or PT. Each morning, he would call the platoon up to the helipad and we would go through a complete routine of running, push-ups and sit-ups. I always got the feeling that the sailors on board thought we were completely nuts to be doing this in the heat and humidity of Vietnam, but obviously Lt Debruler thought otherwise.

First Assault Operation Medina

The word finally came down that we would be leaving the next morning for another operation, the first for us new guys. Many new activities took place, most of which we had never experienced. There were numerous weapon checks to make sure either your M-16 assault rifle or M-60 machine gun, whatever you were supposed to carry, was ready to go. Then came the ammo: bandoleers of M-16 ammo, M-26 grenades, claymore mines, 60-MM mortar rounds: they seemed to never end. It was mandatory for each one of us to carry a claymore anti-personnel mine, a 60-MM mortar round, two smoke grenades, and 200 rounds of M-60 machine gun ammo. There were also trip flares and pop-up flares that we had to pack.

On top of that, we had to carry own needs. I had 12 magazines of M-16 ammo, each with 18 rounds, and 4 fragmentation grenades. On top of that, I carried 3 additional bandoleers of M-16 ammo, just in case. Then add your C- rations, poncho, poncho liner, canteens of water, entrenching tool, letter writing stuff, helmet, flack jacket, and M-16 and you're all set. Our outfit was always prepared for the worst because you never wanted to run out of ammunition.

Morning came and everyone was a nervous wreck. The more seasoned troops were very quiet, their minds were somewhere else, possibly reliving past assaults and what had taken place. The name of the operation was Medina and it was in the rolling hills of Vietnam somewhere, I'm still not sure where we were.

For this operation we were transported by helicopter as it was too far inland for any other vehicles. You had to wait on the edge of the helipad for the loader to give your group the signal to move forward before loading onto one of the available helicopters. Each chopper could only take 4 or 5 combat-ready troops and even then it was very crowded.

We were using CH-34's, also called flying grasshoppers, which were not new by any means. From a distance they looked ok but when I actually ran up to the one I needed to load onto, I couldn't believe my eyes. All the windows had been taken out, but that was for good reason- it was an attempt to increase the number of escape exits that were available. But what really caught my eye were all the bullet holes that were un-patched. I couldn't believe this thing could still fly.

We climbed on board and within a few seconds, we were on our way. During the varied phases of Marine training, you practiced loading and unloading from helicopters and ships but it was always simulated. The real thing is quite different. Getting on the helicopter would have been interesting enough just in jungle fatigues but combat- ready was an experience all its own. The sheer weight of your own body plus all the gear you were carrying made it difficult to climb the two metal steps to get on the chopper.

Once inside, you needed to work your way around the door gunner, move inside the cramped interior and then somehow turn around and to try to sit without smashing all your gear into the Marines around you. The thing I remember vividly was the air rushing around you while in flight. With all the windows missing and the side door open for the door gunner, the fresh air flooded the rear compartment. The other immediate change was the air temperature; you immediately went from dying of the heat to being cold. The altitude we flew at was always much cooler than ground level and the coolness always woke us up.

I can't remember the flight over the water but I do remember looking down as we began to fly over the Vietnam coast. The deep blue-green of the foliage was striking and quite beautiful, but it was the devastation that really caught my eye. There were bomb craters everywhere, visible with either white sand or clay red and they looked like huge sores. Everywhere I looked, I could see the scars of previous battles and firefights. All solid structure buildings, mostly built during the French occupation, were roofless, the ends and sides splattered with hundreds of sores made by bullets and shrapnel.

My fire team leader's name was Corporal Waight and he was one of the few seasoned men in our squad. My other fire team members were Mike and Ralph, and the three of us all arrived in Vietnam at the same time. It was interesting that they put us together. We all first met while going through staging training in California and had become quite close. Mike and his twin brother, Bill, had joined the Marines together and had both volunteered for Vietnam. Normally they wouldn't allow two brothers to be "in country" at the same time, but they had signed a waiver saying they wanted to serve together. Bill was also in our platoon but was assigned to one of the other squads. They were from Watertown, New York and both were very funny. Mike had a more dry sense of humor, and Bill was goofy but still a sharp Marine.

Ralph was a country boy from Duncansville, Pennsylvania. Ralph was very religious, but not in the way where he pushed it on people- he just had very strong beliefs and read the bible daily. He was already married and his wife was pregnant with his soon-to-be son. He chewed snuff or tobacco, whichever he could get his hands on, but his preference was Scoal, the one that came in the green tin. Within our immediate group, Ralph was the best shot with a rifle- we all had pretty good marksman scores, but Ralph had that extra knack and it was good to have him as part of our team.

28

Other than Waight, none of us had any idea what we were in for. We were very nervous and I'm sure scared at some level, but we hadn't been introduced to the different levels of hell in Vietnam, all of which would keep us very scared in the future. From our formal training, we knew the basic fundamentals of what we needed to do when the helicopter landed. From the time it touched down or the door gunner told you to jump, you would be on the move. Once on the ground, immediately your fire team leader would fan everyone out, attempting to create a hasty perimeter around the landing zone, or LZ.

Each group touching down would increase the size of the perimeter, eventually making it relatively secure to land in. On this first venture, we listened and did everything Waight told us to do and as quickly as possible. Over time, this all became second nature and very few instructions were needed

Fortunately for us, this was not a hot LZ and the landing went without incident. Once everyone was on the ground, we got somewhat organized and began to move out in patrol formation. Again this was new to us. Practicing in the states and in Okinawa was one thing, but the real thing had a completely different atmosphere. There was no talking except by the radio operators, only hand and arm signals to minimize our presence and hide our location.

The area that we were in wasn't a village or rice paddy areas or the jungles, just rolling hills with periodic areas of vegetation, mostly on the hilltops. The day went without incident and we eventually got to an area where we were told we would be spending the night. The process of setting the lines began. The squad leaders worked with the fire team leaders, picking positions that needed to be manned. Once they were set, two men were assigned to each designated spot. Mike and I were assigned to one where we put our gear down. Waight came back eventually and told us which direction to have the fighting position face, and also to set up the left and right fields of fire.

Fields of fire were designated for each position. Imagine two Marines standing in the foxhole facing outward. Everything directly in front of them was open game to shoot at. The person on the right would aim his rifle at a right angle from their hole that would intercept with the left angle of the Marine in the foxhole to his right. You would take a stick and drive it into the ground at that point. That would tell the Marine on the right where he needed to stop, if he went any further he would be shooting into the position to his right. This sounds pretty lame for fighting during the day, but at night you couldn't see two inches and these sticks really came in handy, these brackets were each position's field of fire.

Eventually, Mike and I got out our entrenching tools and shovels to begin digging our first foxhole. We took turns digging for numerous reasons. One was the confined space of a foxhole, and also the other person needed to stand watch to make sure there was no enemy movement out in front of us.

There are textbook foxholes and then there are textbook foxholes, but when we were done, ours needed to be included in the next Marine infantryman's manual. It was perfect in every way and we were completely exhausted, drenched with sweat and very sore. Our bodies were definitely not used to the physical demands of Vietnam and our hands were bloody with broken blisters, but most importantly, we were done and it wasn't even dark yet. Much to our dismay, we were in for a rude awakening. Corporal Waight came around and said they needed to shift the lines, though Mike and I had no idea what that meant. It meant they wanted us to move to another location and dig another foxhole; Mike and I couldn't believe our ears.

Again we began to dig in and this time we were halfway through digging a textbook foxhole when Waight came by- they were shifting the lines again. This time, Mike and I wound up on the top of a knoll, overlooking a small stream to our left and open ranges to our front and rear. It was getting
dark as we began digging in again, but there wasn't much dirt, mostly rock and shale.

All you could hear was clinking and clanking as our shovels hit the rocks. Eventually, the foxhole to our left yelled over to us and said it would be a good idea to stop, they could see the sparks coming off our shovels from where they were. To our dismay, we didn't have a textbook foxhole; you could hardly call it a hole at all. Laying flat on our stomachs or backs, there was barely enough depth to be out of sight.

In general, the setting of the lines had been a success even though Mike and I, as well as others, had to move twice. During all of this, the enemy stayed quiet, which wasn't the norm. We didn't have any time to eat while digging, so we both sat there, half laying back in our pathetic fighting position and choked down some cold C-rations. Now it was dark and we began a whole new experience: night watch.

You would think a watch that could display the time at night would be general issue, especially for combat troops, but this wasn't so, at least in the Marines, because neither Mike nor I had one. The basic rules at night were be 100% alert for the first two hours, then trade 2-hour shifts with your hole mate until early morning when the last two hours were also at 100%. I can't remember exactly, but I know that darkness came early and the nights were very long. Periodically the fire team and squad leaders would walk or crawl the lines, making sure someone was awake at each position.

The night watch began with everyone on watch and normally lasted for about 2 hours. Eventually, Waight came by and told us to start rotating our 2 hour shifts, which was easier said than done. With no watch to tell the time, you sat there and guessed how much time had gone buy. We traded shifts, one after another, and the night was going without incident.

After numerous shift exchanges, we guessed it was somewhere near the early morning 100% alert and waited for word to come down. We heard some activity at the hole next to us and assumed it was Waight passing the word. Waight got to our hole and asked if everything was going ok. We said it was and asked if he knew the time, and he said it was just 11 P.M. Mike and I were really annoyed at this and we were both still completely exhausted. We continued on through the night taking turns, guessing the time as we went.

Somewhere in the early hours of the morning, something really bad happened on the far side of the perimeter. All four companies of our battalion were joined in a big circle and Charlie Company was directly across from our positions. I had a very good friend in Charlie Company so when I learned it was them, I was really worried for his safety. His name was Tom and we met shortly after boot camp in June of 1966.

All hell broke loose on the far side of the perimeter. We could hear M-16s firing as well as numerous M-60 (American) machine guns. At night, it was easy to tell an American machine gun from an NVA gun. In machine guns, every fifth round, or bullet, was a tracer, which left a glowing yellow orange trail.

These trails allowed the gunner to know exactly where his rounds were going so he could make adjustments. NVA machine guns had tracers with different colors, mostly a blue- green color. The tracers flying that night were all yellow. At one point, there was an American machine gun and all it was doing was going around in circles spraying bullets both inside and outside the perimeter.

It was total chaos. We could hear American voices yelling directions and at the same time there were Vietnamese, or what we called "Gook," voices everywhere. From the beginning of the fight, we launched 60mm mortar flares and eventually called in flares launched from 105 and 155 howitzers. You could hear these artillery rounds streak their way across the sky and hear a loud pop. Within seconds, a parachuted flare would begin its descent. As these flares made their way to the ground, they would swing back and forth, making illusions on the ground appear and disappear with the wavering shadows. Once we had enough flares in the sky, you could see activity on the ground and people running everywhere, but exactly who they were we didn't know and at that point, we didn't want to find out.

Mike and I were lying in our shallow hole with just our eyes appearing above the rim. We had no idea how much of our bodies could be seen, but we really had no place to hide.

There were bullets of all kinds flying past us and the intensity of the battle had us in awe. We could hear splashing in the small stream to our left and Vietnamese voices shouting "Lai dai," which means "come here" or "this way" in Vietnamese. We noticed that the Marine fighting position to our left chose not to do anything and we followed suite, the last thing we wanted was any of them coming up the hill towards us. It needs to be said that the nights in Vietnam are very dark, most often you couldn't even see your hand in front of your face. Moonlit nights were different but the cloudy nights of the monsoon season were very dark.

The battle raged on, but as daylight came, the enemy broke contact and headed elsewhere. We later learned that an NVA division was on the move and had accidentally walked through our perimeter. No surprise to me, there were some positions they walked by where both Marines were asleep, I know how hard it was for me to stay awake that night and how easy it was to let your eyelids fall. Eventually their lead elements noticed they were in the middle of Charlie Company, but it was too late. Someone in Charlie Company spotted them and opened fire, beginning the long battle.

As luck would have it, Tom was on an ambush that night and once the battle began, they were given strict instructions not to make contact and stay hidden- the enemy was everywhere and they would have been easy targets. There were numerous casualties and the morning was spent getting the wounded and dead medevac'd out. I can remember lying there in that crappy foxhole with Mike, waiting for the sun to come up. This was our first night in the field and what an intro we got. While we were lying there I said to Mike, "Mike, just think, only 395 more days of this shit." On the surface we both laughed, but inside the events of the early morning battle had left a mark.

That morning once we were more organized, they sent our squad out on patrol. This was not good- obviously the enemy was very close and for us new guys, this seemed like a suicide mission. We headed out and cautiously made our way to the top of a nearby hill that had some vegetation growing near the top. We literally crawled the last few hundred yards up this hill, making sure our silhouettes would not be seen by anyone.

We were instructed to crawl into bushes and face outward, and to pass the word along if we saw any movement down below. I looked and looked but I had no idea what I was looking for. If they expected me to be able to see something or someone walking down by the river, they were in for a rude awakening. I had very good eyesight but I couldn't see anything that far away.

Apparently someone within the squad had binoculars because around midday, someone spotted something, but initially it was kept very secret. Eventually, Waight crawled back to us and said they had spotted a column of NVA soldiers walking along a path by the river, entering a village directly across the river from the hill we were on.

The good news is we had spotted the enemy on the move, and Waight's update continued on to say we were preparing to call in artillery on that village and the surrounding area. I was impressed at all this, thinking it would possibly be a little payback for the previous evening's attack. Waight also said that as soon as the artillery began, the enemy would know that the sighting had been made from the nearby hills and they could come looking.

I couldn't believe what I was hearing. Here we were, all 10 of us, calling artillery in on the enemy and expecting them to come looking. Waight continued to say that our squad leader had called our platoon and company to explain the situation and they were currently packed up and on the way to give us the support we needed if the enemy chose to come after us.

This all played out as expected. The artillery began to fall on the village and its surrounding areas across the river. For some reason, the enemy didn't respond, at least not in our direction.

Other than the firefight that took place the night before, this was my first encounter with our artillery being called in on an enemy position. The barrage that was to begin was under the control of Bruce, our squad leader. Using our squad communications radio, he had made contact with one of our rear area firebases. A firebase was a Marine or Army compound somewhere nearby that contained both 105 and 155 howitzer artillery pieces. These firebases were protected by infantry troops and periodically came under attack too.

The first round that was called in was white phosphorus, what we called Willy Peter or "WP." When these exploded, they sent out a white billowing cloud that was easily spotted by the person controlling the firing, Bruce in this case. If the round is way off target, he would give correcting adjustments and ask for another WP round. When the spotting round was close, he would give final adjustments and then say, "Fire for effect." With that order, the barrage would begin.

From where we were, we could hear the guns going off far in the distance. For the first time, I could hear the artillery rounds as they screamed through the air and the vivid
"crumping" sound as they landed in and around the village. Each round would send up a gray cloud, which I'm sure was the gunpowder used in the round mixed in with dirt and sand from the village.

We watched and watched and never saw any of the enemy make their way across the river in an effort to search out whoever had called in the artillery. I was thrilled at that, because with no fighting position, we would have been at a severe disadvantage.

Our squad leader called in a report stating that there was no enemy movement in our direction, and the rest of our unit began moving back to their original positions. Eventually, we made our way back to the company perimeter and began preparation for another long evening. During the day, they had adjusted the lines again so Mike and I had another opportunity to dig that perfect hole, which we did. This time we got a chance to use it, so much for bonuses.

Early in the evening, while there was still good daylight, supply helicopters came in with more ammunition, C-rations and other supplies. Mike and I were sent up from our squad along with others to the LZ to get the supplies that were designated for 2nd Platoon. We each grabbed 2 cases of C- rations and began the trek back to our area of the perimeter, a sizeable distance. Immediately these two cases became heavy and awkward to carry and we both struggled to find the best way of carrying them.

As we walked back, we were walking along the perimeter of some of the other platoons to reach the area where 2nd Platoon began. On our way, we saw many familiar faces, mostly of the men that we had gotten to know in California at Camp Pendleton. Over the many upcoming months, you saw fewer and fewer recognizable faces, and you never wanted to find out what had happened to the ones that were missing. If there was one thing that you learned quickly in Vietnam, it was a subconscious way of ignoring your inner feelings and emotions.

It was the beginning of the monsoon season and the rains came more often than not. That night, we were standing hole watch and I had just changed shifts with Mike when I tried to get comfortable for my two-hour nap. It started to rain and I chose to grab my poncho and curl up in the bottom of the foxhole- what a mistake. The rain got heavier and heavier and before I knew it, the water was pouring into the foxhole from numerous little waterfalls. Now I was completely soaked and couldn't get warm no matter what I did. All I could think of was the heat of the day and how good it would feel. Other than the rain, the long night was uneventful, unless you want to count the millions of attacks from mosquitoes with what seemed to be 4-foot wing span.

These nights go by so painfully and so filled with fear. Whenever you say that you stood hole watch at night or you went out on a night ambush or a listening post, these all sound like simple words. There was nothing simple about any one of these activities and this was your basic rotation. One night you would stand general perimeter watch, another night you would be out on either a squad or platoon-sized ambush and the next a two-man listening post, the most terrifying of all.

Regardless of the activity, nights were long and very dark, and the fear of Charlie's presence was always there, the fear for the enemy was always deep within your gut. At night, your mind followed the ghosts of what was out in front of you. What was a small bush during the day was a VC or NVA soldier crawling along in the darkness, your mind and its incredible imagination was somewhat your worst enemy.

Being exhausted was something that you needed to try to get used to. The days were long, hot and physically exhausting. There was always something you were involved in and sleep or napping wasn't in the Marine Corps manual, so you went without. During the day, if you could close your eyes for the briefest second, it felt like a 3-hour nap. Grabbing those precious seconds was very difficult; you always needed to be as alert as possible.

Your body was really taking a beating as well. Your pack and essential gear weighed in from 60 to 80 pounds and more often than not, you were on the move with your pack on your back. Your back and shoulders were in constant agony and you were always trying to shift the weight of your pack to relieve the pain from one specific spot or another. Your legs had to support all this extra weight and also to allow you to climb and descend. More often than not, descending was more painful than climbing and this is where the majority of the foot and ankle injuries came from.

Your feet took the worst beating of all. They were either hot and sweaty or completely soaked with rotting, flaking skin that would literally roll off under the slightest pressure. Being in the field, we were not allowed to take our boots off at-will. We needed to wait for the word to come down to conduct foot checks. This was always done when we had a few quiet minutes and our leaders were somewhat confident that the enemy was currently not around.

You would team up with another member of your squad and take turns taking your boots and sock off and letting your feet air out. Your partner was basically there with their boots on and their weapon to guard you while you aired your feet. When you were done, it would be your turn to guard him while he did the same thing. Sometimes this was a painful process. At times, it had been so long since the last time you had your boots off that your socks were imbedded into your skin, especially if you had what was called emersion foot where your skin was rotting from the constant moisture.

When your feet were like this, you needed to pour water on your sock to allow it to loosen its grip on your skin and then you could slowly peel your sock off your foot. Keeping your body healthy was not easy and your corpsman was always on call for ailments you had no idea on how to handle.

Even going the bathroom took on a whole new process and quickly became very natural. When you were out in enemy country, or what we called "Injun Country," which for us was always, you needed a personal guard even when you went the bathroom. Not so much when you urinated, you could do that just about anywhere, but when you needed to defecate, you needed a guard. It became a very natural process. When you had to go you would just get up and walk by someone in your squad and you'd say, "I gotta go."

With no questions asked, your squad member would get up and follow you while you carried your rifle and your entrenching tool, which you needed to dig your cat hole with. A cat hole is a small hole, which you dug with your entrenching tool, enough to go the bathroom in. He would follow you a short distance out in front of the perimeter, wait while you dug the hole and would sit alongside you, rifle at the ready while you went the bathroom. As strange as it sounds, you would even have a conversation during all of this. Normally you would think this is something that was to be very private but in Vietnam, privacy took on a whole new role. This sounds so foreign in this society but that is exactly what we needed to do.

Eating was also something that you needed to learn how to do. In the field we mostly ate C-rations. C-rations come in cases of 12 meals; 4 created for breakfast, 4 for lunch and 4 for dinner. All cases contained the same combinations, so you needed to be very creative in how you prepared your meals, 13 months was a long time to be satisfied with 12 meals.

When I first got to Vietnam, in the field we were receiving C-rations that were left over from WWII. Many of the meals were bad, you could tell because the ends of the cans were swollen and bulging, a key indicator that the meal had spoiled.

Even the tins that seemed ok produced unpredictable results. Peanut butter, which was common in most meals, was separated. You would open the tin and find the peanut oil on top and the butter packed on the bottom. You would need to take your spoon and stir this up to reactivate the natural texture of the peanut butter. The old C-rations created many challenges and many times you wound up with something that was unsuitable for eating.

Out in the field, it was not that easy to have a hot meal. Before you entertained having a meal, you needed to create a stove to cook the meal on, this alone was a learning experience. Within each C-ration meal, there were all different sizes of cans, some tall, some short. You created your cooking stove from one of the shorter cans, something that would be low to the ground. You would take this tin and cut it in such a way to create a tin that would allow you to cook something if it was placed on top.

There is a basic tool that comes with each case of C-ration called P-38s. A P-38 was this small device that you held between your index finger and thumb and allowed you to open any type of can. I'm sure that pure military genius made this device available and if you asked any veteran that served in Vietnam what a P-38 was, they would pull their original one out of their pocket. Minimally with this small tool, which most troops carried around a chain on their neck, allowed you to open any can better than any automatic can opener could do.

To create your cooking stove, you took your P-38 and a small can and put numerous breathing holes in the sides of the can. You also put cuts in the can which would enable you to push numerous areas of the can in, creating ample breathing passages to allow the stove to work properly. These really became a work of art, each person creating their own style of cooking stove.

Once you created a good cooking stove, you saved it. At the end of each meal, you would let it cool down and then you would pack it away in your pack for safekeeping. Cooking in the field was always a challenge even if you did have a good cooking stove.

You had two sources of heating fuel. The basic fuel was called Trioxane, which was a blue tablet that came in a tin foil wrapper. Trioxane was a fuel that you lit with a match that would burn without displaying a flame, a must for any infantryman out in what we called Injun Country. You could heat your meal with Trioxane and it was very effective.

Unfortunately we needed to cook many of our meals after dark and we would normally cover ourselves with a poncho or other material that would hide what we were doing from the enemy while trying to cook. The toxic fumes that Trioxane gave off were enough to make you cry for a year. It went straight for the eyes and disabled your vision, that is if you were foolish enough to do all of this under a poncho and without letting the fuel get enough oxygen. Painful as it was, we needed to do this time and time again because we had no alternative. We needed to eat and we wanted our meal warm so we put up with just about anything.

Unfortunately we were the infantry and we didn't always get the supplies that we deserved, quite often we would not get any Trioxane tablets to cook with. Because of this, we became very creative. Early on we learned that many devices contained Charlie-4 or what was better known as C-4. C-4 is a solid, moldable plastic explosive that is most commonly found in satchel charges, land mines and claymore anti personnel mines.

We learned very early on that you could take C-4 and light it with a match or cigarette, and it would burn but not blow up. You had to take chunks of it and roll it into little balls that would fit in the base of your stove and then touch it off with a match or cigarette. It burnt with a bright flash and very fast so we couldn't use it at night but it was still a viable alternative for what we could use to cook our meals. Many times, we would leave some defense perimeters and all the defensive devices on that perimeter that contained C-4 would be empty of the key explosive. We hated to do this but it was the survival of the fittest and we were attempting to be the fittest.

Eating was always a challenge, regardless if you were in an enemy-infested area or not. Sometimes you ate while you were humping along, other times you ate when you could actually cook your food and enjoy it, enjoying your food was a rarity. On a rare occasion, they would bring warm chow out to us but it was truly a rarity.

During these early days in the field, I can remember watching some of the more seasoned troops and observing some of the things that they did. I can remember watching them squatting around their cook stoves brewing a cup of C-ration coffee. Some of these men had sores on their arms, what we called jungle rot, caused by scratches that got infected. They would squat there, stirring their coffee like nothing was going on.

The climate and living conditions in Vietnam took everything to another level. There were millions of insects and other pests, the two most irritating were the mosquitoes and the flies. During the day, the flies were around you by the hundreds.

They were the smaller black flies that actually feel like they bite and they were merciless. I watched this Marine preparing his coffee and there were two or three flies on each sore on his arms as well as on the lip of his coffee cup. Naive as I was, I couldn't understand why he wasn't at least attempting to shoo them away; he just sat there stirring his coffee. Eventually I learned. There were so many flies that as soon as you would wave your hand to shoo one batch away, a new group was already in place, why waste the effort?

The third day of Medina was quiet for 2nd Platoon. We took part in a company-sized patrol and fortunately there were no enemy sightings and no contact. Even with a unit this size, the patrol was conducted with strict rules about noise and talking. The unit was spread out in multiple V formations, which was one of the safer formations.

A point person would be in the lead and the following members would begin the reversed V with a good space, or interval, between each Marine. The command unit would be in the middle of the V, well protected by the point elements, and the remainder of the troops to their left and right. One fire team would be positioned in the back of the V as rear security, ensuring that no one was sneaking up from behind.

During these patrols, we would stop often. Sometimes, it was to check out areas of concern or to check the actual progress of the patrol using a map and compass. Whenever the formation stopped, each individual would face outboard and usually kneel on one knee. Each individual was responsible for scanning the countryside, looking for enemy movement or areas that should be searched.

If the intense sun was out, you needed to be careful on how you were sitting, kneeling or standing. If there was a baggy part of your uniform that was directly exposed to the sun, it would get very hot, as if it had just been ironed. When you stood or moved and this material would touch your leg or arm, it would actually burn and you had to move quickly to lift it off of your skin. It was just one more discomfort that you needed to learn how to deal with.

We made it back to our positions and began getting ready for another long night. At one point during the night when Cpl Waight was checking the lines, I was on watch. While he was there talking to me, we heard a single shot fired from somewhere inside our perimeter. Waight immediately squatted down, possibly thinking that another battle was about to begin. There was no additional gunfire, so we were both somewhat confused.

Early the next morning, Waight came by our position and filled us in on what had happened. Two days earlier when the helicopters came in with supplies, they also brought out some new troops. One of these men was a navy corpsman that had been assigned to our platoon.

It seems that after being in Vietnam for two days, he had enough and used his 45 caliber pistol and shot one of his toes off- a definite way to get out of the field. Of my 13 months there, I think that was the most drastic measure I heard of anyone taking to get out of the field. There were many other less drastic attempts, but that was the worst.

On a daily basis, the new troops would do things that would cause a chuckle among the older troops. Simple things like brushing your teeth or washing your hands in a stream made them chuckle. Eventually, you began to change as well. I personally don't think it was because of the chuckling, it was just something you did. After a short period of time, the toothbrush got used less and less and washing your hands was something that was almost worthless.

Although it was quiet where we were, you could always hear the sounds of war off in the distance. There were always planes and helicopters flying around; not necessarily for you, but on their way to another unit out there somewhere. You could always hear artillery being fired in one direction or another and the distant crumping of the highly explosive (HE) rounds crashing to the ground.

One afternoon, we were on patrol and had taken a break on the side of one of the rolling hills. It was sometime in the afternoon and it was very quiet around us. Somewhere out in front of us, not too far away, a Marine unit got into a major
battle. It's hard to describe the intensity of a fight like this, but it is very intense. All at one time, there were M-16s, M-60 machine guns, grenade launchers, mortars, and many other firearms going off and a lot of bullets flying.

The fight went on and on, and Cpl Waight was sitting next to me, picking his teeth with a piece of straw grass. I leaned towards him and asked him why we weren't going down there to help. He looked at me and took his time in saying, "It's not our fight. When it's our fight, we'll be on our own as well." This didn't make much sense to me, but I wasn't going to say anything. Later I learned that the firefights and battles that you got involved in were bad enough, you didn't need to be a John Wayne and start looking for more.

The remainder of Operation Medina went without incident and before we knew it, there was a rumor that we were going somewhere north, and I didn't like the sound of that.

Jungle fighting, Operation Granite October 1967

Early one morning, we were instructed to pack up and to get ready to move out, not on patrol but permanently. We took what little trash we had, dumped it in the bottom of our foxhole and shoveled all the dirt back in, trying to minimize the number of foxholes the enemy would have a chance to use.

By midday, the CH-34 helicopters were coming back to pick us up and ferry us to a base camp somewhere up north. When we got out of the helicopters, we were just outside the firebase called Camp Carroll, which was slightly east of the area known as the Rockpile and further west was Khe Sanh. Like stray dogs, we weren't allowed inside the perimeter of Camp Carroll, so we had to dig in outside of their concertina wire- that's the razor-edged wire that comes in rolls and is strung between metal fence posts. The intensity of battle sounds was much greater here than where we were during Operation Medina. There were air strikes and artillery bombardments going on constantly to the north and west of us all day and night.

We stayed here a couple of days and supplies came in, telling us that we were getting ready to jump off on another operation but we had no idea what or where. This operation was called Granite, and we were going high in the mountains for this one. Again, the helicopters came and picked us up and flew us somewhere, but this time it was like landing on Okinawa, where we trained for jungle warfare. The helicopter I was on came in and hovered about 5 or 8 feet off the ground, forcing us to jump. Fortunately, the landing zone was not jungle, it was a marshy area with tall elephant grass. We were also fortunate that Charlie wasn't there to greet us-this was another quiet landing.

We immediately moved out of the marshy area and began a climb up the backside of a jungle-laced mountain. It was very eerie moving out of the sun-drenched marsh and into triple canopy jungle, almost as if someone turned out the lights. In comparison to the sunny area, the jungle was cooler but much harder to travel in.

We climbed and climbed and eventually began to dig in for the night. I thought being on open ground at night in Vietnam was scary, but boy was I mistaken. If it was dark in the jungle during the day, imagine how dark it was at night. The only thing you could do on hole watch was listen. At times, you tried to listen so hard it almost hurt. Fortunately the first night Mike and I stood regular perimeter watch, which was bad, but not as bad as an ambush or a listening post. The second night we weren't as lucky.

The second day was as uneventful as the first, which was a very good thing. By mid-afternoon, we were digging in again for yet another night. Somewhere during this process, one of the men in our squad had a minor accident.

There's a weapon called an M-79 grenade launcher, which looks like a sawed-off shotgun with a barrel that could shoot a pool ball. These were single-shot weapons but they fired miniature grenades. Once fired, the grenade traveled approximately 50 feet before it was activated, somewhat of a safety measure.

The nickname for this weapon was Blooper, because when the round was fired, it sounded exactly like "bloop." This guy Ray, who was our grenadier, was digging his foxhole and he had his grenade launcher leaning against a tree- it needs to be said that the launcher was loaded with a high explosive grenade.

Just as it was getting dark, either Ray or someone else bumped the tree and his launcher fell, landing butt-first in the bottom of the foxhole. The jolt released the safety and the gun fired, sending the grenade skyward. Everyone dove for cover and the grenade came down outside our perimeter and exploded safely in a gorge. Needless to say, Lt Debruler came marching down the lines to find out what happened and even though it was an accident, he was really pissed at Ray.

Ray arrived in Vietnam with us and I felt bad for him getting off on the wrong foot. One thing that you don't want to do is give your position away or to let the enemy know you were there at all. Although we were a large unit on the move, until now everything had been very quiet. With Ray's mishap, the enemy would know for sure the Americans were out there somewhere.

That night, Mike and I were designated to go out on a listening post. A listening post is a two-man task where you crawl out in front of the lines 50 to 80 meters with a communications radio and find a relatively safe place to hide. Your task is to simply stay awake and listen. You don't do any talking; all communications are done by pushing buttons on the communications radio's handset. Someone would ask you to press the keyset once if everything was alright or otherwise press the keyset twice, that's all there was to it. Sounds easy, but emotionally you were terrified, out in front of the lines, all alone with who knows what crawling around you.

I think it was terrifying because it was mine and Mike's first listening post. For whatever reason, Bruce, our squad leader, was going to join us. Believe me- Mike and I were not complaining. It was getting dark and the three of us were near the perimeter. Bruce was checking out the radio and making sure that Mike and I were carrying the proper gear. Somewhere out in the darkness came the growl of what we were assuming was a tiger. The three of us just looked at each other and Bruce said, "Shit, we don't need this kind of aggravation tonight!"

Off we went, first walking then crawling through the jungle. Bruce was in the lead, Mike was carrying the radio and I was in the rear. We went much further than I thought was necessary and eventually, Mike and I crawled up alongside Bruce. Bruce had found a huge thorn bush and with much effort, the three of us crawled deep into the middle of it. As bad as it was, none of us were complaining.

The tiger, even if he did come near us, would think differently about coming into that thorn bush after us and the NVA wouldn't even assume we would be in there.

Still, none of us slept at all that night. Here we had a wonderful opportunity to catch up on some sleep with three of us taking turns at watch, but that tiger made it impossible!
I can't say if he was ever really nearby, but he was on the prowl all night and periodically let out a growl. The night went without incident and the three of us took turns answering the status calls on the radio. Early the next morning, we made our way back to the perimeter, the three of us pissed off and tired.

On one of the upcoming days, the unit was on the move in the mountains. We didn't make much headway each day; in the dense vegetation, you couldn't travel in the V formation and had to use existing trails or create your own. There were numerous pre-made trails that showed signs of being well- traveled, so we knew Charlie had been here recently. As usual, there were always rumors as to where we were and the current scuttlebutt said we were somewhere in the A Shau Valley, a known hideout of the NVA due to the dense jungle. They felt so safe here they used it as a rest and recuperation, or R&R site.

On this one day, we were making slow forward progress and there were at least one or two platoons ahead of us on the trail. All of a sudden, there was this tremendous release of gunfire quite a distance to our front. Everyone took immediate precautions to get down and alternate facing to the right and left. The battle up ahead raged for an few intense minutes but then fell silent. Quickly the word came down the line that our lead elements had reacted to what they thought was an ambush. It seemed that the path they were on had some very dense vegetation to their left and apparently there was another path directly on the other side. At one point, one of our Marines caught sight of something moving in the opposite direction on the other side and yelled ambush left.

There are times when the intense Marine training comes back in your favor. For days, weeks and months, you are taught how to react in certain situations- ambushes being one of them. If someone in the patrol sees something that could be an ambush or an ambush is actually triggered against the unit, someone will yell to alert everyone of the ambush and which direction to focus the reaction in, like "ambush left" or "ambush right."

As part of your response, you held your weapon at waist level and aimed just above the ground, slightly out in front of you. Any enemy in ambush formation will normally be lying on the ground, so any bullets fired straight out would be a waste. While firing, you would fan your fire from left to right, making sure that you are creating interlocking fire with the Marines to your left and right. In an ambush, whoever gains fire superiority first will be the victor. Marines with M-16s, M-60 machine guns and M-79 grenade launchers can put out a tremendous amount of firepower; enough to overwhelm most units. Our reaction to the sighting worked, but the results were not exactly what we expected.

When the lead elements felt everything was over, they began searching the other side of the hedgerow. The reality of what they found impacted everyone, but at the same time made you realize what we were up against. What they found were 8 NVA bodies who were believed to be on a search patrol looking for American aggressors. What was different for us was they were all female, it was a female squad we had ambushed.

They didn't go down without a fight, as two of our Marines were wounded but with only minor flesh wounds. The impact of fighting females was dealt with at an individual level and I don't think any one of us were comfortable with this news.

Our unit moved on and we eventually stopped and dug in for another long dark night. We went on for a couple more days with no major contact, just periodic sounds of the war going on somewhere in the distance. One morning we had just moved out and our forward elements came under fire, this time not by a single squad.

As the battle raged, we were moving forward slowly, trying to make our way up to where the enemy had made contact. At this point, we had all moved off the trail and were moving side-by-side as much as possible but the heavy vegetation made this difficult. We were trying to run at some points and then diving for cover as bullets went cracking by our heads. We moved as far forward as we could and the battle was taking place right in front of us but we couldn't see anything, the dense jungle blocking our view.

The smell of the fight caught me off guard. When you mix the smell of gunpowder, vegetation being destroyed by high explosives and the heaviness of the air in the jungle, it gave off a smell all its own. It wasn't disgusting, just unique enough where you would never forget it.

Finally, the enemy broke contact and everything was quiet. We had taken some casualties, which was difficult to deal with in the jungle. There were numerous injuries in addition to a couple of deaths. We learned that the unit involved in the action was from Delta Company.

The Marine, John, who I knew from Charleston was in Delta Company and unfortunately he was one of the men wounded. He was a machine gunner, a position that was one of the primary targets in any battle. A few of us from 2nd Platoon were told to go up to were the casualties were and help carry down some of the bodies. We walked up there very slowly, everyone was still on edge because the enemy could come back at any second.

I can't remember who I was with, but the two of us picked up the ends of a poncho with a dead Marine inside. I know at one level we were both dealing with the fact that we were carrying a dead Marine, but I know what surprised me was how heavy the dead body was. It was a real struggle to keep the poncho off the ground as we made our way back down the trail. On top of that, jungle trails are seldom dry. It was a very painful, slow process of trying to keep the poncho off the ground and make headway.

My personal feelings were of unexpected emotions. This was a detail that none of us ever trained for and the emotions that were wrapped up in it at a personal level were gripping. I didn't share any of these feelings with the person who was trying to carry that poncho with me, I was assuming he was dealing with this in his own way. My frustration over not being able to carry this dead Marine with any kind of respect almost brought me to tears. Neither of us knew who he was, but it didn't matter, he was a Marine, one of us and he deserved better. For the first time in my military career, I wished I was a huge strong person, someone that could carry this precious load with ease, but unfortunately that was not the case.

The Marines did an excellent job of preparing their own for combat at many different levels. You were taught to work as a team, you were taught to follow orders without hesitation, and all of this worked as it should. But there were numerous things they didn't prepare you for and caring for your own dead was not addressed at all.

Usually under the triple canopy, there was always dripping moisture that kept everything on the jungle floor damp, if not wet. Slipping on the trail, especially with this awkward weight was something that was happening more often than not, and it was a very difficult trip. We cussed and swore every time we slipped, not for ourselves but more out of respect for the dead Marine we were carrying. Each time we would move a few feet with some confidence, one of us would slip, pulling the other down with him. We were really pissed; we had gone through numerous levels of training trying to get ready for Vietnam but nowhere did that training come close to this, how could it?

No one offered to help, this was an assignment that was yours until you reached your goal. On our way, we passed many Marines and there was always dead silence. Everyone knew it could be them in the poncho instead, and we had total respect for the dead.

We didn't even know where we were going, all I know is that we were being told to continue lower and lower down the side of the mountain. Eventually we got to an area where all the casualties were brought. There was a break in the trees above us and they were trying to get the helicopters in for medivac extractions.

We were told to stay around to help the corpsman any way that we could and also to help load the wounded. This was far uglier than I ever imagined. The only way that the helicopters could get these men out was by dropping a device called a jungle penetrator, which was a folded chair harness on the end of an extraction cable. While we waited for the choppers to arrive, we sat back with not too much to do. The chaos of the corpsman working on the wounded was enough to shock me. They were a wonder to watch, patching these men up temporarily, hoping that they would make it to the better medical facilities in the rear areas.

I was really taken aback when I saw John, my friend from Charleston, propped up on the side of the trail, obviously he was one of the Marines who had been wounded. I went over and sat on the ground next to him and luckily I could see that his wounds were not life-threatening. I can't remember exactly where he was wounded, but he was hurt bad enough to be medevac'd.

I knew he was somewhat short and hoped that after he was better, they would not return him to the field, but that was something neither John nor I had any control over. He was very calm and quiet, possibly thinking about what was going to happen next and how they were going to get him and the others out of there.

We heard some choppers in the distance and someone popped a smoke grenade in the clearing- a visible signal to the pilots as to where we were. As the first chopper came into view above the trees, they signaled to John to get ready to be loaded. John could walk, so he got up and moved to the general area where the penetrator would be coming down.

The device made its way down through the exposed branches and we worked with John to get him into the seat as best we could. I remember looking at him just before they began to pull him up and there was a look of distance, it was hard to determine where he was at that moment. My only guess was that it was of someplace safe.

They began to raise John and he went up slower than I thought he should have. Maybe that was because he was wounded or maybe it was the normal speed of the winch, but it did seem quite slow. We couldn't see everything that was taking place up on the choppers, they were above the trees and the trees in the mountains were very tall. Eventually the penetrator began its way down again, and we prepared the next wounded Marine for his trip. I didn't know this man at all and he was quite chatty, probably more from being nervous than anything else. He was also able to stand and getting him into the seat was as easy as John.

We were just finishing strapping him in when we started receiving small arms fire from slightly up the ridge. The enemy had heard the choppers and determined where they were coming in. Now they were coming down the ridge to do some damage.

The radio operator communicated to the chopper that the Marine was ready and the winch was started slowly, pulling the chair upwards. By now the Marine was not chatty at all. He was scared shitless, bullets were flying everywhere and here he was, strapped into a chair and slowly going skyward. The NVA had worked their way down the ridge and were starting to lay down some very effective volleys, keeping everyone around the LZ pinned down. Some of our other troops were making their way over to where the NVA had positioned themselves, but moving in the jungle was making their progress slow. The chair was halfway up when the NVA moved into a position where the chopper was in view, and they were opening fire on the bottom of the chopper. The pilot indicated to the ground crew that they were taking hits and he needed to move. These were some of the unfortunate events that went on day after day and you never wanted to be on the bad side of one.

Unfortunately in this case, it turned even uglier. The chopper needed to move to get away from the ground fire, and was dragging the Marine in the extraction chair through the trees by doing so. It wasn't long before everyone knew that the Marine never had a chance. When they did get the chair up to the helicopter, he was definitely a mess and had died from being dragged through the branches.

It wasn't over yet, there were still more wounded and dead who needed to be pulled out. By now, the reinforcements had made their way to our side of the ridge and were starting to lay down some return fire down on the NVA. The size of the NVA group had grown and this began to be a considerable battle.

The trick was to keep them busy or pinned down while the remainder of the medevacs were completed. All the Marines who were wounded and still on the ground were completely terrified of what was going to happen to them. Its one thing to be on the ground and being able to fight and to defend yourself, but these men were going skyward with no protection, something very unnatural for a Marine.

One by one, the remaining wounded were put in their chairs and hoisted upwards to the helicopters without another nasty incident. The ground crew was having a very difficult time kneeling or standing to get these men into the chairs while still receiving incoming fire from the NVA. It took two Marines to hold the chair and assist the wounded Marine into place. When it got to the dead, it was even more difficult. It took four Marines to complete each one of these and sometimes all of us were standing in a tight group waiting for the helicopter to raise the chair. Eventually they had all been extracted and we had not incurred any additional wounded.

With the helicopters gone, the NVA broke contact and things became quiet again. I made my way back up the trail to where all this began and found my squad. They had already started setting the lines and we needed to dig in, but this time it was much different.

Periodically, we were getting ground fire from sporadic areas out in front of us while we dug in. We purposely did not return fire, we didn't want to give away where our positions would be. From now on, this operation was going to be a challenge. Charlie was out there and he was plenty mad. We had killed some of their female NVA soldiers and I'm sure we inflicted some casualties on them this day as well. Each night from now on was going to bring the feeling of being scared to another level.

This night I was assigned to dig in with Ralph, who always had a good sense of humor. The position we were given was very near the edge of a cliff. After we had dug our fighting position, there was only a foot or two between our hole and the edge.

Ironically this was the end of October and we all knew that it was Halloween back home, trick or treat. Right from the beginning of the night, Ralph and I could hear activity down at the bottom of the gorge and we were confident the enemy was trying to make their way up the side of the cliff. We had one of our shift changes right around midnight and it was Ralph's turn to take watch.

Before I began to try and sleep, I heard Ralph rumbling around for something- remember, it is completely pitch black where we are. I said, "What the hell are you doing?" Ralph responded, saying that he was getting ready for a celebration and he had dug out two M-26 fragmentation grenades.

He gave one to me and kept one for himself. At the same time we pulled the pins and held the grenades over the side of the cliff, releasing them at the same time. We could hear them clink and clank as they fell, having 4 seconds before they would blow.

Eventually they both exploded. I heard Ralph chuckle as he said, "Happy Halloween, mother fuckers." In the dead silence of the night, the two blasts from below sent a jolt through everyone and immediately someone crawled over to our hole to find out what had happened. At least this time, what we did was legit and there were no further questions. For the remainder of the night, we heard thrashing and moaning from deep in the gorge: payback.

A number of days had passed since we began this campaign and getting re-supplied with food and ammunition had become a major task. Because of the triple canopy, the helicopter pilots couldn't see the smoke grenades that traditionally marked a drop zone. Basically, they had no idea where we were below them. Periodically, they were instructed to drop their loads when we thought they were directly above us. Sometimes we wound up with some smashed supplies and other times we had no idea where they wound up. Needless to say, we were running very low on food and anything that moved or an attractive berry became an enticing meal- we were becoming exceptionally creative with our attempts to find food.

I don't know if it was because of the supply situation or if it was the planned duration of the campaign, but we eventually began to make our way out of the mountains. Unfortunately, Charlie was still really pissed at us and followed behind us every step of the way.

I don't know if it was because of the dense jungle, but for some wonderful reason they never worked their way around to our front and ambushed us, they were always attacking our rear elements. Each day, one of the four companies took over the rear guard responsibilities, which meant that you minimally had a fight on your hands once every four days, sometimes more depending where they were hitting us from. Casualties were mounting, but now we had no way of getting them out by chopper so we needed to carry the dead and help the wounded, which slowed us down considerably.

Eventually we made our way back to what appeared to be the same place we landed many days earlier. Initially it was nice to get out of the constant darkness and dampness of the jungle, but within minutes we were dying from the intensity of the merciless sun. At least at this point we could call in the choppers, which came in dumping out cases of C-rations and ammo, and carried away our dead and wounded.

At first there was no time to eat, we just tore open the cases and made sure everyone had at least one meal before we were on our way. We were forced to hump back to Camp Carroll which was a considerable distance from the base of the mountains, and the first task was to get out of this marsh, laden with elephant grass. All through the marsh, we were in numerous columns, a point person with a machete in the lead. Elephant grass is very tall and strong, and the edges of the long stalks were like razor blades.

The lead person's responsibility was to try to hack, stomp, or fall on the stalks in order to create a path for everyone behind them. In the heat of the sun, this was a painful undertaking. Humping normally was hard enough in the sun, but with this additional physical effort, you got so hot you thought your head was going to explode inside your helmet.

With all the hacking, stomping and falling the lead person needed to do to make any headway in the elephant grass, his body took the brunt of it. The razor-like edges of the grass cut time and time again and each Marine's arms were covered with blood. The sweat running down our arms would bring additional pain to these tiny slits. The route out of the marsh seemed to take forever and the point people were thoroughly exhausted.

The marsh floor was wet and muddy, causing us to stop every half hour or so for leech checks. Everyone would stop and take turns stripping with another Marine close by standing guard. Time after time, there were numerous leeches found crawling everywhere and were carefully removed either by a burning cigarette, a drop of insect repellent, or salt out of a C- ration salt packet. This took more time than you can imagine; we each needed to strip not only out of our fatigues, but our packs and other gear as well. Standing in the tall grass, we were completely isolated even from troops 3 or 4 feet on either side of us, and the heat and humidity was unbearable.

Eventually we made it out of the marsh and began the long trek back to Camp Carroll, which we could periodically see way off in the distance. At least in the open we could get in more secure formations, and walking on firm ground again was a treat. I can't remember how long it took before we got back to the camp, but I do know when we were approaching the perimeter, it was quite dark- not a good time to be out in front of a defensive perimeter with nervous Marines at the ready.

Camp Carroll had numerous gates and each one was protected by what were called Dusters, which looked like small modified tanks. On either side of the turret, there were quad 40mm cannons that could put out many destructive rounds in a very short period of time. When they were being fired, they reminded me of the "Pom Pom guns" we all saw in the movies on the big battle ships of WWII. The crew would drop a sleeve of rounds down a chute and the guns would blare away.

We were slowly making our way up the access road to the camp and someone said they could hear the turret of at least one of the Dusters turning. At that point, we stopped and someone in our command section got on the radio to say there were friendlies coming in and to let the Dusters know immediately. Eventually, we got the go-ahead and made our way into the compound. Maybe it was because we got there after dark, but for some reason they let us stay within their perimeter, at least for the first night.

As hungry as we were, we set up camp but didn't have any major responsibilities with line watch or ambushes- tonight we had someone else protecting us, what a nice feeling. In the morning, we were sent out on patrol, scanning the rolling hills just north of the camp to ensure that Charlie didn't follow us all the way back.

We came back around midday and were told we would be served hot chow at one of the mess halls within the camp. In this part of the country, a mess hall is an area where they serve you food and you can eat either outside on the ground or under tents with standing tables.

I hadn't seen my friend Tom since we left Da Nang at the beginning of all this, but we bumped into each other while we were getting ready for chow. We only saw each other a few times during our 13 months in country, and each time it was like a mini reunion. Over the years and months of knowing each other, we had adopted each other's families. My grandmother along with my sister and all her co-workers were writing to Tom, and his parents and family were writing to me. When we got together like this, we would try to get caught up on what was going on back home. Most importantly, it was good to see the other was still there and in one piece. We never talked about it, but I knew it was on each of our minds.

We made our way over to the mess hall area and got in line for some hot food. When we got in front of the Marine that was serving the food, he looked up at the two of us and asked us where our mess gear, or food tray was. We couldn't believe our ears but it was obvious that we were not going to be able to eat unless we had something; mess gear was not something that grunts in the field ever carried or used. Tom and I got out of line and began searching everywhere for something that we could use, and eventually we came across some garbage cans in the back of the mess area that had some large, empty fruit cans in the trash. We each grabbed one and wiped it out with the shirttail of our jungle fatigues and got back in line. This time when we got in front of the server, he just looked at us. He said, "You're kidding, right?" We said, "No way, just start dumping the food in one on top of the other."

I can't remember what kind of meat it was, but it came with vegetables and mashed potatoes, though all together in the can it didn't look like much. I even think we got a container of milk, something we never saw. Through all our time together, Tom always accused me of eating too fast, saying with the way I ate, it would be very difficult for my body to digest the food properly. He ranked on me all the time about this and I must admit I did eat considerably faster than he did.

When we both had our meal in a can we went under the tent and found one of the standing tables to eat at. I can't remember what I was doing, but whatever it was prevented me from starting to eat right away. Eventually when I turned around and looked at Tom, he was shoveling his food into his mouth faster than I ever saw him eat before. I actually began to laugh and fed him some of the proper food etiquette that he had been dumping on me for years. Unfortunately he didn't take this lightly and actually got a little pissed at me.

Over the next couple of days, we made our way down both sides of Highway 9 to just north of the fire base at Cam Lo. This is the early part of November and we were running patrols in the area between Cam Lo and the next base further north, Charlie 2 or C2. These bases were all part of what was called McNamara's Wall.

At the very top of South Vietnam, there was the demilitarized zone, better known as the DMZ, also called "The Trace." The trace was a swath 600 or so meters wide that had been swept clear of all foliage by a group of engineers in the early phases of the war. There were some patches of new growth but for the most part it was a 600-meter clearing the width of Vietnam.

On the far western border of the DMZ was the infamous base of Con Thien. Traveling east, the next base, which they had just begun building, was Alpha 3 and further to the east closer to the coastline was Gio Linh. These three base camps, evenly separated, were the initial observation posts which tried to ensure no large enemy unit attempted to come straight across the DMZ into the south.

A short distance behind them were the base camps of Charlie 2 or C2, in the middle was Charlie 3, and on the coast Charlie 4, which we wouldn't begin working on until December. These bases constituted McNamara's Wall; I guess he thought with these in place, enemy troop movement from the North would be diminished to a trickle. Unfortunately, Vietnamese ingenuity and years of fighting a guerilla type of warfare showed their genius when they began developing what was to be called the Ho Chi Minh trail, a spider web of trails that ran along the border of Vietnam slightly to the west.

For the most part these were rolling hills with patches of vegetation, and the area was better known as Leatherneck Square. Running these patrols just North of Cam Lo was going pretty well and we hadn't had much contact. We had gone through the first few days of November and we were currently focusing on November 9th. For many people this is truly an insignificant day, but for Marines, it is the eve of the Marine Corps' birthday. Unlike other branches of the service, our heritage, our tradition focused on the almost holy day of November 10th. Although it was called Highway 9, it was nothing more than a dirt road, barely wide enough for two trucks to pass each other going different ways. On the eve of the 9th, we were split on both sides of Highway 9 with all companies sending out their own listening posts and ambushes in the evening. 2nd Platoon had theirs out and the ambush that night was positioned just in front of my fighting position, which was facing back towards the Cam Lo base. My foxhole was on one side of the road and directly on the other was a two-man position manned by Marines from 3rd Platoon. The night was going well, the only presence of war was the sound of distant artillery, an occasional flare and tracer bullets skipping their way across the night sky.

Early in the morning of the 10th, all hell broke loose directly out in front of our positions. The ambush had been triggered and the intensity of the battle raged on, seemingly endless. As usual, this was just before dawn and the smell of the gunpowder began to drift back over our foxholes.

As the day began, our squad was asked to join the squad who had triggered the ambush and search for enemy dead and wounded. We were exhausted, seemingly much more than usual. I was drenched with sweat and my hands were sticky, almost as if someone had sprayed tacky glue on them.

It was still mostly dark and we crept forward, moving slowly in the early morning ground fog. We moved out slowly and linked up with them to form a line, walking very slowly side by side to make sure we had a safe interval between one another. The intent was to sweep forward and force out any remaining NVA from wherever they were hiding. Initially, we had to move very slowly because the ground fog prevented us from seeing the detail we really needed.

Eventually, the early morning light began to help us and we could at least begin to see shadows. We finally got to what we thought was the ambush sight. It was obvious that a significant battle had taken place, there were spent cartridges everywhere. As we moved forward, we saw numerous pools of blood, dropped weapons and other pieces of NVA gear.
There were blood trails everywhere but no bodies. We searched and searched but there were none to be found.

This was one of our enemy's most significant traits. More often than not after a battle or firefight, we would never find the bodies of our victims. The enemy made a very powerful point by dragging their injured and dead away. Without the physical evidence, it always seemed as if we were fighting ghosts. There were always plenty of blood trails but usually our night activity seldom showed any KIAs or WIAs.

Now with a little more light, I looked down at my hands as they held my M-16. Everything was covered with blood. The M-16 was smeared with it, it was drying on my hands and my jungle fatigues were literally saturated with it. What the hell had happened? I looked around at other squad members and most were in the same visible shape. The numbness of the previous encounter was really setting in and now I was totally confused; why was I covered in blood?

I approached Ralph but he was in very bad shape, avoiding my eye contact and initial approach for conversation. As I went by him, I noticed he had fixed his bayonet to the end of his M- 16, though I don't remember getting word to do that. I glanced at the end of my M-16 and my bayonet was fixed as well, and I definitely didn't remember doing that. What ever had happened in the past few days for some reason was not recorded in my memory- nobody ever talked about it, and I never did find out what took place. Eventually, we all cautiously made our way back to our platoon's perimeter, frustrated that there was no proof of the outcome of the early morning ambush and now totally lost as to what really took place during the past eight or so hours.

We had taken some casualties and wounded, some more seriously wounded than others. A call went out for medevac choppers and as usual, when they began their decent, they started drawing ground fire from the enemy in the surrounding hills. Three choppers came in, one after the other, and Marines scrambled to get the wounded aboard.

By the time the third chopper was leaving, we had a mini battle going on towards our right flank. Parts of each squad were moved over to that flank and we began our assault on the hidden NVA. Regardless of our current attempt to quiet the NVA, all remaining medevacs were called off.

The ensuing firefight lasted until midmorning and by then, we had made our way to the hill where all the enemy fire had been coming from. There were definite signs that we had wounded numerous NVA but again, no bodies. After clearing the area, we made our way back to our positions close to Highway 9.

Because the last few choppers were not allowed to come in, we had some wounded Marines to tend to. One was our platoon sergeant, Ken Bouchard, who had been wounded in the leg. He was stuck out there with us for the remainder of the day and by the time he did get to Dong Ha for treatment, some serious infections had already set in- the climate and dirt of Vietnam was very good at escalating things like that.

That day, our platoon had line watch while other elements were out on patrols. During the course of the day, numerous trucks were coming north on Highway 9, bringing out supplies. Not just the normal stuff but more importantly, all the ingredients for a Marine Corps birthday celebration, and most important of all: mail. There were the special insulated buckets which, meant we were going to get hot chow, cases of soda and even a birthday cake, all lined up on both sides of the road directly behind my fighting position. We couldn't wait for all the patrols to get in so we could begin this annual celebration.

The squad leaders were called up to our platoon command post or CP, and we all assumed it was to discuss how to distribute all the goodies while keeping everyone safe and still protecting the perimeter at the same time. Woody came walking back down the lines with a look of disbelief on his face. We all looked at him and waited for him to share what his instructions were. When we heard what he had to say, we couldn't believe our ears and we were all so pissed that I'm surprised no one flipped out. What he needed to share with us was the most unpopular phrase to any grunt in Vietnam: saddle up. That meant break camp, pack your packs, draw any ammunition or C-ration supplies needed, because we were going to move out.

And move out we did. Our entire battalion saddled up, got in operational formations and humped past all the goodies stacked up on the side of the road. Not one bit of it got touched, even the mail was left behind. It's hard to describe the psychological impact of a move like this. We were all in disbelief that they would do this to us, the grunts of all people. We all knew, far too well, that all the rear areas would be having a wonderful party which would last long into the night

Off we went into another operation, one that would take us through the next couple of weeks. We humped straight up Highway 9 until we got to the outer perimeter of Con Thien, which was laced with the traditional concertina wire. By the time we got there, we had a good number of hours to get madder and madder, and we were thirsty, hungry and grumpy.

I can remember being near the wire and someone from our unit yelled in to a Marine within the Con Thien base, asking if we could get some water from their water buffalo, which is a water storage tank on wheels.

The little shit had the nerve to yell back that he couldn't help us and for us to get our own. Water was a precious commodity in Vietnam, one you never had enough of. This guy really ticked us off and he had no idea on how close he came from something very serious happening. There were times I couldn't believe how much crap we took and never took revenge, and there were times that it seemed like the crap issue would never end.

After all of that, our excursion north turned out to be a real waste of time. There were days and nights when we made contact, but nothing of significance and it seemed to me as if we had made one very large loop around the northern area. One day we were humping along, completely exhausted, and we were told to hold up, so we all took our normal positions facing outboard.

We had stopped alongside a base camp, and as I was looking, I was facing directly into the perimeter and I couldn't believe it! We were back at Con Thien. There were some Marines walking around inside the compound and some of them came over very near to us just inside of the concertina wire. They were asking questions of us and none of us would answer, not one word in response. All we did was give them this very cold look, one that would cut through someone with the thickest hide. We were so pissed at them. They didn't deserve anything from us, we all hoped they got the message.

Much to our surprise, there was a convoy of trucks coming to pick us up; we weren't going to have to hump all the way back to Cam Lo. We all packed onto the backs of the 6-by's for a most pleasant ride to somewhere. We really didn't care where- getting a ride was wonderful.

We went right past Cam Lo and continued on to the larger base of Dong Ha. The engineers had set up platoon-sized tents for us and we had a wonderful night without obligation, but with very little partying. The sergeant in charge of the mess hall had kept his facility open even though it was very late by the time we got there. We all took turns going in and we were fed a wonderful steak dinner with all the trimmings, even some fresh Italian-style bread, what a treat. It had started raining, so we made our way back to our tents to start what we thought was going to be a dry night with no watches.

It wasn't long before we were all laying down, using any parts of our gear as pillows to get a long overdue nights sleep. When the engineers set up the tents, they forgot to dig irrigation ditches to funnel the runoff from the roofs away from the tents. I don't know how long we were asleep, but the runoff began to make its way into our tent and before long, the water was ankle-deep and rising.

Most of us were completely drenched and we were now standing, trying to stay out of the water. The tent sides were down and someone had a squad flashlight that we used to look around for our gear. Someone noticed Ralph, who had fallen asleep next to me, still asleep on his back. The water had reached just above his chin; fortunately, he breathed through his nose when he slept. He just laid there on his back sleeping, as if nothing was wrong- none of us could believe our eyes, but he slept most of the night while the rest of us stood.

As it became daylight, we were all milling around our designated tents completely miserable. The rain had let up somewhat but we were all still soaked and cold. The word came down that our captain wanted everyone to fall out in company formation. This even created more grumbling- very seldom did we ever have this type of formation, and as a matter of fact, it was the first time we had since we left the ships.

With some hesitation, we took our respective positions within our squad and platoon, and waited to hear what the big man had to say. He came out of his tent and we were all called to attention, and he began reading us the riot act. He was accusing us of robbing the mess hall of everything that wasn't bolted down and was edible. He had been reamed by the commanding officer who was in charge of the mess hall and apparently, many things had been stolen.

In our defense, we all learned very quickly in Vietnam. When you are a grunt out in the field, you literally got the leftovers. All the clerks and other staff in the rear had all the comforts of home: clean fatigues, hot chow and many other perks.

Whenever it came to us, we got the bottom of the barrel. Every now and then, we were provided an opportunity to acquire some things that we could use out in the field, usually food items but we were very flexible and creative.

We all knew what took place the night before. All night long, you could hear men coming and going, and usually when they were making their way back into our tent they were snickering. Some had made off with food stores, others cooking items and utensils. The food would always go to good use, but I could see the metal items being discarded shortly after we moved out because nobody would really want to hump the extra weight.

Our captain was really chewing us out but I had a feeling deep down he was ok with what we did; after all, we were his grunts. Part of the reason for the formation was an announcement that we were going back to the ships for Thanksgiving, which was wonderful news for everyone. Eventually, he released us from formation and we began getting our gear ready for transportation. We were to take Mike Boats back to the ships, and they had come up the Cua Viet River to pick us up at Dong Ha. We humped down Highway 9 for a short stint and came to the docking area.

Slowly but surely we were all loaded onto Mike Boats for our journey down the river.

Finally a break, early November 1967

Ralph and I had been standing together and we were some of the last people from 2nd Platoon to get on our boat. Everyone in front of us had taken what seemed to be the prime locations and us stragglers didn't have much choice of where to go. Before we got in the boat, they had loaded a 6 by, which had a 105 howitzer in tow, and the back of the 6 by was filled with empty 105 howitzer casings. One of the few places left was actually standing on the wheels of the howitzer, leaning on the gun barrel; these were the positions that Ralph and I chose.

Eventually, all the Mike Boats pulled away from shore and began the long trek down the river. Everything seemed so peaceful. Off in the distance you could hear the sounds of war, but it was somewhere else, not here.

The river was dead calm except for the minimal waves the Mike Boats made, and it was almost surreal. On both sides of the river there were numerous Vietnamese villages- some fishing villages, others rice harvesting villages, but all beautiful. Everything seemed to move in slow motion.

Watching the villagers plow their rice fields walking behind slow-moving water buffalos with the rich green of the bamboo bordering village was like watching a travel log, it was simply beautiful.

The rain had stopped and for the time being, the sun was out and it was very hot on the boat. Ralph and I were standing directly in front of the naval crew who was piloting the boat and they had a million questions for us smelly, disgusting Marines. Ralph and I shared what we were willing to share as long as they kept giving some of the food they had stored on board. Ralph and I were talking about the 6 by and the artillery piece and we were wondering why they were chained down to the deck with heavy chains- we both thought it was over kill.

It was a slow process getting down the river, but eventually we made it to the mouth where it flowed into the South China Sea. From our observation post on top of the gun, Ralph and I didn't like what we saw. The turbulence ahead created some of the highest waves I have ever seen. Some of the other troops were standing, looking over the sides of the boat, and no one was saying a word. The sailors didn't seem overly concerned- if anything, I think they were entertained with the looks of worry on every Marine's face. Now things started to happen quicker and we were swiftly swept away into the heavy waves. Ralph and I held on to that gun barrel for dear life.

The Mike Boat would go struggling up the backside of a wave just to go roller coaster-style flying down the other to what seemed to be a bottomless pit. There were times when I swore that I looked up and all I could see was a wall of water all around us and a speck of blue sky way above. Once the boat was at the bottom of each swell, it began its climb up the next wave and you could feel the boat struggling to make it up each one.

As the boat climbed, I noticed the front wheels of the truck lifting off the deck and I poked Ralph to make sure he saw what was going on, too. At this point of our ride, we had a different appreciation for those reinforced chains. This seemed to last forever and all the gear on the boat was thrown every which way. Waves were coming over the bow and the sides, and everyone below was completely drenched. Ralph and I seemed to have lucked out; we were both very dry and at this point, having a wonderful ride.

Eventually the boats made it out of the mouth of the river and into open ocean, which was somewhat calmer than the mouth, but not much. The ships were nowhere to be found at this point, they were most likely positioned just over the horizon. It took most of the remaining day for the boats to make it to the main ships.

By now, almost everyone on board had gotten seasick from the constant motion. It was truly a mess down below Ralph and I. Everyone was throwing up and most of them were not making it to the sides of the boat. The water in the bottom of the boat was almost knee-deep and most of the Marines didn't care, they just sat there, washing back and forth with the water.

Ralph and I were still hanging in and we could see our ships off in the distance. The sailors were still feeding us and they offered us sardines on crackers which Ralph took eagerly and I hesitated, but still took them. It had been so long since I had decent food that I went ahead and ate it, not really caring what it was.

Everything was going fine until the sailors needed to make a maneuver prior to going into the hold of the ship. Our ship was sitting there and the back end was slowly opening, exposing the internal docks that the Mike Boats needed to come in to. For some reason, all the Mike Boats needed to come alongside each other prior to coming into the hold and to do so, our boat needed to go backwards.

It didn't hit me at first, but eventually the change in direction threw off all the measures I had in place for not getting sick. It hit me like a punch in the stomach and I still blame it on those sardines. I jumped off of the gun and landed in the water next to where Cpl Waight was sitting, pale as a ghost. I was really sick and grabbed his helmet from the gun carriage and pulled out the helmet liner. With that, I sat alongside Straight, throwing up in his helmet, which I thought was somewhat better than in the water that was already a mess.

Slowly the Mike Boats made their way into the hold of the ship and when in position, lowered their ramps onto the metal deck. I felt so bad I couldn't move, maybe it would have been better to get sick when everyone else did- they seemed to be moving much better than I was. I was sitting there, one of the last Marines on board and I felt like a wet dish rag, I had no energy.

I found my pack which was floating in the water, grabbed the rest of my gear and began making my way towards the ramp. Even though you were inside the ship, you were still in ocean water and both the Mike Boat and the ship seemed to have their own rhythms. One of the fears of getting off a boat like this is when you try to run off the ramp, it could be in the air. If you slip on the wet deck and slide backwards, the ramp could come down on top of you and it would all be over very quickly.

I was standing there, trying to figure out how to time it and there didn't seem to be any constant rhythm to work with. I looked up at the ramp, there was a sailor standing there and he yelled to me to go on the count of three. I nodded and with that, he began to count; when he reached three, I ran forward and jumped just as the ramp began to rise up off of the deck again.

The sailor grabbed me and pulled me forward onto the flat part of the deck. I said thanks and just stood there, not knowing which way to go. The sailor didn't say much but pointed to the port side of the ship and I began to shuffle off. I remembered the look on his face when he was helping me and it reminded me of how I felt when I was watching the combat troops come out of the field for the first time. My guess was it was his first time as well.

I made it back to our quarters not realizing I was in a safe place, but that feeling quickly came and I could begin to relax for the first time in many weeks. Everyone was stripping their fatigues off and heading down the gangway towards the head for a nice hot shower. The shower felt wonderful, but everyone was also trying to regain their sea legs and the rocking of the ship was a real challenge. When everyone was cleaned up, they focused on getting their weapon and gear clean before they could really begin to relax. Once I had everything squared away, I made my way up to the mess decks. It was early evening and we had eaten a few hours earlier.

Very few people were there and I was just walking around, enjoying the peace of not needing to be on 100% alert every second. I was looking around at the varied vending machines and enjoying the quiet time. From the other side of the mess hall, someone entered and began walking to another bank of vending machines on that side of the room. We began looking at each other and I realized it was the sailor that helped me off of the Mike Boat.

He came over to me, said hi and asked if he could buy me a soda, and I said sure. We sat at one of the metal picnic style tables that were bolted to the floor and he had a million questions. This was my first experience with this and I was surprised with how reserved I was. Everything seemed so personal, not just for me but for all the men I represented and even more importantly, the ones that didn't come back. I tried to answer his questions, but my responses came with great hesitance and I know he felt as if he was asking things that were much too sensitive.

He was new to Vietnam- as a matter of fact, most of the crew was new, and on top of that, the ship was brand new. I can't remember the exact order of ships. I think the first ship that I was on was the Cleveland and this new one was the Duluth, but it could be the other way around; at any rate, this ship was brand spanking new.

He shared with me how scared he was when he found out that he was going to Vietnam, and how that feeling quickly disappeared when he saw us coming off of the Mike Boats.
He immediately felt embarrassed that he felt in danger on board a ship when here we were, covered with mud and blood having been in the bush for almost two months. Overall, it was very nice of him to think to by me a drink, and I felt odd not being able to answer his questions.

Somewhere in the midst of all of this, I found myself on mess duty. I can't remember if I volunteered or was assigned to it, but it turned out to be more of a blessing than anything else. It really helped me to acquire some in-demand ingredients that the troops in the field crave. We had a few days until Thanksgiving, and being on mess duty got you out of doing all the PT and the regular Marine stuff.

I had to report to the mess decks two hours before each meal and I found the sailors to be wonderfully accommodating, they all treated me like royalty and we had a ball together.
Everything was going fine when we heard that orders were coming down for us to leave the ship the morning of Thanksgiving; we were really tired of being screwed and this took the cake.

The night before and that morning, we went through the drill of getting all new ammunition and everything else that went along with going into the bush. This time there was no light chatter anywhere- there were very few new guys and we all had other emotions swarming through our heads. We had actually saddled up and we were waiting in line in the hold of the ship to disembark on the Mike Boats when an announcement came over the intercom. It was very brief, but sweet to the ears. It was the captain of the ship and he said he had reviewed his decisions with the Marine leaders and said that no Marine aboard his ship was going into battle until they had a Thanksgiving dinner. What wonderful words to hear, there were shouts coming from every corner of the ship- it was about time we caught a break. I made my way back to our compartment and grabbed my mess duty apron and headed for the mess decks.

Beach Assault Late November 1967

It was time to go eventually, so we saddled up again and awaited our departure. This was to be a beach landing or an assault. Word had come down that this was our last assault from the ships, our battalion was coming off of SLF and would be replaced by another grunt unit. From now on, we would be ashore in what we called the bush or Injun Country, no more chances for hot showers and beach parties.

One company from our ship was to go ashore on the Mike Boats, the other company in the Amtrack's. We were the company chosen to go ashore on the Mike Boats. We feared two primary things: one was getting caught on a sand bar and needing to get off the boats and swim or wade ashore, the other was to be under enemy fire as we made our way to the beach.

We all feared for the company going ashore in the Amtrack's. These were huge rectangular boxes that had a loading ramp, and each one could hold a good number of combat ready Marines. There was a pilot and a co-pilot who sat up high and navigated through miniature periscope or through a hatch they could open directly above their head.

When fully loaded, the ramp would close, making the interior compartment airtight. These things were huge and when they were in the water, the only thing that kept them afloat was the air in the main cabin and the air trapped in the track wells. This alone is scary enough- this huge machine is floating just by the air inside. When these machines leave a ship at sea, much bigger issues come into play. The Mike Boats are launched and then we board them, but the troops who are going in the Amtrack's board while they are still inside the hold of the ship. They then power up to the edge of the landing dock and drive off the edge, falling bow-first straight down.

With the tremendous weight of the vehicle, they descend to some considerable depths before leveling off. The only thing that brings them to the surface is the captured air inside. During all of this, the pilot and co-pilot are looking out their mirrored periscopes, looking for light and a certain kind of air bubble, all while a clock is running. If they don't see light above in a certain amount of time, it means the vehicle is still descending and everyone will need to get out. Believe me, we weren't overly happy about making a beach assault in Mike Boats, but the alternative seemed much worse so none of us were complaining. Fortunately, the launch went without incident and all the Amtrack's came to the surface, even then they were barely visible in the water.

Once everyone was afloat, we began making our way to the shore. The section of beachhead we were headed for was just north of the mouth of the Cua Viet River, near the coastal village of Gia Liem, a fishing village slightly inland from the coast. The Mike Boats we were on took over the right flank as we all headed ashore. Every now and then, I peeked over the side of the boat to see what lay ahead.

From what I could see, it was an endless stretch of beach soaked in the turquoise waters with some scattered pine trees slightly set back from the water- no sign of any major enemy fortresses.

We were quite a distance from the beach when our boat went aground on a sandbar. The sailor at the helm kept working the boat first in forward then in reverse to try to force us free, without any luck. Lt Debruler was trying to get the sailors to lower the ramp and let us walk or wade onto shore, but the sailors were adamant they could work the boat free. I was on the side of the sailors, and the last thing I wanted to do was to get into that water and be a sitting duck all the way to shore.

They finally did get it off the sandbar and we made our way to shore. When the ramp went down, we all ran off the boat following our fire team leaders' instructions. Initially, we were side by side up on the beach, lying with our weapons aimed towards the pine trees, waiting for something to happen.

Each platoon was instructed to send one squad ahead to see if there was any evidence of the enemy or, if anything, to draw their fire.

One of the other squads went up, and after a period of time, we were all moved forward by our squad leaders in what were called fire team rushes. The squad leader yells out the number of the fire team randomly, and when he does, that fire team would get up, sprint for a few meters, and then dive for the ground. It was important to keep the order of advance random so if the enemy was out there, they wouldn't know who would be getting up next.

Shortly, it was obvious we had no greeting party—again, another quiet landing. The sand was damp and very fine, sticking to everything and it was a struggle to keep your weapon clean. Eventually, the entire company, all four platoons, got up online, which meant they were standing side by side one Marine next to another with a safe interval between each person

Little by little, we kept moving forward with no enemy activity at all, which at times could be just as unnerving as having some action. All day long, we continued forward in our online formation, waiting for something to happen. After we worked our way through the few pine trees near the coast, there were just rolling dunes of sand for us to cross, almost like a desert. At one point, I had come up an incline and there was a sandy, flat area directly in front of me and more dunes further on. Directly in front of me was a pool of water, which seemed quite shallow but its color was one of the prettiest blues I have ever seen.

86

One of the rules of being online is that you don't break your forward direction to go around anything, no matter what it was you had go through it. So go through it I did, walking at the same pace as the Marines to my left and the ones to my right. I wasn't a quarter of the way across the pool when I felt my feet begin to sink in the soft sand. I quickly realized that if I didn't move quickly, I was going to go very deep in this stuff. I yelled out that I was sinking, at the same time I gave it everything I had to try and run forward quickly, keeping my feet moving forward.

With all the gear I was carrying, this was very tricky and I know I didn't do a very good job, as I almost didn't make it to the other side. Some Marines ran around the backside of the pool and barely grabbed the end of my M-16, using it to pull me the rest of the way.

To this day, I swore it was quicksand; I don't know what would have happened if I just stood there and let myself sink.

We continued on, but now I was completely soaked and the sand was everywhere. Inside and outside my fatigues, inside and outside my boots- everywhere. A dune or two later and I was faced with another pool, but this time I didn't take any chances. I told the Marines to my left and right what I was going to do and they moved forward to help me if needed. A few feet before I actually got into the water, I began to run and continued until my feet were not pushing off of anything.

I was going down, again. This time I was much closer to the other side and it wasn't that hard to get me through the rest of it. We began to move slowly out of 100% sand and into a combination of sand and soil, and we could see a sizeable village off in the distance. Fortunately, there was still no action and we continued with our cautious approach.

We got to one point where a small stream was directly in front of us and on the other side some thick bushes began running up and into the village. We were told to hold up, and we all stood there side by side with our weapons aiming at the bushes just above the bank of the river. We stood and stood, and finally someone told us we could sit, which we did and continued to face the bushes. Now we sat and sat, with no sign of moving forward. No one could understand why we were waiting so long.

I was sitting there with my M-16 cradled in my lap, the barrel facing the bushes, when I thought I saw something move on the other side. I carefully moved my weapon towards the general direction where I thought I saw the movement and waited. Again, I saw something move, but still no aggression. Corporal Waight was behind me and slightly to my left, so I turned my head very slightly and slowly, and whispered his name. He whispered back and without turning, I told him what I thought I saw. He in turn whispered to Mike and Ralph, who then slowly and carefully turned their weapons and waited.

There was something there and whatever it was, it was right in front of us- this was not good. I saw something and was trying to squint to make it out. I think everyone else was doing the same thing. Within seconds, Waight whispered a strong command for us not to do anything and to take our fingers off of our triggers. Slowly out of one of the bushes, a long black cylinder came into view about 4 or 5 feet off of the ground.

Corporal Waight stood up and was mother effing quite loudly while the rest of us had no clue of what was going on. Then we saw one face and then another, and yet another, and slowly they made their way out of the bushes.

It was a media film crew taking our pictures and the black cone was the microphone. Waight called our lieutenant who came up quickly and he went berserk and started screaming at the film crew. Just like my stupid move when I first came in country, these jerks had no idea how close they were to going home in bags.

To this day, I'm still not sure who knew the media was waiting in the village and it left a sour taste in our mouths. Most of the older guys didn't have anything good to say about the media and they were already off to a bad start with the rest of us. We continued our sweep of the area and individual reporters came up to some of us, asking questions and taking pictures with their still cameras.

At one point, one ventured up to Ralph, Mike and me and wanted to ask us some general questions. There was a short period of silence and then Ralph finally said that we really didn't have too much to say. It didn't take to much to turn these guys off and he moved quickly to another likely target for what I'm sure he thought was going to be an incredible scoop. The village that we had entered was the first of many I would visit on the Cua Viet River. This village was on the north bank about a mile or so up stream from the mouth.

The Vietnamese name for the village was My Loc, but over time, the Marines named it Camp Big John for some obvious reasons. For some miraculous reason, this village had escaped the war that was raging all around, and it was as beautiful as it was quaint. The village was split in two by a stream, both sides connected by a sturdy cart bridge. The part of the village south of the bridge had a catholic church, which was positioned on the north side of the path that ran through the village. On the opposite side of the path was a steep embankment with the Cua Viet River flowing just feet away. Everything seemed very peaceful here; somehow there were no signs of war. We began the ritual of setting our night defensive positions, also know as our foxholes, and Mike and I were lucky enough to be positioned directly in front of the church.

We dug in on the south side of the path, giving us a beautiful view of the river, which was quite wide at this point. We finished digging in and were trying to organize our gear for the night while attempting to heat up some C-rations. If we were anywhere near civilians, this ritual always brought a flock of kids, all looking for handouts.

There was a standing rule that we all took quite seriously: if we gave any canned goods out to the civilians, we needed to put at least one puncture hole in the lid. This was to ensure that they would eat the food immediately and not be able to store it for possible use by the NVA. This gesture usually made most of the civilians irate, but others took the food and made their way back to their hooches and used it in their evening meal.

We finished eating and were just milling around the hole when a very young boy came down the path with the Vietnamese version of a fishing pole. There was a small trail leading from the main path down alongside our hole to a flattened area on the edge of the river-obviously a favorite fishing spot. We let the boy walk down to the river and we were drawing odds on who could go down there first; I lost.

Mike went down and brought along some C-ration chocolates, one of the biggest treats of all for the kids. Mike stayed down there a while, trying to teach the boy the New York version of perfect fishing and when I got there, I showed him the Connecticut technique. Neither one was very effective, but relaxing with the boy was wonderful.

It was almost as if we were far away, possibly at home, definitely not in the middle of a raging war. This was my first time being able to completely relax and interact with a Vietnamese person; all my other contacts were during patrols or search and destroy missions where we took everything very seriously. It was incredible to see how relaxed and natural the little boy was being with us, knowing the war was not too far away. For the brief minutes that Mike and I spent with him, we felt that here in this place, there was no war. For those brief minutes, it was a wonderful feeling.

Evening came and the boy needed to go back to his hooch, which was somewhere further north on the other side of the footbridge. This was somewhat of a treat. In front of us we had a very wide, swiftly running river, which would be very difficult for the enemy to use for any type of attack. Behind us we had the main footpath of the village, "Main Street" in our terms, which was very easy to monitor. At last we had caught a break and we weren't has nervous or scared as we usually were on hole watch.

Somewhere around midnight, Mike and I were changing watches as a battle was unfolding on the opposite side of the river. It seemed so strange to be sitting there with the swiftly moving river in front of us, a Catholic church behind us, and a peaceful, sleepy village all around us, while just over there, men were dying. We watched the battle rage on- the intense firing of the M-16s, the machine gun tracers skipping through the air, the grenades and the artillery making their deep crumping sounds, and the illumination flares dropping slowly from overhead, allowing our troops to get a glimpse of the enemy.

Although the action was across the river and we knew we were relatively safe, we still had a nervous, yet sad, feeling for the men who were in the heat of the battle. Fighting during the day was bad enough, but when Charlie was out there angry and in the dark, it took on a whole new perspective. We never did hear who they were or how they made out- you learned some questions were never asked, and your turn could be next.

We ran patrols out of My Loc for a few days with no significant contact, and the battalion moved out, heading northwest initially and staying along the northern bank of the river. Periodically, we would run into some resistance, but no major battles

Although there was no significant contact, our nerves were not spared. Patrols, ambushes and listening posts were as dreaded then as any other time. A key factor in Vietnam was the element of surprise; someone was always hiding, waiting to inflict devastation on their adversaries. There were always sounds of war somewhere nearby and if Charlie was that close, he could be in your face at any time.

Sometimes the quiet times were the most painful. In the heat of the action, your body took on the roll of responding instantaneously to the events unfolding in front of you, and it's amazing what you can do when presented with the right situation.

Many times, new guys, or Fucking New Guys (FNGs), would say they would never be able to do this or to eat that. It was only a matter of time until they were pushed to their individual limits and they had to adjust and accept this abnormal change.

Little by little, we were making our way further north into an area called Leatherneck Square. This area was basically the width of Vietnam and started at the Demilitarized Zone (DMZ) in the north and continued down to the Cua Viet River: this was our turf. Along the way, we would occasionally come across dead NVA soldiers lying in varied stages of decay. Some were no more than skeletons inside a uniform. These soldiers were either killed in a skirmish and never buried or killed at night by an ambush, with random artillery rounds or overhead assault from Puff.

We had worked all the way up to the actual trace where the new defensive base A-3 was being developed. At this point it wasn't much, just a bunch of foxholes scattered around the large perimeter and some engineers attempting to build the main underground structures in the middle of a muddy mess. The monsoon rains were pretty constant now, making the entire base a huge mud hole. Up there, the ground was deep red clay and when wet, it was almost impossible to walk in. Minimally it was very slippery; secondly it was like stepping into a suction cup. If both your feet were stuck in the mud, you were in real trouble- getting out on your own without a full clay bath was hard to avoid.

We went through the process of setting the lines and by a wonderful stroke of luck, they put our foxhole right next to a machine gun position. My hole mate at this location was Lenny Tuckett, another Marine who came to our unit the same time I did. Lenny's original home was one of the Caribbean islands and he had a wonderful accent. Just inches away from Lenny and I was the machine gun position with a crew of three. We took it upon ourselves to combine the positions and to dig one big defensive fighting position that would fit us all if needed.

Having done that, we took the opportunity to dig a hug rectangular crater that would become our home for the next few weeks. We all took turns digging and didn't stop until we had this very deep hole that would keep us safe from everything other than a direct hit from artillery. When you weren't digging, you were out scavenging for materials to cover the hole and to keep the rain out. We kept raiding the LZ where the engineers had most of their supplies stored, and eventually acquired all the needed materials to cover the hole and make it as secure as possible.

The good news was we had a fighting position staffed by five Marines, the downside was our fighting position was aimed directly north. As you sat there in the fighting position, you were looking directly out at the trace. This was a very eerie feeling, knowing that the 600 meter wide stretch of land in front of you separated the good guys from the bad guys. While we were at A-3, we took on responsibilities other than our normal day and nighttime patrols and ambushes. While here, we were to be laborers to help establish it as a formidable defensive base.

Some of these activities were just physical: filling sandbags, digging trenches, helping drive metal posts, stringing concertina wire, and more. Other activities required us to work in and around the LZ. No one wanted to be assigned any of those details. It was bad enough when you needed to go to the LZ, which was in the center of the base, to pick up C- rations and other supplies.

As soon as the enemy would hear the choppers coming in, they would start with the artillery, rocket and mortar bombardments of the perimeter, hoping to interfere with the daily supply run, knowing there would be people out in the open unloading the helicopters. Even on supply runs, you needed to dart from one spot to another to get to where the supplies were while trying to anticipate where the incoming shells would land. Unfortunately, not everyone was all that lucky and more often than not- there were numerous casualties and deaths just from supply runs.

While on work details, you were required to be out in the open more often than not. Numerous times during the course of the day, Charlie would lob a few artillery rounds or rockets into the perimeter, hoping to catch some of us out in the open.
Wherever you were, whether you were on a work detail or not, you could hear the artillery being fired off in the distance.
When a gun like this is aimed in your direction, it has a different sound and everyone would know we were going to get some incoming and would run for cover. Rockets, on the other hand, didn't give you a distant warning. They wouldn't begin to make noise until they were almost on top of you, so they were much more difficult to get away from. Regardless of what was being fired, no one knew where they would land and it was literally a crapshoot choosing where to hide.

The Marines used small-wheeled vehicles called Mules for many different reasons. They were handy for carrying supplies, but they also had a built-in mount that would allow for a 106 Recoilless rifle to be mounted. In and around the base camp and LZ, they were mostly used for carrying supplies and construction equipment.

One day, I was up at the LZ on a work detail and a stream of helicopters came in with the daily supplies. As usual during their run, the enemy began their traditional bombardment and we all scurried around, trying to unload the helicopters while dodging the incoming rounds. Even in the mud, I managed to stay out of harm's way and made it through the initial onslaught.

At one point, shortly after the main barrage, we began our chores: digging, moving equipment, whatever. In the supply run, there was a delivery of pint-sized milk containers, a rarity which were tremendously enjoyed whenever they did come. Being at the LZ made it easy for us to ensure every worker assigned to the LZ got at least one carton to enjoy, even while working. It was always amazing how quickly everyone got back to work after the devastating pounding from the artillery- it was just something that you got used to. This day, there were numerous people in the middle of the construction area, everyone going their own way. Two Marines were on a Mule, heading across the area and they were sharing a container of milk, passing it back and forth as the Mule moved along.

Periodically, the enemy would wait a few minutes for us to get back to our work tasks and then they would lob in a few rockets just for good measure, which is what they chose to do today. Many of us were caught out in the open and the rockets, giving very little warning, hit pretty much on target. There were screams coming from everywhere and mud flying through the air.

The man on the back of the mule was reaching back, attempting to give the container of milk to the driver, and when he didn't feel the other Marine grabbing the box, turned to get his attention. As he turned, he was looking at the headless driver rolling to his left to fall lifeless in the mud. The mule rolled forward a few more feet and came to a stop. The Marine on the back of the mule quickly jumped off and crawled in the mud until he was under the mule. He lay there with his arms holding his helmet down, staring at his friend lying a few feet away. I ended up face down in the mud, having been blown forward by the blast of one of the exploding rockets. When I dared to raise my head, all I could see was the horrible mess in the center of the construction site- some things we will never forget.

That was the end of our work for the day in and around the LZ area, as we were all released to go back to our respective fighting positions. I walked in silence. I remember that I had a cigarette in my mouth while I was walking back to the perimeter with my M-16 slung under my right arm. In the chill and dampness of the monsoon, even cigarettes would go out. I was so pissed that I couldn't keep the damn thing lit and after frequently touching it with my damp fingers, I finally threw it down in the mud in disgust. My frustration over that damn cigarette has stuck with me and I'm sure it is somehow associated to the horror that took place only minutes before.

With the monsoons, the daytime and nighttime temperatures were considerably cooler than normal. Normally when you slept, you slept alone and only one other person was on hole watch with you. Regardless of the season, your body automatically began to sleep curled up in the fetal position, your hands together between your legs. This allowed your body to retain as much natural heat as possible. With this crew of five, we got more sleep each night but we also had a chance to sleep together. With one man on watch at the foxhole, the rest of us would be below ground, curled up side- by-side. The person on watch next would be on the far right; the person just coming off watch would lie down on the left.

There were so many things that we did that would never be accepted in our society- this being one of them. Here we were, men of all races and ethnic background, sleeping side- by-side. Not just side-by-side, but what we called "nuts to butts," meaning snuggled up to the man in front of you. Not a word spoken, mostly because you were warm and warmer by having someone in front of you and at times, behind you. Try to imagine four men doing that in today's world without numerous insinuations or assumptions being made.

Standing hole watch during normal weather was difficult and challenging enough; during the monsoons it took on a whole new dimension. The rains during the monsoons were torrential, making hearing and seeing almost impossible. They at least gave us permission to wear our ponchos while on watch, but you still had many challenges if you wanted to stay dry. Whether you were standing or sitting, you tried to adjust your flak jacket, helmet and poncho in an attempt to get the water to go around you. Somewhere under all of this, you needed to have your M-16- after all, you were on watch. Once you found a position that worked, you tried to freeze in that position because any slight movement would open a channel of water coming in from every direction. While doing all of this, you needed to try to penetrate the pitch-black darkness in an attempt to identify any movement. Between the wind, rain and the cooler temperatures, it was very chilly, and you were usually chilled to the bone regardless of how dry you stayed. Staying awake was much easier; there was always a cool, chilling breeze and sufficient dampness to keep anyone awake.

It was here at A-3 where we were first introduced to the Starlight scope. It was a wonderful device, normally issued to our snipers, which allowed you to see in the dark. The scope we used looked like a large rifle scope, which is exactly what it was. When you peered through the scope, everything in front of you was in a hazy, pale green image.

The Starlight technology took advantage of any available light in the night, mostly being the moon and the stars. On moonlit nights, the images in the viewfinder were much brighter and clearer. Less available light drastically diminished what you could see, but it was better than nothing. Every now and then, you would hold the scope up and slowly scan the area in front of you, trying to keep your movements very slow. Unfortunately there were very few of these and it was seldom available for use by the grunts on the line.

The other nighttime activities of ambushes and listening posts were much more difficult in the rain. Whenever you needed to go outside the perimeter for one of these activities, other restrictions came into play. The most uncomfortable one was that we were not allowed to use ponchos on either activity.
There was a concern that they would glisten too much in the rain and there was a chance they could give your position away.

Without the poncho's protection, you were completely drenched before you left your fighting position, never mind the perimeter. Even though you had all these men on an ambush, and normally it would be a good opportunity for most to get a decent night's sleep, when you were this cold and wet, nobody got any sleep. The monsoons made life very difficult in many different ways, sleep deprivation was just one.

One afternoon, our platoon was standing line watch on the perimeter and for the most part, it was an uneventful day. Our platoon command post, or CP, received a message that they needed a couple of men to help provide security for some tanks and trucks. Some supply trucks had left the base camp of Gio Linh earlier in the day and one of them had become entrenched in the thick clay mud halfway between the two bases.

They had asked for some tanks to be sent out to help pull the trucks out of the mud, and two tanks were sent. I can't remember how I was chosen, but Sgt Butler from our platoon and I went down to the location where the tanks were getting ready to leave. Other volunteers from different platoons were there, and Sgt Butler and I were assigned to bow security on one of the tanks. The forward corners of the tanks were lined with sandbags and we positioned ourselves behind the small fortifications.

I had never ridden on a tank, so this was somewhat of a treat, and anything was better than walking. We set out on our mission, one tank behind the other, heading east towards Gio Linh. We eventually got to where the two trucks were and one of them was up to the truck's body in the thick mud. After some discussion between the tank drivers and the truck driver's it was decided to offload all the supplies onto the back of the other tank. It took some finagling but eventually the tank backed up close enough to the back of the truck and we all took turns helping move the supplies to the tank.

When everything had been moved, the tank pulled forward and got on the road heading in the direction of A-3. Our tank backed up to the front of the truck and they attached the tow chain. The truck driver decided now that all the supplies had been moved, he preferred to have his truck turned around to head back to Gio Linh. To accomplish that, our tank needed to pull the truck forward and then make a wide turn to get the truck back on the road heading in the direction of Gio Linh.

Seemingly, everything was going fine. We were in the midst of the turn, relatively on solid ground, when there was a deafening explosion. I can't remember flying through the air, but the first thing I remember was being on the ground, scrambling for cover, as was Sgt Butler- we both thought we were receiving incoming artillery. I found a mound to hide behind and I looked around for Sgt Butler, who I located some distance away, we both had a very puzzled look on our faces.

We looked back at the tank, which was ok, but the truck that had been in tow was completely destroyed. Apparently, we had run over an anti-tank mine which missed us but struck one of the wheels on the truck. The driver and co-driver of the truck were killed instantly, as were the two Marine guards that were positioned on the back of the truck. All we got was a deafening ring in our ears and some scrapes and bruises from when we hit the ground.

It took some time to clear everything up. Medevac choppers were called in to remove the four bodies and the remaining gear on the truck was removed and placed on the back of our tank. All this was done in dead silence, there was no conversation from anyone- we were all somewhat in shock and numb from what had just happened. We left the carcass of the truck where it was and we cautiously turned our tank around to get back on the road, now heading for A-3.

Eventually, we made it back to our base camp just before dusk and Sgt Butler and I began to make our way back to our side of the perimeter. As we approached our CP, we were getting some unusual stares from the Marines in our platoon who were at their fighting positions. Something was up, but neither of us knew what was going on.

We got up to the CP and the Lieutenant came out of his hooch with an awkward stare on his face. He was stumbling for words and it eventually became clear that somehow in the chaos with the tanks and truck incident, my name had been called in as one of the casualties. Apparently one of the Marines who had gotten killed was either Polish or may have had a last name which sounded like mine.

There was a scramble within the CP to get the word back out to everyone that I was still alive. They needed to get through to the Red Cross and our Battalion headquarters to clear that up quickly. One thing they didn't want was a death notice going home to the wrong family.

A new lieutenant was at the CP and everyone knew he was the replacement for Lt Debruler. Officers in the field were required to be out in the bush for six months and then they would rotate back to get a rear echelon job for the remainder of their 13-month tour. The two officers would work together through the transition period in an attempt to teach the new lieutenant as much as possible before being left on his own.

The new lieutenant's name was Lewy and he stood about 6- foot-4. He was quiet and he made a sincere attempt to get to know everyone as the days went by. Sometimes at night, he would come down to our underground bunker where it was dry. We had taken many precautions to ensure we could burn candles at night without any chance of the light slipping through the cover- Charlie would love something like that at night. Quite often, Lt Lewy would come down to visit and take advantage of the light to write some letters.

One thing that was needed out in the field was respect at all levels. The way Lt Lewy worked his way into our platoon showed that he was trying very hard to gain our respect, and along with that would come trust. He would walk the lines at night, taking the opportunity to stop and visit with the Marine on watch, taking the time to get to know everyone a little bit better. While on patrol, he would simply observe what we did and what instruction Lt Debruler needed to give us. He learned quickly, and over time, we all felt comfortable with his ability to lead us. One day, without any fanfare, Lt Debruler departed 2nd Platoon and went back to Quang Tri, where our battalion headquarters was, for his new assignment. 2nd Platoon was now the sole responsibility of Lt Lewy.

Heading to Charlie 4 - Early December 1967

Fortunately, our stay at A-3 was relatively uneventful other than a few nighttime skirmishes with very little impact on us. Sometime in early December, we got word that we were moving out for another assignment down by the water. We humped part of the way back, and eventually got on a convoy for the remainder of the trip to Dong Ha. The Mike Boats were waiting for us and again we loaded for a trip to the mouth of the river.

The ride down the river was uneventful and surprisingly beautiful. The flow of the river was in the same direction of the Mike Boats, so they gave off little if any wake. For the most part, it was like gliding over a mirror with deep rich green river banks at the edges of the murky water. Occasionally, you could see a village off in the distance and there were also a few on the riverbanks. I recognized a couple from our previous operation that started in November, and now I could see what they looked like from both sides. Fortunately this time, we didn't need to go all the way out; we offloaded on the northern bank just before the mouth of the river.

Morale wasn't too bad. We had gone through some rough areas and had come out basically unscathed. Although the LZ was dangerous, at A-3 we got our mail and supplies more often than not- out in the bush, the frequency wasn't that promising. At times you would think that getting mail on time was everything. People who haven't traveled away from home may not have an appreciation for getting mail, but believe me, it was the all-important event. Being away from home is one thing, but being in a place where no one knew what might happen next, that all-important communication from home meant everything. Regardless of where you were, there was always a focus on the mail. Whenever a supply helicopter would come in, everyone's eyes would focus on the open hatches of the helicopters, searching for the colored bags that mail came in. If anyone spotted the bags, the word traveled quickly and then everyone waited to see if they would be lucky enough to get something.

One of the villages I recognized was the one where Mike and I had the foxhole in front of the church. Before I saw the church, I saw the footbridge and the small river, and then I began looking for it. Everything was still peaceful and the village seemed to be unscathed. As the Mike Boat came in front of the church, I moved to get a clear view to see if I could find the foxhole that Mike and I had dug. We had filled the majority of it in when we left the village, but you could still see the indentation of where it had been. I quickly looked around to see if I could find any sign of the little boy walking the path without any luck. There were villagers walking the numerous paths, but no one seemed to have the build of the little boy.

Eventually the Mike Boats arrived at the north bank of the river just before the mouth and approached the shore to let us off. There was no ground fire and our landing was very quiet. We all spread out and took some cover, but it was obvious that Charlie was not in the immediate area.

Someone with some insight passed the word that only two companies, Alpha and Charlie company, were sent down to the coast. Nobody was really sure where Bravo and Delta companies had been sent.

Eventually, some Amtrack's from the base across the river came rumbling in and we were instructed to throw our gear inside and climb on top. The Amtrak's began their journey up the coast, keeping the ocean on their right side. Many of us began to take notice of the area we were traveling in. This was where we made our beach assault the day after Thanksgiving- it already seemed like a lifetime ago.

The Amtrack's rumbled along for quite some time and then eventually began to make their way slightly inland. They had traveled a short distance when they all came to a stop and we were instructed to get off. We were looking at an area of white sand, small rolling sand dunes mixed in with huge pine trees. There were Marines scattered around the area in front of us, all standing by their gear, obviously ready to move out. We basically traded places with them.

We climbed off the Amtrack's and grabbed our gear, moving to one side. In turn, they grabbed their gear, threw it inside the huge machines and climbed on board. Most of us were still at a loss about where we were and what we were supposed to be doing. Eventually, we were separated by platoon and moved around an already-formed perimeter. We came to learn that we were in the base camp called Charlie Four or C-4, another piece part of McNamara's Wall. The camp was comprised of numerous platoon-sized bunkers, all of which were underground and complex fighting positions around the outer perimeter.

We were here to guard the base, but at the same time, we were grunt labor to help with the continued building of the base.
Each day we ran our patrols, night ambushes, listening posts, and observation posts but there were always other work parties you would find yourself on. This was quite like being up at A-3 but with slightly different terrain. The base camp of C-4 was slightly south of the Gio Linh base which was up on the DMZ; basically directly behind it but with a good deal of open ground between the two.

If you weren't out on patrol or other daytime assignments, you were on a sandbag filling detail. Every other day, you would climb on board the Amtrack's and they would take the work detail out to the beach area. We would scatter out among the sand dunes and get our sentries positioned. Once secure, teams of two would begin filling hundreds of sandbags. The work was quite easy. One Marine would hold the bag, the other would use his entrenching tool to shovel the damp sand into the bag. Each team was given a set amount to fill and as soon as you were done you could start the next phase.

The second phase was to load your sandbags into the hold of the Amtrak, still a manageable task. As soon as your team was done, usually by mid afternoon you could join the others to get a swim in the South China Sea. Sentries would be stationed up and down the beach and in the palm trees, keeping a sharp eye out for Charlie.

Charlie wasn't the only foe in this area- there were numerous sharks that the sentries in the palm trees strained to see. If you had finished your chores and you weren't standing sentry watch, you could strip off your jungle fatigues and enjoy the water.

Having grown up on the water in Connecticut, I thought this was wonderful. The water was beautiful, as was the sand and the immediate surroundings. Each day it was like getting a mini R&R and for us who enjoyed the water, it was even nicer. Every now and then a sentry would yell out, "Shark," and everyone would get out of the water. If they could, they would concentrate and open fire to encourage the shark to move on. If they actually killed it, that was even better.

Charlie Company was there and every now and then, I would get a glimpse of Tom. More frequently than not there were supply choppers coming in, so in a short period of time, Charlie knew the Americans were somewhere close by. As time went on, we started to get more and more action both during the day and at night. Our lines were being probed on a nightly basis and our nightly ambushes were getting triggered more often than before. Scattered around the perimeter, we had 106 recoilless rifles that were very effective guns. They could fire a devastating high explosive (HE) round just as an artillery gun could do. Based on their design, they did not give any recoil, which enabled them to be quite accurate, shot after shot.

One day a 106-gunner nick named Hippy noticed a flash, like a small mirror in the sun, out to our northern front in a grove of pine trees near the ocean. He got on the communications radio and asked if we had any friendlies in front of us. He received the word back that there were no friendly patrols out in front of our perimeter. A short time later he noticed another glimmer as he had before. Again he got on the radio to check, he got the same answer no friendlies out in front of us.

With that he loaded a "beehive" round into the gun. Beehive or flechette rounds were not necessarily high explosive rounds. The projectile was filled with thousands of small metal arrows. The projectile could be set to go a certain distance from the gun after being fired. When the projectile got to that distance it would blow up sending thousands of arrows out in a 360-degree path, almost impossible to hide from. Hippy loaded the shell and yelled the appropriate
command, "Clear the back blast area," and shot the gun.

On a recoilless gun, the design prevents the gun from jumping. Instead it creates a tremendous blast of air behind the gun that could cause permanent damage if you were directly behind the gun. The projectile traveled out towards the pine trees by the water and exploded with its usual yellow vapor. This all happened so quickly-no one was really sure what was going on.

Officers were jumping all over Hippie's case because he fired the gun without asking permission, and a patrol was being hastily formed to go out and search the pine tree area. As luck would have it, 2nd Platoon got the call to go out and check out the tree line. We got ready quickly, got into a V formation and made our way to the coastline. Just prior to the tree line, we held up for a brief period and then we sent 3 fire teams in to check out the immediate area around the first few trees.

We moved in fire team rushes to the sand dunes just prior to the trees. Team rushes in the sand are difficult and you make slow progress. Once we got to the tree line, we moved more cautiously. Our squad was closest to the trees and specific fire teams were instructed to move forward to start the initial investigation. Ralph and I moved together and slowly crawled over the sand dune to the side where the trees were exposed towards the perimeter of C-4.

We couldn't believe our eyes. There were no less than 20 NVA soldiers lying in their positions, as if frozen in time. After realizing they were all dead, we quickly moved towards the backside of the grove. There were numerous blood trails moving out into the sand dunes to our north and some signs of bodies or wounded being dragged.

We passed this word back and other teams were sent north to track down the wounded. As they moved out, you could hear the sporadic M-16 gunfire as they came across the wounded NVA and brought the issue to a close. We moved back to the bodies we initially found and they were all filled with the little arrows, they never knew what hit them. Propped between two of the more prominent pine trees was a 75 recoilless rifle they had trained on our perimeter. One of the bodies on the edge of a sand dune facing our perimeter was an officer with a set of binoculars, it was obvious to us they were what Hippie saw flashing in the sun.

Over the next few hours, we provided our input to the after action reports. Once done, we all helped sweep the area and removed any weapons and other NVA equipment, then made our way back to C-4. Many of us knew Hippie from staging and as we went passed him, we yelled out our appreciation for his quick action. Unfortunately Hippie would pay a price for what he did. Although we all believed that he saved many of our lives for taking immediate action, he didn't follow procedures. Eventually he was removed from the field and rumor had it he got a court martial for what he had done. No mail wasn't the only thing that affected our moral-bullshit like this did as well.

We were getting close to the end of the month of December and everyone was hoping we would be getting some large mail deliveries, including packages. Packages didn't always get the same attention as letter mail. As often as possible, letter mail would be ferried by chopper, but packages came much more seldom. But now, the holidays were upon us and we were all getting anxious for some packages.

Finally Christmas Day was here and there was a very cheerful atmosphere around the camp. Around midmorning, they announced that church services were going to be held in the center of the compound and I slowly made my way there.

The church pews were made up of ammo crates lined up in rows, a rough attempt to keep you from sitting in the sand. I looked around and saw Tom milling around the area and I caught his attention. We picked out an ammo crate and sat and began a nice visit, one that didn't happen very often.
Everyone was milling around, waiting for the protestant chaplain to come out to begin the service.

There was some commotion in the far side of the clearing and eventually a sergeant from Alpha Company made his way to the front of the makeshift church. He stood there and announced enemy movement had been spotted north of our perimeter and Alpha Company was being activated to go
conduct a search and destroy. I sat there numb as I'm sure everyone in Alpha Company did, we could not believe our ears. I looked at Tom and said, "I don't believe this shit," and stomped away, I was really pissed.

All four platoons saddled up and after the usual confusion, we moved out gradually making our way north. We periodically heard contact being made further north from where we were
but as far as we knew, it wasn't any elements from our patrol. All day, we moved cautiously north looking for the elusive NVA. You need to remember that all this was taking place during the time when there was a cease fire in effect all over Vietnam.....cease fire my butt.

Periodically, we would take breaks and have a chance to look around. We could hear the choppers coming in and we could see the mail bags and containers of hot chow in the open helicopter doors as they flew by. This was bad enough, but sooner or later, we would be getting back to the perimeter and would join the others in some long overdue packages, hot food and your basic holiday celebrations.

The daytime patrols turned up nothing and now it was getting late in the afternoon. We were becoming impatient about getting back to the others. Finally the word came down to head back, everyone except 2nd Platoon. We would be staying out for a platoon-sized ambush. They were still expecting the NVA to hit our camp and what better time than during a big holiday like Christmas. Again I couldn't believe my ears. It seemed like every time we turned around, we were getting the short end of the stick and everyone in 2nd Platoon was very angry.

We sat there in the sand and watched the other three platoons begin to make their way back to the camp. We eventually moved out and continued moving until dusk. We began to move into position as it got dark, minimizing the chance of the NVA seeing where we were setting in. To make matters worse, we got some rain that night and there was no way of staying dry. We lay there all night, waiting for the NVA to move through the kill zone but nothing happened.

Eventually daybreak came and after a safe period of time, we began to form for our hump back to the camp. Everyone was a soggy mess of wet fatigues layered with clumps of wet sand. We slowly made our way back to the perimeter and they had opened some space in the concertina wire for us to come through. I was coming through the wire and I caught a glimpse of Tom standing off to the side with a fresh cup of C- ration coffee. He didn't need to say anything we both had the look of disgust on our faces. I was very appreciative of the hot coffee but I was in no mood to talk, we were all exhausted and basically fed up with everything.

We made our way to our squad bunkers, where our mail and packages had been stacked. Of course all the hot chow was long gone, there was no sense in saving us any when we had no way of heating it up. During the course of the day, we had mail call and we all sat back and got caught up with our contacts from home.

There were always sad moments during mail call, there were many men that got mail very seldom if any at all. We all lived for these brief moments of hearing from our loved ones back home and I couldn't imagine not getting any mail, it was very painful to watch them each time. I was lucky, I got some great mail from my family as well as Tom's and numerous packages, mostly to help celebrate Christmas. I sat back and got caught up on everything that was going on in Connecticut as well as the mountains of North Carolina.

Enemy activity around the camp had picked up and daily and nightly skirmishes were becoming more common. New Year's was only a few days away, which would mark me being a third of the way through my tour. New Year's Eve day, I was in a fighting position with Ralph, one of the ones that faced north. We had received word earlier that they didn't want any flares to be fired to celebrate the coming of the New Year, due to the cease fire. We didn't have any major activities scheduled for the day and during the afternoon, I told Ralph that I was going to the other side of the perimeter to visit with Tom. I made my way through the compound and asked around to get the location of Tom's fighting position.

The perimeter was considerably different on this side of the compound and I needed to walk on wooden planks to get to a fighting position out in the middle of a bog. Tom and I didn't have the opportunity to get together very often so we always made the most of it. After the usual attempts to get caught up on what was going on back in the world, we sat back and I had a smoke while Tom had a chew. We shared the combined mail we received and got caught up on what was going on back home.

The afternoon went on and we eventually grabbed some C- rations and had a nice relaxing meal. Sometime in the latter part of the day, Tom broke out a bottle of Seagram's 7 Crown. None of us were sure if was the real McCoy, but if it gave us a buzz that's all that counted. Tom said one of their scouts purchased it one day when they were on patrol and he said it was the real thing. We sat and drank and chatted, chatted and chatted some more.

Before we knew it, the bottle was empty, it was pitch dark and we were all completely shot. I realized that I needed to get back to Ralph before it got too late and after some quick good- byes, I slowly made my way back to my side of the perimeter, it was a long and messy walk. I finally got back to the fighting position I was sharing with Ralph and all he could do was let out a groan when he saw me

I was a mess and all I wanted to do was talk but I'm sure I wasn't making any sense at all. Eventually he made me lay down at the back of the bunker and told me to go to sleep. By that time we were hearing some noise from further north and there was evidence of flares and pop-ups being fired in celebration of the New Year.

A pop up is an aluminum tube about 12 inches long and 1 inch in diameter. On one end, there is a cap that can be removed which is then placed on the other end of the tube as you would a cap from a ballpoint pen. Inside the cap there is a sharp tip. When you slam the pop up down on something hard; the ground, your helmet, anything hard; it drives the sharp tip into a firing cap which ignites the rocket flare inside the tube. These flares were different colors and we used them for signaling at night: red- danger, green- friendlies, white- all clear. I could see the distant flares from where I was lying but no one from our perimeter was doing anything.

Ralph couldn't see everything that I was doing and before he knew it I had grabbed a pop-up and my helmet. I came to the front of the bunker, put my helmet on the ground in front of the sandbags and slammed the butt end of the pop-up down hard on the helmet. The white flare shot upwards and popped high overhead. That's all everyone in our perimeter needed, and flares began being fired from all around the camp.

Ralph grabbed me and threw me to the back of the bunker and told me to lie down, which I did. He took a chance and crawled out in front of the bunker and dug a quick hole in the sand by hand and buried the flare tube, getting rid of the evidence.

Within minutes, Sergeant Hall, our platoon sergeant, was up on the lines asking a million questions as to who set off the pop-up. Ralph responded first by complaining about me getting shit faced and then said the flare had been launched from somewhere to our left. I don't know if they ever found anyone to pin it on, all I do know is they never came back to us.

Although it was the middle of winter back in the states, it was the monsoon season for us. Even in monsoon season, the temperature stayed in the 70s, so it was still mild compared to home in New England. The terrain around our camp was mostly rolling white sand dunes with an occasional clump of pine trees. If the moon was out at night, the sand could almost be mistaken for fresh fallen snow, and some nights were absolutely beautiful and really made me think of home. I was not missing the cold, but everyone and everything else that was there. With New Years came yet another change. The following day we were told that we would be leaving the coastline camp of Charlie 4 to head up to the main Marine base of Quang Tri, which was currently being developed.

Moving To Quang Tri Base - January 1968

As usual, there was much confusion with our move. We were instructed to dump everything that wasn't critical—basically, just bring your combat gear. This was very upsetting for us in Alpha Company. When we got screwed out of Christmas Day and other patrols between then and New Years, we had little time to go through our Christmas packages. Now we were forced to rummage through everything quickly and pick out only a few things we were willing to hump to our next destination. With much emotional pain, we all went through our gifts and selected a few choice items to take with us.

By midday we heard the distant diesel engines of the Amtrack's. Just like when we got here, our replacements were traveling atop the Amtrack's. Without much fanfare, they removed their gear from the tracks and we were instructed to load our packs inside and to get aboard.

The Amtrack's made their way down the coastline towards the Cua Viet River in a convoy formation. We didn't encounter any resistance on our way, only a periodic view of some Vietnamese fishermen casting their nets into the ocean. From here, you would never think there was a war going on, just some primitive fisherman trying to scrape a living. We arrived at the river and were pleasantly surprised to see numerous Mike Boats lined up waiting for us. We disembarked the Amtrack's, removed our 782 gear from inside, and started the loading process onto the Mike Boats.
Once loaded, the boats backed away from the riverbank and one by one headed north. This was a much longer venture than our two previous ventures, this time we were cruising against the river's current.

Although we didn't encounter any direct enemy activity, we could hear the sounds of war in the distance, seemingly in all directions. I always found it hard to get used to ignoring these distant sounds of intense combat, knowing that it could be us just as well as some other infantry unit.

The distant sounds of the artillery crumping mixed in with the sporadic sounds of small arms brought back instant images of the intensity of a firefight or battle. There are smells associated with battle as well the intense sounds and when all of it is mixed together with the personal emotions of fear and pending death, it makes for an intense feeling. You
experience them once, and it doesn't take much to rekindle the feelings; these sounds, although they were off in the distance, were doing just that for everyone on the Mike Boats as they headed north.

After what seemed like an endless ride, we could make out the loading area of Dong Ha. One by one, the Mike Boats took their turns unloading their combatant cargo and eventually we were all ashore. It was an overcast day but so far we were still relatively dry and staying dry during the monsoons was always a treat. Again we were surprised when we found out that there was a convoy of 6-bys waiting to transport us to the Quang Tri base.

We got everything loaded on the trucks and made our way slowly up Highway 1 towards our new division headquarters. We arrived without incident except for the surprise of finding an airfield that was already operational.

The base itself was still in its infancy; at this point the 3rd Marine Division was living out of tents. As usual, being grunts we were assigned to man the outer perimeter of the base but that was ok, we were getting used to these types of assignments.

A few days after arriving at the Quang Tri Marine Combat Base LT Lewy was called up to the company command post to talk about an upcoming short term mission. Apparently a Marine helicopter containing crew and officer passengers went off course in the fog and smashed into the side of a mountain, killing all on board.

We were told that they wanted a unit to get up to the mountain top, retrieve all dog tags from the Marines on board and all material thought to be sensitive.

When LT Lewy first went up for the meeting we heard that one of the other platoons was asked to take on this mission but for some reason that fell apart and 2nd Platoon got the honor.

The squad leaders were briefed on this short term mission with an emphasis on not knowing what kind of enemy resistance we could expect. The word spread quickly and everyone was uneasy with the whole idea. We were to leave early the next morning with hopes that it would all be over in one day.

Early the next morning the choppers arrived and we boarded for our trip to the distant mountain. As with other insertions none of us knew what to expect when the choppers approached the LZ. Fortunately for us it was a quiet LZ and once the choppers were gone we blended into the dense coverage. I was fortunate to be assigned to help establish a perimeter around the LZ while the remaining part of 2nd Platoon would venture down the mountain side to locate the downed chopper.

We set in our positions around the LZ allowing the others to go on their search party. Later in the day they made their way up to the LZ having recovered all the dog tags and anything that the Lt thought was something that should not be left behind.

Although I didn't go with the search team I got this description of the effort from Mike Muldovan.

"We were tasked to go up to the crash site where the choppers and the bodies had been there for about a week in the hot weather. When we arrived, about a half mile from the crash site, we could start smelling the decay in the air. We were told to put on dust masks and rubber gloves when we got on top of the mountain to the crash site. It was pretty gruesome to see all the destruction and the bodies that were like goo from all the heat from the fire of the crash. We were told to get as many of the dog tags as possible no matter how we did this

Like I said this was no easy task, we improvised by the use of sticks to try and pull the dog tags away from the necks of the departed. In some cases we could only get a few teeth to put in a plastic bag so that they could be identified.

They even had a larger chopper come in to try and lift it up off the ground, they attempted this it was one of worse things that I had ever seen. We learned that the chopper had crashed and that there were important papers showing our defense locations on several of the base perimeters that we were holding. We did get the briefcase and as many dog tags and anything we could to help identify the remains of the fallen Marines. After we got back down to our LZ we could hear the roar of the jets coming in low so that they could napalm the whole top of the hill. We were told that this would eliminate anything that we might not of found.

I will never forget this image for the rest of my life."

After getting this description from Mike I am happy to have been assigned to guard the LZ.

By the end of the day we were on our way back to Quang Tri Combat Base to continue with patrols on the out skirts of the base

2nd Platoon was assigned a section of the northern perimeter, some rough terrain with thick patches of brush. As luck would have it, our first night there 2nd squad got assigned to the night ambush, and none of us were very happy about this at all. With dusk came a heavy drizzle and eventually a gentle but steady rain. We made our way out of our perimeter, slipping and sliding in the thick red clay mud, another memory that any infantryman who served in Vietnam would not forget. We moved out in front of our perimeter a hundred yards or so and began setting in. It was a miserable night, very wet and very few of us got any sleep at all.

An hour or so before daybreak, we heard some different sounds, something that I had not heard before. It sounded like the bottle rockets that you set off as a kid but louder. There were some visible flashes occurring at the same time as the sounds and they were a good bit further north from our position. Within seconds, there were the distant sounds of the crumping of high explosives, somewhat like artillery landing. None of us were sure what just took place, but it was only a matter of time before we found out.

When it became light enough, we were instructed to move north and search where the lights and sounds came from. We spent an hour or so searching the thick brush and finally we found a clearing that looked like a mortar pit. There was evidence of some equipment being set up, possibly to fire a rocket or something, but it had since been removed. We reported our findings and did some further searching to ensure that we didn't miss anything, and made our way back to our perimeter. Our squad leader gave a detailed description of what we found and our lieutenant drew a diagram that was relayed to the division intelligence group. I began the process of digging a foxhole to get our new position established.

Sometime later that day, our platoon sergeant came by and asked if there was anyone that wanted to volunteer for mess duty. I had done this on the ship and knew it wasn't as bad as everyone made it out to be. I was with my friend Mike, and quickly said to him that we should take them up on the offer, which we did. We were instructed to grab our gear, walk down to the lower perimeter by the airstrip and look for our division's mess tents, and he gave us the name of a corporal to report to. We quickly grabbed our gear and set out for the lower perimeter.

Although the base was relatively new, it was already quite large and it took us quite some time to make our way down to the mess tents. We asked for the corporal by name and he was expecting us. As expected, we didn't get a lush job, all those were reserved for the full time mess crew.

Mike and I were assigned to the work of cleaning the hundreds of mess trays and to keep the emersion burners going during mess call. An emersion burner is a burner that gets submersed into a 55 gallon barrel that burns kerosene. The burner keeps the water in the barrel boiling and there were 3 or 4 of these barrels.

When you are done eating your chow, you scrape your tray into a trash pail and then you dip it in each of these boiling barrels. Supposedly this cleans the trays and you then place them in a drying area.

We also worked with the other mess men to clean the entire area at the end of each meal. The mess area was still relatively new and everything was still in tents. The enlisted personnel had to eat outside but the officers had the luxury of eating inside a tent, but there was nothing elegant about the mess area. With all that aside, it was very nice to be off the front line and into somewhat a rear, secure area.

The normal mess crew was absolutely nuts. They spent long hard hours doing their job but at least they were always in a relatively secure area. They had a million questions for Mike and me and some of them were so trivial or naive that Mike and I felt foolish answering. There was a big difference between grunts from the bush and anyone that had a rear echelon job, and we were beginning to get a better understanding of it. They partied very hard each evening but they were up bright and early each morning to start the process all over again.

It didn't take long before Mike and I really started to enjoy this rear echelon type of work. We had only been there a few hours and it began to sink in that we wouldn't be running any patrols, ambushes, observation posts or the most hated two- man listening post- that alone was a tremendous relief. Before we started in with our new chores, they showed us what tent we would be sleeping in and which cots were ours.

Cots, real cots, we wouldn't be spending the night in the mud, not even on the ground and if it rained, we were in a tent, and we would be nice and dry. We started in with our chores, which compared to our normal duties were nothing, actually enjoyable. The regular mess crew was quite cheerful and the attitude was catchy, it was a feeling that we hadn't had for quite some time.

Darkness came as we were finishing up with the big pots. Being the new guys, we did what there was as far as shit jobs, and the regular crew started in with the nightly partying. We knew that as soon as we were done we could join them, so we made short order of what was left. We sat on the ground leaning back on empty ammo crates and drank ice cold beer. It was that crappy 3.2 Fallstaff, but it was cold nonetheless.
We all needed to get an early start the next morning, so we didn't stay up all that late. Mike and I were actually looking forward to getting to our cots and the opportunity to take our boots off for the first time in a long time. We stored our boots, flack jackets and M-16s under our cots and lay down for some long overdue sleep.

Crack, crack, crack! What in the hell was making that cracking sound? I lie there on my back looking up towards the tent ceiling, watching orange fireflies streak through the tent. What the hell are fireflies doing in our tent? Shit, shit, shit, hit the deck we've got incoming!

The silence was broken with screams and total chaos inside and outside our tent. The fireflies were 50 caliber tracers going through our tent, something was dreadfully wrong. Mike and I were on the deck, actually really pissed at ourselves for letting our guard down, we never should have taken our boots and equipment off. We were scrambling around in the dark trying to get our boots on, then our flack jackets, helmets, our cartridge belts and finally our M-16s.

Everyone else had escaped out the tent and made their way to their fighting positions. Unfortunately being the new guys, Mike and I didn't have any. We made our way to the tent opening and tried to see outside, although there was fighting going on it was still pitch black. We made our way outside and moved towards the front of the tent, the end that faced the open area with the eating tables. Someone was shouting orders to move away from the tents and to dig a hasty fighting position in the open table area.

Mike and I moved out into the middle of the area and initially just stayed there trying to figure out exactly what was going on. Bullets were flying everywhere, orange tracers crisscrossing every which way. In the distance we could hear the heavy thumping of the 50 caliber machine guns pumping out their rounds. Every fifth round in a machine gun, regardless of type or caliber, was a tracer, so for every tracer we could see there were four bullets in between.

It was obvious to Mike and I that the outer perimeters were getting hit and had possibly been overrun, which gave credence why some of our guns were shooting inside our base instead of out. Each minute the intensity of the gunfire increased, and Mike and I realized that we needed to do something about a fighting position. Our entrenching tools were up at our regular positions so we lie there with nothing to dig with but our hands, which is what we started to do.

The ground was pure sand so we made some headway but our hands were taking a beating. We took our helmet liners out of our helmets and used the outer shell to scoop up the sand. Now we were making some progress and we took turns digging, the other would lay there on watch. We had dug down a few inches and were disgusted to see water seeping into the shallow hole. With that we gave up, there was no use trying to dig any further. We were lying there facing north, listening to the machine guns pump away. Behind us was Highway 1 and a little further the airstrip of Quang Tri base, both very quiet in comparison to what was going on up on the front lines.

Mike and I were lying there in the damp sand, watching and listening to what the Marines out in front of us were going through. There were Marines running everywhere, trying to create hasty fighting positions and figure out what was going on. We couldn't hear any enemy voices, so we were relatively relaxed- all things considered. We knew that we couldn't go anywhere, our front line positions were too far away and it
didn't sound like that was any place we wanted to be. Not having a fighting position was bothering us but we didn't know of anywhere to go, so we stayed put.

We were lying there looking north when we both saw something that we had not seen before. Off in the distance we both saw what seemed to be sparklers or something like a roman candle. We both made a comment about it and then we saw another one, we were still muttering to ourselves when we heard swoosh, first to our left and then to our right

Huge explosions followed the sound, there was shrapnel and debris flying everywhere. More swooshes followed, this was our first introduction to rockets and we didn't like it at all.

Over the past few months, we had become quite accustomed to incoming artillery and mortars, and we could tell by the sounds of them being fired about where they were going.

Rockets don't give you much warning at all. It's only in the last few seconds before they hit when you can hear the swooshing sound. More and more rockets were coming in. We were confident that they were actually aiming for the air strip, as many of them were falling short of their targets and landing in our area. Mike and I felt completely helpless against this.

We still had no protective position. We pushed sand back as fast and as hard as we could with our hands in an attempt to create two troughs, one for each of us to lie in. We never did get very far, as it wasn't easy to dig and duck at the same time.

Chaos was everywhere, the rockets were taking out tents and bunkers, and there were screams of pain and panic coming from all directions. Mike and I knew that directly to our right front was our battalion medical tent; again, there were no permanent buildings, just tents. Numerous rockets had landed in that area and we could hear men scrambling and yelling but we could not make out what was going on. The guns on the front lines continued to pump rounds in all directions and the rockets continued to pour in.

Eventually the infantryman's best friend, sunrise, was on its way. With the beginnings of daylight the enemy broke contact on the front lines and with their rockets. From what I remember, I don't think they ever made it through our lines and their rockets never hit the targets they were destined for, but there was considerable damage none-the-less.

128

With daylight, we got a better idea of what damage we had taken, at least near where we were. The positions along Highway 1 really took a beating. We knew their real target was the airstrip, but everything on both sides of the highway really took a beating. Although the mess area was relatively unscathed, nearby tents and positions were completely destroyed.

The battalion aid tent was completely destroyed, it took either one or two hits, though one was probably enough. Some of the rear echelon personnel were walking around the area, scanning for some of the hundreds of pills that had been blown into the surrounding areas. The tent itself was only used during the day and was unoccupied when it was hit. but there was still some tentative bad news. Being our battalion aid tent, all of our staff's medical records were, or had been, on file there. Wherever they had been stored didn't matter any more, at this point they were nonexistent. Medical records might sound trivial, but ours were more complex than most.

Troops going to Vietnam needed numerous shots just to get there and others periodically while there. With records destroyed, the individual documents needed to be recreated. Here is when you began to realize how you were personally being perceived. Over the next few days everyone needed to meet with one of the company corpsman to recreate a new shot card.

Most of us had it easy, the corpsman basically asked you what shots you were given with some approximate dates. We smiled when some of the real jerks were forced by the corpsman to get all their shots all over again as part of this process. What was even better was the fact that each of these individuals realized that they were being singled out and they needed to face the reality of why. The front lines for the most part were relatively unscathed as well. Other than some minor injuries the long night's battle was almost soon forgotten.

What we didn't realize was that this was the best a tenacious enemy had for us, with the beginning of the soon-to-be famous Tet Offensive of 1968. We were truly lucky with the outcome of our battle, as other areas were less fortunate with numerous serious overruns documented. Little did we know that this was just the beginning of more serious fighting, which would last my remaining time in Vietnam. Days were spent getting the base camp back together and launching numerous patrols into the surrounding countryside looking for the NVA troops that had attacked. Our patrols were confined to the immediate area just outside the Quang Tri base. We learned later that the main force that hit our perimeter was part of the same unit that took over Hue City which culminated in one of most famous Marine battles of the Vietnam War.

Our patrols encountered numerous NVA units, possibly split from their main force by other battles. These firefights were always intense, these NVA soldiers knew that each fight for them was a fight to the death. They were all trying to make their way north towards the DMZ and a safe haven on the other side.

The monsoon weather had set in and numerous days of bad weather were upon us. Days, weeks, and months went by without even a glimmer of sun, talk about depressing. The constant rain made the daily patrols even more dangerous. The dullness of the constant rain could put you into a psychological slump and you had to keep yourself above that, your quickness was still the one thing that would keep you alive. During the bad rainy season, the NVA we were pursuing were at best trying to stay out of our way, all they wanted to do is make it back north to safety. Our daily patrols ruined this dream of theirs.

One day in mid-February, we were beginning to set out on a platoon-sized patrol. Frequently, we had Vietnamese Popular Forces troops accompany us on these patrols, but on this day, they stayed behind to man our positions. We had set up a perimeter around a large village to protect the local residence from the severe tactics of the NVA.

One of their tactics was to make their way into a village undetected and to murder and decapitate the village chief or any high official. They wanted to create the feeling that if they cooperated with the Americans, they would all eventually be killed, and the NVA were very effective in delivering this message. The patrol was designed to take up the entire day. 2nd squad took the point position and I was the lucky one to actually be walking point for the entire platoon. We were traveling in a platoon wedge formation just as you would see a flock of geese fly through the sky. On a patrol, the lead person was called "walking point." This person had the responsibility of looking for land mines, booby traps, signs of enemy activity, and numerous other defensive tactics.

Walking point was never fun- you had a lot of responsibility, not only to yourself but to everyone behind you. There was no talking, all communications were conducted with hand and arm signals, and silence was critical. Patrols move like snails, every footstep calculated, every movement slow and controlled. My squad leader was directly behind me with our radioman who kept the platoon commander a little further back informed with what was taking place.

On this day, we were navigating over some rolling hills covered with low, thick, patches of bushes. The morning phase of the patrol went uneventful and we took a short pause to get our bearings and grab a quick bite of C-rations to eat cold. Even this was done without any noise. During the break, everyone faced outwards and did their job of making sure that there was no one on our flanks. Eventually, the patrol continued and we were coming down a long, gradual slope towards what looked like an old rice paddy in a small valley.

As I was coming down the slope, I could see thick vegetation growing on my left flank, much different from the bushes on the upper hills. Looking out over the flat ground, it looked like what once was a rice paddy that hadn't been worked for quite some time. I was moving very cautiously out towards the open area, not a place that you would normally like to be.

As I moved forward, I kept looking towards my left at the unusual vegetation and I could see that down towards my left front it came to an end. In time, I came to the end of the vegetation and took my time scanning all avenues around me. I turned and looked to my left and saw that at the end of the vegetation, there was a stream which had obviously been on the other side. At that point, the stream took a left turn away from me, heading towards the other end of the small valley.

That's when I noticed a Vietnamese man standing there, naked. It was obvious that he had just come out of the stream, most likely from taking a bath. My hand went up slowly behind my head, instructing everyone behind me to stop and I just stood there waiting to see what was going to happen. The man hadn't seen me yet and I was sure that he was an NVA soldier even with the absence of a uniform.

We weren't in a free fire zone so I couldn't just open fire on him, he had to make a move. We had to live within numerous very stupid rules while I was there, and at this time there was a standing rule that you couldn't shoot at someone unless they physically had a weapon aimed at you. I know it sounds crazy, but that was some of the BS that we put up with, all of which was an outcome of the protests back in the states.

I should probably go on to say that there was also a standing rule that we couldn't shoot water buffalo either. In the eyes of the Vietnamese people, most of whom were Buddhists, water buffalo were reincarnated relatives. There were numerous times when American soldiers would be searching a village when a water buffalo would go berserk and charge the troops. We took no hesitation to empty our M-16s into the charging bulls rather than getting trampled by them. We tried to make peace with the angry villagers, they instructed us not to shoot, but under certain circumstances we still did.

Getting back to the immediate situation- the soldier stood there drying himself off, unaware of my presence. Just in front of him there was a small tree and I could see something leaning up against it which looked like a rifle. I slowly turned in his direction and even slower, I squatted down into a kneeling position. As I crouched down, my arm went down, which instructed everyone behind me to do the same.

I slowly brought my M-16 into position and aimed down the barrel at the naked soldier. I can't remember my breathing, but it seemed as if everything was in slow motion. Eventually the soldier heard something, possibly one of the many Marines behind me made a noise, I still don't know. Whatever it was, it made the soldier turn to search the area. It seemed like an eternity, but eventually he saw me, kneeling there staring directly at him, waiting. At first he just froze, and I could tell he was trying to figure out what to do, he was definitely in a tough position.

I'll never forget the look in the soldier's eyes. Later, my experiences in Vietnam would put me in the same position. Here he was looking down the barrel of an M-16, knowing that any second a bullet was going to rip through his chest, and now he was looking into the eyes of the man who was going to terminate his life.

This is the moment in your life that you never want to come, the one that you never want to experience. The feelings are not one sided. I as the shooter was faced with the unwanted decision to terminate someone's life or to let him live. Although letting him live would be an unwise decision. That split second when my rifle fired, two lives changed forever. I lived and unfortunately the NVA soldier did not, and I need to live with that fact the rest of my life.

Over the next number of months, this scenario would change sides often. Numerous times I would be looking down the rifle barrel of an NVA soldier knowing that in seconds I would be dead, but somehow I survived each of those instances. Although I survived, I know the deep personal feeling of how it felt to be facing imminent death. As soldiers, we respected this level of death, we all knew that survival was sheer luck and having luck was a crapshoot.

Slowly he began to make his move towards the tree, which was a few steps away. He got close enough and began to reach forward, and I saw him grab the object to pick it up. I let him get as far as showing me that it was definitely a rifle, and that was good enough for me. I let three quick shots go and he went flying backwards. I didn't move, I was waiting to see what else might take place over there, not really sure if there could have been others.

All of a sudden, I heard yelling coming up behind me. Lt Lewy was coming up behind me in a rage. "Jesus Christ, what did we tell you about shooting water buffalo? Don't you realize how much crap we're going to get for doing this? These villagers really have a fit and report it right to the main base!" All the time he was yelling at me, I was trying to tell him that it wasn't that at all, and instead of yelling at me he should be taking cover. At this point, I had no idea how many more of them there were and we should have been getting our act together.

I was not surprised when I heard small rounds fire coming at us from the hillside. With each second, it got more intense and we needed to get into a formation where we could do something about it. The Lt gave some signals to tell the other Marines to begin moving down the hill while he and I moved out further towards the bend in the river. The rest of second squad had moved up with us and we were in some thick, tall hay grass and if we kept low enough, we had cover but no protection. The rest of the platoon had moved down the hill, giving some return fire as they moved but they were instructed by the Lt to stay put and not to move out into the open.

The enemy was now beginning to intensify their fire and we were in a real predicament. It was obvious we needed to get out of there and we couldn't go back the way we came. It seemed that the only way out was across the open area where the rice paddies had once been. On the other side, the elevation began again back to rolling hills.

Ralph, Mike and I were lying there, frustrated that we couldn't even get up and return fire. We had no protection other than the dried grass that we were hiding in. The Lt told us to run across the open field and get into position on the other side.
While we were running, our troops would provide covering fire.

Once we got into position we would lay down some covering fire which would enable the other to make it across the clearing. We initiated the plan quickly and the three of us began our zigzagging run across the open area. The others gave us some covering fire but even with that, the earth was kicking up all around us during our run. Our scramble was successful and we made it safely to a protective area.

We quickly got into position and radioed the Lt that we were all set. From our new position, we could see some of the NVA changing position, getting closer and closer to the other Marines. We opened fire and began to sweep the area where the NVA were, attempting to keep them down and prevent them from shooting. The other Marines began their journey, running in team rushes across the open area, attempting to get to cover and safety.

I remember glancing to my left, watching some Marines at a full gallop while one of our new Marines must have gotten hit square in the back. He was at a full run when hit and he did a full forward flip, landing solidly on his back. I knew him, he was one of the newest men to second squad, and I had just taken his picture a day or two before. Other Marines coming up behind him grabbed him and dragged him the rest of the way up the hill. I know there were more casualties as they came across the clearing, but that's the only one that I can remember clearly.

Eventually everyone was across, but we still had a long way to go to get back to our village and now time was against us.
Once organized, the Lt instructed us to take the lead again and gave us instructions on which way to go. Unfortunately, our pace needed to be a little quicker because of time and this was always a dangerous way to advance. One of the biggest fears for any patrol is to be ambushed. This is bad enough when you are doing things correctly, but when you are acting hastily, you are more vulnerable to getting hit. Ambushers normally let the point elements through their trap, which gives a false sense of security or success. This is what happened to us this day. The NVA, guessing the direction that we would be moving in, moved hastily out in front of us and set up an ambush.

Again, Ralph, Mike and I made it through the critical area and were continuing cautiously down the main path. All of a sudden, we heard screams of "ambush left" from the Marines behind us and the beginning of very intense gunfire. Months of training paid off and when the NVA went to trigger the ambush, one of our Marines saw something out of the norm and yelled an immediate reaction command, and we beat them at their own game. We still had wounded that we needed to carry out, but we left many dead NVA behind us as well.

In basic terms, this was a bad day and everyone was dealing with their own personal emotions. We came back to the village and went back to our assigned positions. I for one was thinking about the new guy, the one I took the picture of, he was with us this morning and now he was gone. I can't even remember his name but surprisingly I can remember his face and how awkward he looked in all-new jungle fatigues and flack jacket, being completely new to Vietnam.

We had been in this village for a while and we had sporadic contact with the NVA. It was still the tail end of the monsoon season, but Charlie was out there and he periodically came after us. From our fighting positions, most of us had good fields of fire, or a clear view of what was in front of us.

Each position put out numerous protective devices that would help if the enemy ever tried to approach us during nightfall. Minimally, everyone put out a variety of trip flares that would be ignited if someone broke one of the trip wires. Booby- trapped grenades were set up the same way. If someone pushes too hard on the trip wire, the safety pin on an M-26 hand grenade will be pulled out and the grenade would explode, hopefully catching its prey. We also put out claymore mines.

These were concave-shaped devices the size of a good reading book. Half of the insides were filled with Charlie 4, or plastic explosives, and the front was filled with hundreds of small bearings. It was a common problem, figuring out which side contained what, and they printed "This side towards enemy" on the bearing side of the device.

Claymores were manually detonated by what we called a clacker. The clacker was on one end of a wire that would go all the way out to the hidden device. To prevent us from setting one of these devices off accidentally, you had to squeeze on the clacker three times in quick succession to have it go off. The concave shape created a wide swath for the bearings to be blasted; you would not want to be out in front of one of these when it went off.

The NVA were no dummies though. They took great pride on finding one of these and making their way to it under the cover of darkness and then turn it around, facing our lines.
With the claymore now facing towards us, they would create a noise or a situation that would make the troops manning the lines press on the clacker, and the results were quite ugly. To help prevent this, we always placed something white or bright on the backside of the device. During the night, we always kept close watch on the patches of white to try to ensure they were facing the right way. Nights even in good terrain were a very difficult time even with these protective and warning devices out in front of you. There were many times at night when creatures would trip our flares or grenades, and they were in for a real surprise, almost always deadly.

I was in a fighting position with Ralph that was at the end of a nice, wide trail and we had a clear view of the open field out in front of us. The next position after ours was a few feet around the corner, with a good bit of bamboo and ground cover in between. Even though the nights were somewhat brighter with the diminishing monsoons, it was very dark at this corner of the perimeter.

When we had returned from our patrol that day, we were all exhausted and we struggled through our evening C-rations while we waited for nightfall. Someone else had the responsibilities for the ambush and listening post; we were manning the lines for the night. During any given night, the squad leaders had the responsibility of checking the lines by going from hole to hole to make sure everything was ok.

Periodically, the platoon commander would do the same, especially in good terrain like this. At some point during the night, I was on watch and had sat down in a seat that we had carved out of the back of the foxhole. This gave us the ability to sit on something like a chair and still be able to look out over our area of responsibility

I was doing what we all did to try to stay awake- looking at the stars, thinking of people back home while keeping an eye on what was out in front. At one moment I remember sitting there, completely still, opening my eyes to look out in front of the hole. I hadn't moved and I was deep within the shadows of the foxhole.

I felt the presence of something to my immediate left and it took everything in me to turn my eyes to see if I could make out what it was. At first, everything was blending together in the pitch darkness- there was something that was not right but I couldn't tell what it was. Within seconds, my eyes started to adjust to what was in front of me and I realized that I was looking at a pair of legs. Without moving anything else, I scanned upwards with my eyes not knowing what I would find. I strained my eyes to try to make out who or what it was and I was terrified with what I saw.

There stood Lt Lewy staring out over my foxhole. He didn't say a word but just stood there for what seemed to be a lifetime. It was pitch black where I was sitting and he would need to look straight down to even have a chance of seeing me. Eventually he turned slowly and walked down the path to check on positions on the other side of the perimeter.

140

I was furious at myself, I had fallen asleep while on watch, the one thing that was never permissible. I don't know how long I was asleep but it was long enough to scare the hell out of me, it was long enough for Lt Lewy to walk down the path to where I was. I never fell asleep again after that. Fortunately, the night went without incident other than the normal fears of standing watch. The Marines that had been there longer took great pains to teach us the basics and some of the basics were more important than others, learning how to stay awake was very high on the list.

The NVA had been periodically probing our lines but they never came at us hard. Early one morning we found out why. Somewhere around 4 A.M. there was a lot of commotion in the central part of the village. During the early hours, a small team of NVA soldiers had made their way through the Marine defenses and paid a visit to the village chief. When they were done, they had made their point very clearly.

They had taken the village chief into the open area, just outside of his thatch house and beheaded him with a machete. They then dismembered him and scattered the pieces in the open area just outside his hooch while the rest of his family looked on. The message was clearly meant to discourage the villagers from working with the Americans. There were no obvious signs as to how the NVA infiltrators had made their way into the village, or out afterward.

Surprisingly, this horrible act did not change the overall feelings of the village residents. I always found myself completely surprised how determined they were to live their lives the way they wanted, regardless of the actions of the NVA. I found the Vietnamese to be some of the most determined people that I had ever met and they were very simple farmers. We always feared what would happen to the residents of a village after we had left and were no longer there to give them protection from the tactics of the NVA. Months later, we would learn more about exactly how far the NVA would go to make their point.

A night or so later, Mike and I were assigned to go out on a listening post, the scariest assignment of all. We got our gear together just before nightfall and got the PRC 25 communications radio that we would use to send in situation reports, or "sit reps" as we called them. The men on the listening post didn't do any talking when they were in position.

The platoon radio operator would call your call sign, ours being Alpha-2-bravo, and then he would say, "If everything is ok, press the send key on your handset once; if there is trouble, press the send key twice". When he was finished with the message, you would respond accordingly. For night activities, the squelch on the radios would be modified so that when the send key was depressed, it would send a "pshhhht" sound and that was what the radio operator would be listening for- either one or two of those sounds.

The men on the LP would share two-hour watches throughout the night and normally you wouldn't be able to move at all once you had found a good hiding place. Whoever was on watch would need to keep the handset up to their ear to prevent anyone else from hearing the messages coming from the platoon radio operator.

When you went out on an LP in the jungle areas, it didn't really matter where you went as long as it was out in front of the lines somewhere- after all you were there to listen. In the village areas it was different. There were numerous paths and cart trails that needed to be monitored and you usually found a hiding place either along side a path or better yet, an intersection of paths.

For this night's watch, Mike and I left our lines and moved cautiously alongside a very wide cart path. We knew that further out, there was an intersection where two cart paths came together. We didn't move on the path itself; instead, we made our way through the vegetation off to the side of the trail. Keeping out of sight was very important but you still needed to move slowly enough so you didn't make any noise. With these rules, it took us quite a while to get to the trail intersection. There, the trails came together in the shape of a "T," the main trail went straight and the other trail came in from the right. We found a nice place to hide about two feet in from the main trail, directly across from where the other trail came in.

The moon was out, which gave us a good view of the trail coming straight at us. We could only see a few feet of the main trail, just the section visible through the vegetation in front of us. All things considered, this was a good spot. It wasn't raining and everything around us was fairly dry, we had been on much worse listening posts and ambushes.

The first half of the night went by without incident, but that changed drastically in the early hours of the morning. It was somewhere after midnight and Mike was on watch; on a listening post, you never had the luxury of sitting up, you were always laying down, making sure you were out of sight. We were both lying side-by-side with our heads facing the trail that came into the main trail.

I was lying there in the usual half sleep state when all of a sudden, something was squeezing my right arm. I opened my eyes to see what was going on and Mike had his face directly in front of mine with his finger up to his lips, making sure I knew not to talk at all. When he knew he had my attention, he pointed to his right ear and then pointed down the main trail towards our left. He was trying to tell me that he had heard something coming from that direction.

This was not all that uncommon. There were hundreds of wild animals which were hard enough to deal with, but at least they didn't carry weapons. Our initial thoughts were that it was a wild pig, a boar or possibly a mongoose. We lay there for quite some time and didn't hear a thing. I had started to drift back off to sleep when Mike grabbed my arm again.

This time I had heard something as well and whatever it was, it didn't sound like an animal and it was very close. Immediately our senses were alive, both of us were wide awake and nervous sweat was running down our faces. We couldn't change our position to see what was coming from our left, we needed to lay there and let it come to us. One thing we knew for sure- it wasn't a squad of Marines out on a night patrol.

In a few minutes, which seemed to be an eternity, a soldier's leg came into view. He was taking one very cautious step after another. From our position, the best we could do was look up with our eyes, trying not to move our heads or anything at all. What we saw was an NVA soldier in full gear; he wasn't out on a patrol, he was on the move. After a few steps, he had moved out of our sight to the right.

Each second was like an hour and we had no idea as to how many of them there were. There was quite a gap between the first soldier and the next one. Mike and I both assumed they were taking advantage of the moonlit night and the first soldier was walking point.

Eventually the next soldier came into view and made his way slowly past our narrow opening. Before he was out of sight, another came into view. The main formation was moving very close together, not necessarily a good way to move. If we were scared before, we were well beyond that now. From where we were lying, we could actually reach out and touch them as they went by. Even though the moon was out, where Mike and I were lying was very dark but at this point, I was thinking, is it dark enough? If we can see out, they could just as easily look down and spot us.

Just like any patrol, there were times when the whole column would stop, and this is when it got really scary. Seeing them walk by us is one thing but now here they are, two sometimes three of them directly in front of us. We were sure their rules were the same as ours; when the column stops, it's everyone's responsibility to keep an eye out for the enemy.

All Mike and I wanted to do was to melt into the ground beneath us. We were sure that one of them would spot us eventually. During all of this, Mike had the handset up to his ear terrified that when a situation report request came in, the enemy soldiers would hear it no matter how hard he tried to muffle it. He did a good job, when the first sit rep came in, I couldn't hear it from where I was, just inches away from the hand set.

Mike listened to the radio operator's words and eventually pressed the send key on the handset twice. This didn't happen often and the radio operator came back immediately asking for verification of two key presses. With that, a million questions began to come in. We could envision the entire platoon command post, awake and nervous, trying to put the questions in order by priority.

Were the soldiers NVA or VC? Were they on patrol or on the move? Were they carrying any heavy equipment? Did they have mortars? Did they have big machine guns? The questions went on and on. During all of this Mike and I were trying to keep count we knew that would be a question they would eventually ask.

We had no idea what to expect from the Marines in our platoon and company. Minimally we knew that the word had been passed that there was a large enemy unit moving in the direction of the perimeter and I was very confident that the foxholes alongside the trail were being reinforced with additional Marines and machine guns.

The air was dead still and it was a very warm night. We could smell them as they went by, the Vietnamese had a distinct smell that we could identify easily. We also knew that we too had a distinct smell and we were terrified that one of them would smell us and begin looking, especially during one of the periods when the column had been stopped. Numerous times, the soldiers took advantage of the pause and took a leak into the bushes alongside the trail. They peed to our left and to our right but somehow no one ever peed directly on top of us.
Boy did their urine stink, the only good thing about that was now they wouldn't be able to smell us, and we felt somewhat better about that. This was a very large unit and they were carrying some very heavy equipment, mortars, machineguns the works.

The NVA soldiers didn't have many of the luxuries that we had. Each day or so, we had helicopters flying in to bring us re-supplies of food, ammunition, combat gear, anything or everything that we needed. The NVA soldiers had to carry everything with them, they had no re-supply channels. The troops out in front of us were heavily laden with extra ammunition, bags of rice, hand grenades. We knew what it felt like to have a heavy pack on, but they were carrying a lot more than we ever needed to do. There were times that they would talk softly when the column was held up, but Mike and I had no idea what they were saying. I could only guess they were complaining just like we would under the same circumstances.

The trail they were traveling on went straight to the village where our company was dug in and there were no other trails that we knew of for them to turn off onto. Somewhere between where Mike and I were and the village, they turned because they never got to the village. Before the early twilight came, the unit had passed. I know that I had counted more than 100 of them, but now I can't remember the exact number.

When it was light enough to see clearly, Mike and I crawled very slowly forward and stuck our heads out of the bushes, I looked to the left and Mike looked to the right. The only thing I saw was a white chicken walking way down on the trail, and the trail was empty on Mike's side.

In the light of the morning, we made our way back to our perimeter. I think if it was a different day, we would have walked back on the trail, but we both agreed that it would be safer to walk back the same way we had taken on our way out. When we got back to the perimeter, there were a million questions from our squad mates. None of them had heard the questions that were asked of us over the radio the night before and they wanted to know everything. We were initially wide awake, with our adrenaline running fast and furious.
Eventually it went away and Mike and I were left exhausted, we hadn't slept all night.

Heading to the Qua Viet River - Late February 1968

Within a few days after our exciting LP, our unit was on the move again, making our way back past the Quang Tri base, out further towards the larger Marine base of Dong Ha. As usual, we had no idea as to where we were headed but we had made our way back towards the river where we had loaded onto Mike Boats before.

Slowly the word trickled out that we were going to get onto Mike Boats and head down the Cua Viet River, but not all the way to the mouth. About halfway down, the Marines had set up a supply point on the riverbank, which we eventually called the supply depot. The boats finally arrived and we took turns climbing on board.

This was a larger-sized boat than we were accustomed to. The cargo area was much larger and there were crew quarters down below for the sailors who manned the vessel. It had a loading ramp like the other boats, which allowed us to walk on with all of our gear. Towards the back of the cargo area, there were two pallets of C-rations that were obviously going with us. I was one of the last ones on and found a comfortable corner up forward just to the left, or port, of the loading ramp. Eventually the ramp was raised and we began our slow journey down the river. Sitting at deck level with the cargo area it was very hot, it was late February and the monsoon season was slowly leaving us, being replaced with the hot, scalding sun.

Shortly after we had left, I needed to make a head call, knowing that there was one down below. I signaled to the Lieutenant that I needed to go and he nodded his head ok. I got up and walked toward the stern of the boat trying to find the hatch, which would get me below. As I was walking by the two pallets of C-rations, I saw a group of our platoon busily at work carving holes into the sides of the cases, allowing them to grab some of the cans and put them in their packs for later.

I found my way inside and a sailor pointed the way to the head. I took care of my business and was walking back and I was in an open room which was basically their mess deck. A sailor was walking through and asked me if I needed any food supplies, not knowing what he meant I said sure. He took me to a refer door and opened it. There on shelves were canned
hams, packages of cheese foods in quantities that I hadn't seen in a long time. I went over and picked up a canned ham and turned to look at him and he said, "Go ahead take it, when we get to Cua Viet base after dropping you guys off we'll stock up with everything we need." With that, I took the canned ham and slid it up under my jungle blouse.

149

Now I had to make my way back to my position without getting caught. I walked as quickly as I could to where my gear was. I had made it all the way back and at the last second, the Lieutenant looked at me and saw that I was hiding something under my blouse. He signaled me to come over and softly asked me what I was hiding and why. I told him that it was completely ok that I had permission from one of the crew and he said ok. Somehow the word got around and before long everything the crew had on board was in the hands of the Marines.

The boats made their way to the supply depot and we cautiously disembarked, not knowing what was waiting for us. Initially it was quite eerie, we had the river behind us and a huge, flat, open area in front of us with villages way off in the distance. We spread out to make somewhat less of a target and waited for the powers that be to get their act together. In time, we began to move out very slowly, heading out towards the villages in the distance.

Stealing something the size of a canned ham is one thing, humping it for thousands of yards is something else. Infantry packs were heavy enough and added weight such as this was not easy to manage. Many of the guys in our platoon knew that I had the ham and now I was everyone's best friend. As long as I carried it and not them, what did they care?

By late afternoon we had made our way to a village called Gia Liem, what was later to be named Place Guard, our headquarters village. With the usual shuffling we set the lines in for the night, and Mike and I wound up in the irrigation trench directly in front of the hooch that the Lieutenant was setting up as the platoon command post or CP. Mike and I dug in and surprisingly, this time our position didn't get moved. Behind us to the right, our forward observer was
calculating positions for night D's. Night defensives or D's were calculated positions for artillery to be placed during the night outside our perimeter. They were set to be fired at different times throughout the night in an attempt to catch the enemy on the move and out in the open.

Every now and then you could hear the distant firing of one of our artillery batteries and the screaming of the round as it came near us. Eventually the white phosphorus, or Willie Peter, round would go off out in front of us and the forward observer would mark his map. Once we were dug in, Mike and I began to make a fire behind our foxhole and gathered some stones that would hold up the canned ham. We put puncture holes is the can and put it over the fire for what seemed like a never ending cooking job. Someone guessed that it had been on there long enough and we dragged it off and cut off the remaining part of the lid. Within minutes, the entire ham had been cut up and dished out. Many villagers had gathered around and they really enjoyed watching us scramble over the ham and many of them took a piece as well. It was delicious and worth every bit of the discomfort of carrying it.

The area around this village would become our Area of Operation, or AO, for the next number of weeks. The villagers of Gia Liem were friendly but we still weren't
supposed to share anything with them. Even though we were not supposed to give them any unopened C-rations, they would come to our foxholes during the afternoon asking if they could look through what we had. It got to the point where we would let them look through our C-rations and they would take the ones they wanted.

Later in the day, around dinner time, they would come out to our foxhole and ask us to come to dinner. One of us would go at a time and we would sit on the floor of their hooch and have dinner with them.

Inevitably we would see the food that they took from us that afternoon somehow mixed in with what we were eating, sometimes you had no idea of what it was but it was better than C-rations. Things are very different in a country like Vietnam. Quite often later in the evening, we would be back in our foxhole and the papa san would come out to the front stoop of the hooch and light up his opium pipe, not illegal in Vietnam.

We knew that the NVA were trying to use the waterways to get around and many of our patrols were in the villages that resided on the banks of the Cua Viet River. We spent numerous days searching the fishing villages, looking for men that were young and strong. We would always single them out and have our interpreters question them and check their papers. This was one of the most difficult parts of this war, trying to figure out who was the enemy. The NVA could walk into a village, trade their uniforms for farmer or fishing clothes and become what seemed to be a local villager. We would look for soft hands, softer than farmers or fishermen, we would look at their shoulders to look for the redness left by back pack straps, anything that would help us identify them as the enemy; much harder than you would think.

Time to crank up the Heat

During the last few days of February, we were instructed to get ready for a platoon-sized patrol, at first it didn't seem like anything out of the ordinary. We were getting our gear ready in Gia Liem when we heard the distant engines of Amtrack's heading our way. They pulled up on the outskirts of the village and we were instructed to climb aboard. We all split up, climbed on top of the big, hulky machines, and we headed out for another village.

They circled around and around and eventually stopped in front of the village of Phu Tai. We climbed off of the tracks and assembled for a sweep of the village- we were looking for splinter groups of NVA soldiers. We made our sweep without any reactions from the villagers. We had never been to this village before, but the villagers seemed to be pro-American simply based on their actions.

Later in the day we were transported back to Gia Liem to our familiar foxholes. We had a quiet night with the normal nighttime activities. The next day we heard that the tracks were coming back to take us on another distant patrol. We climbed aboard and the tracks began to make way towards the river, going past villages that we knew well. These tracks can go on land and water- they entered the river and started towards the north bank. Just to the right of where we were heading, there was a small river or stream emptying into the river, and a little further right, a village tucked behind the traditional border of bamboo.

We were half way across when we heard a loud whooshing sound at the same time as a loud scream of "Oh shit." Someone yelled, "RPG's," and others were yelling, "No, it's something else!" Mixed in were the sounds of small arms fire and machine guns. We all hugged the tops of the tracks in an attempt to leave a very low profile. Miraculously, all the tracks made it to the north bank without getting hit but we were definitely under attack.

SOME BY AMTRAC—An amphibian tractor car- to launc'
ries Leathernecks of the 1/3 on the Cua Viet river banks. "attacks on ...

On our way across the Cua Viet river to Dia Do
March 5, 1968

As soon as we hit the north bank, we all jumped off and scrambled for cover. As soon as we were all off, the screams which signaled the beginning of an attack began. We moved forward to the edge of the stream and formed into squads and fire teams. Sergeant Alexander was screaming orders to advance across the stream and the squad leaders were moving the men into position.

Things were happening so fast I don't even remember being scared but before I knew it, I was running through the shallow water of the stream with the bullets kicking up the water at our feet. We reached the other bank and dove for whatever cover we could find.

At this point, the battle going on above our heads was aimed at the Marines still coming across the stream. Sergeant Alexander came screaming across and the squads moved forward into the village. For some reason, Alexander felt that Bill Muldovan wasn't moving fast enough and dramatically
put his 45 caliber pistol in Bill's face screaming at him to advance with the rest of us- Alexander was a real jerk.

We moved out of the streambed up into the village of Dai Do and surprisingly, the enemy fire was decreasing. By the time our squad reached the village, the ground fire was coming from a distant village across another rice paddy. We made our initial sweep of the small village to find that the NVA had definitely moved out. We were instructed to burn all the hooches and one by one we set them afire by either a match or cigarette lighter.

This wasn't as inhumane as everyone thought back then. The enemy would hide firearms and ammunition in the thick thatch of the hooches, so burning them down was the only sure way of finding them. Time and time again, you would hear ammunition blowing up from deep within the thatch, which was a very real issue for those of us involved in the clearing of the village.

It was very common for the villagers to have an underground bunker that they would use for their own safety when any enemy was around. They were fairly large underground rooms made to withstand a direct hit from small artillery.

These bunkers were easy to spot, the entrance was seldom hidden- but they were not always easy to clear. One by one we approached each bunker that we found and would yell, "Lai Dai" which meant "come here," numerous times, trying to coax anyone hiding in the bunker to show themselves.

It seemed pretty obvious that this village had been deserted, and we found no villagers anywhere. As most of us searched the village, the rest were busy firing at the few enemy that they could see making their way towards another village on the far side of the rice paddy facing north. The squad leaders were running around, giving quick instructions for us to dig in. Smitty, Mike and I were given a spot on the north side of the village looking out over the large rice paddy where the enemy had been only minutes earlier. It was early afternoon and we didn't get overly excited about digging in- we all assumed that these would be temporary positions.

Word was beginning to trickle out as to exactly why we were sent to this village and why was the higher echelon so confident that the NVA were actually there. It seems that over the past several days or weeks, the NVA were taking pot shots at the U.S. Mike Boats traveling to and from Dong Ha on the river. They were pretty confident that the NVA were using a 75 recoilless cannon when they were taking those pot shots.

A 75 recoilless isn't a huge cannon and it's actually quite portable, but we couldn't find any sign of it as we searched the village. We were also quite doubtful that the NVA had carried it across the large rice paddy without being seen, but wherever they had hidden it, it was still not in our possession.

We were in the process of digging in when we heard some subtle yells from a foxhole somewhere down to our left. PFC MaGee, a member of 2nd Platoon, was helping to dig in at a position next to a pool of water, like a small pond. Somehow Magee spotted something just beneath the water and a couple of Marines waded in to check it out. To everyone's pleasant surprise, they had found the 75 recoilless.

ua Viet Waterway Open

CAPTURED WEAPON—A mounted 75mm recoilless rifle is examined by members of the 1/3 after its capture. *PFC MaGee 3rd Plt A/C.* (Photo by Lance Cpl. P.L. Schackmann)

Captured 75 recoilless in Dia Do
March 5th, 1968

It took a good-sized crew to drag the gun out of the muddy water and eventually it was set up alongside one of the main hooches. Anyone with time on their hands seemed to find a way to come over and get a glimpse of the captured weapon.

We were still digging our foxhole when we heard a familiar sound of a mortar being launched, but the direction of the sound's origination was in question. Within a few seconds, we saw the round land in the middle of the rice paddy in front of us. Seconds later, another round fell- this one approximately half the distance from our position to the first round. Then there was another round even closer to us. Everyone was yelling, "Incoming!" and running for cover.

Our defensive position was not finished, definitely not big enough for three of us and we didn't feel comfortable staying in our shallow foxhole. We glanced around quickly and found a family bunker within a safe running distance, so we took off in a crouched run and made it to the side of the bunker.
Incoming mortars were still making their way towards our perimeter.

It's never good to do something in a rush, but somewhere in the middle of this, we let PFC Wright try to go down the narrow entrance of the bunker. Wright was a very large man and somehow he managed to wedge his huge frame into the entranceway and got stuck like a cork in a bottle. I was directly behind him and Smitty was behind me, and we were both yelling at the top of our lungs, pushing as hard as we could to try to get Wright through the narrow opening. Finally something gave, and the three of us poured into the underground bunker.

None of us knew what direction Doc, our corpsman, went in but he wasn't with us- he might have realized that the distance from the foxhole to the bunker was too risky and stayed at the hole. The mortars had found their way inside the perimeter of the village and now they began pounding away.

We separated and sat in the corners of the bunker, hoping that it didn't take a direct hit. With the landing of each round, you could feel the concussion come through the ground like a dull feeling of electricity. The dirt ceiling of the bunker trickled down with each impact and the mortar rounds kept coming.

Eventually they subsided and we gave everything enough time before making our way back to the bunker opening. Wright again went first and when he got to the top of the opening, he peeked out cautiously toward the open rice paddy to see what was going on. He finally signaled to us that everything was ok and he made his way out into the bright daylight.

We worked our way slowly back to our foxhole and rejoined Doc Bird. Many of us in Vietnam had nicknames, Doc being one of them. His real last name was Peacock and he was quickly labeled Doc Bird. Nobody ever busted his chops seriously, after all he was one of our corpsman and on a day- to-day basis, they were any Marine's best friend.

We got back to the hole and were caught up in some light chatter, trying not to think about the mortar barrage that we had just endured.

At one point, Doc asked Smitty how he got all covered with blood and Smitty looked at Doc like he had two heads. With a quick closer look, I saw that Smitty's backside was drenched with deep red blood and I told Smitty that Doc was right and he was covered in blood. Doc asked Smitty to move to the village side of the foxhole and for him to drop his jungle fatigues. This was no time for arguing and Smitty did what he was told. Doc did a quick inspection and found a short, deep and clean cut on the under side of Smitty's butt.

With a quick cleanup, Doc told Smitty that he was going to put him in for a purple heart. Smitty got very offended and gave Doc very clear instructions that he was not to put him in for a heart. The last thing that Smitty wanted is to get a purple heart for getting shot in the butt.

As Smitty's medical visit was coming to an end, we heard some M-16 small arms fire down the perimeter from where we were. This was accompanied by numerous people yelling and as we looked, we could see them pointing out into the rice paddy where the mortars had just been walked across. We could see some enemy soldiers making their way back into the village on the far side of the paddy. Within seconds, there were Marines pouring out into the paddy, spreading out as they went. Commands rang out and before we knew it, we were being called to join those already in pursuit of the enemy.

We followed our fire team leaders and squad leaders as we fanned out to the left of our platoon commander in a relative line. There was some incoming fire and our platoon radio operator was hit as he tried to enter the rice paddy. Within a short period of time, we had moved forward and we were now about halfway across the paddy.

Off in the distance in front of where I was, there was a Catholic church set back within the perimeter of the other village. We were getting a lot of incoming rounds from that area and were sure that there was a sniper or maybe just some NVA soldiers in the church tower taking advantage of the view. Things were beginning to heat up around us and most of us realized that we were hung out there to dry in the open. Our lieutenant was in a dilemma, he had no way of calling in artillery or air strikes without a radio and his radio operator was back in the village tree line wounded. The lieutenant yelled out to two Marines, one on either side of where he was, to crawl back and to drag the radio out to their current position.

Two men that I knew well were part of this, we had all come to Vietnam together. Mike Muldovan from Watertown, New York was the Marine to the lieutenant's right and James Banning from East Hampton, Connecticut was the one on the left.

They cautiously took off on their mission, making their way to the village tree line and the wounded radio operator. They wrestled the PRC 25 from the wounded Marine and each took one shoulder strap. They tried their best to do a Marine low crawl, using one arm while their other one was dragging the radio. They made it back to the lieutenant's position, deposited the radio and went back to their original positions. The lieutenant went to work quickly, calling in artillery support and numerous air strikes on the village out in front of us.

Things had really heated up on our side of the line. Even though we were well spread out and had relatively good cover, we were all behind a rice paddy dike, and the mud was kicking up all around us. We were trying to concentrate our fire on the church and its tower, assuming that was the vantage point the NVA were using. After numerous artillery volleys and air strikes, the lieutenant announced the charge into the village.
The squad leaders and fire team leaders took charge of their men and we made our way into the village. This time the enemy chose to fight another day. There was some minor resistance, but when we entered the village, the enemy had vanished into thin air, a frustrating and common reoccurrence.

As we made our way cautiously back across the rice paddy, word began to travel that we had lost some men during our charge across to the village. At first I didn't think too much of it, but eventually names were attached to the body count. James Banning was one of the men that had been killed. Apparently after he had returned with the radio and assumed his former position, an NVA sniper had found James and took him out.

This news hit me like a brick, and for numerous reasons. James was one of the first casualties who was close to me, he was one of the Marines that came to Vietnam with our group. He was also from Connecticut, my home state, and that had somewhat of a special meaning to me. But I think why it affected me so deeply was I knew who James was. James was our platoon comedian; nothing ever seemed to faze him. He would do things that would make most of us shudder on one hand and yet laugh hysterically on the other. He was our comic relief in a place where we all needed it.

I didn't take part in carrying our dead out of the rice paddy but I knew they were all put in an area until medivac helicopters could come in. It was still quite light and I told everyone where I was going, I was going to say goodbye to James. I found them laid out, side by side, in an area of hard packed soil, like the front porch of a hooch.

It's hard to describe what a dead body looks like and this was one of my first times to be up close and personal. I found James's body and sat on the ground, inches from where he was placed. When life goes out of a body, so does all control over its muscles. James's body laid there in a position that no one could get into, not even a newborn infant. I can remember sitting there and talking, hopefully not out loud, to James, asking him why.

You learned in Vietnam very quickly that there were very few answers which made much sense- so why not talk to a dead man? It's hard to put into words how much of a loss I felt with James being killed. He was the first of our group, he was from Connecticut, he was the jokester- why him?

Unfortunately, he was one of many close friends that I would see meet that fate and I always asked why. Although it was painful to see Jim lying there and there really was a deep sense of sorrow, there was also a new feeling, one that was very real but it also made me feel very cheap.

Mixed in with the deep sense of loss, there was this voice going through my head saying, "Phew, at least it wasn't me." Time and time again when I would lose someone close, these words would ring very clearly in my mind and I never felt right for thinking that way. I never dared tell anyone that I had this feeling, it never felt right.

I sat there a foot or two away from Jim and just looked at him. Whoever had carried him there had tried to place him on his back. There must have been something behind him or possibly a few panels in his flack jacket had twisted and were bracing his back up.

At any rate, regardless of what was holding him up, the upper part of his body was angled back in an awkward position. His head was tilting back in what would normally be an impossible angle, making his whole body look extremely grotesque. His legs were sprawled out in front of him, also in positions that were not normal. This was my first up close and personal look at a real dead person. There had been many more before Jim, but this was the first time I had ever wanted to get close to them. What I saw during that visit left a lifelong impression on me.

While I was there, I promised Jim that I would look up his family when I got home and would tell them what I knew of their son, how courageous I thought he had been. There would be other such promises; most were never kept, some took most of my adult years to come to grips with, and even then, the deliveries were very difficult and hard.

I finally felt that I had spent enough time there and I made my way back to our foxhole. It was late afternoon, by now all the digging was done and men were starting to pull together their evening meal of C-rations. When we had made the assault on the village, we had left our packs in the Amtrack's to make our physical efforts in the assault somewhat easier. During the afternoon, squads made their way back to the track and picked up the packs belonging to members of their squad. Someone had collected most of ours, but mine somehow was missing. We looked everywhere around the foxholes that belonged to second squad but there was nothing to be found.

I asked my fire team leader and squad leader for permission to walk the perimeter to look for my missing pack. I began walking the perimeter looking for my gear. Although the packs looked very similar we had all made some personal modifications and there were certain things about my pack that would stand out among others. I slowly walked the paths between foxholes, casually greeting the other Marines because I didn't want to forewarn anyone that I was in search of something.

I finally came to a hole and the Marines inside were busy getting their evening meals. I caught a glimpse of a pack that was similar to mine. There was a Marine sitting next to it so there was a good chance that it wasn't mine at all. He reached towards the pack to get at something inside and pulled out a plastic pouch filled with personal writing gear, pads, pens and envelopes. We normally used the plastic bags that the batteries came in for the PRC radios, as it was good thick, plastic and tall and wide enough to hold our writing gear.

As soon as I saw it, I realized it was mine and I was really pissed that someone had claimed it for their own. It wasn't a regular issue pack- I had purchased it from a Vietnamese boy in a village a month or two prior. It had many pouches that were nice for carrying supplies. I gently brought my M-16 around in front of me and I stood in front of the Marines who were sitting on the ground. I stood there until I got everyone's attention and they knew by the look on my face that I was dead serious.

I'm sure that most of them had no idea what was going on. I looked the Marine with my pack in the eyes and asked him where he got the pack. I still don't know if he was a new guy in country or just a complete idiot, but there was one thing that you never did and that was mess with your own people. He was scared shitless and I was equally as mad. I told him to put everything back in the pack and I waited for him to kick it forward towards me. Before I picked it up, I told him and his friends that if something ever happened like this again, I wouldn't be leaving them with a full magazine in my rifle. I looked at all of them and made sure that they realized exactly how close they had come- they realized.

The next morning came without incident, which was a welcome relief. A patrol was sent across the rice paddy to the adjoining village without any action, the NVA had chosen to move on and to save the battle for another day. The patrol came back with numerous pieces of enemy rifles and other
equipment including a sniper's rifle. This was all very puzzling; normally they never left anything behind, especially weapons.

The Battles to oust the enemy continue

On the morning of March 7th, we were told that we would be boarding the Amtrack's again and we'd be going back across the river to a staging area. With no fanfare, we boarded the tracks and made our way across the river, converging on an area near the riverbank just shy of another village.

We were told we were going to make an assault into the village and again we were going to travel light. Squad by squad, we took our packs and carried them inside the tracks for safe keeping while we ran our assault. After I had dropped my pack off, I sat down on the ground and leaned against the tracks of the vehicle, trying to choke down some breakfast.

There was someone on top of the track that I was leaning against who was yelling orders to the other track operators. For some reason the voice sounded very familiar. I let him yell a few more orders before I stood up and took a few steps away from the track so I could look up to see who was making all the noise.

I was extremely surprised to see Sergeant Lewis, who I was stationed in Charleston, South Carolina with, barking out the orders. All I could do was laugh and asked him when the hell he had gotten into country. As soon as he saw who it was, he jumped down and we had a nice, brief, visit.

He was trying to ask a million questions in just a few minutes, he had only been in country for a month or two and he wanted to know what us grunts were up to. I told him what I could about Tom and I and how we had survived so far. He asked me what I thought about the assault on the village and I just shook my head- like I had a choice.

Eventually, the word came down for us to start forming up on the boundary of the nearby rice paddy. From what we were being told, there was a reinforced company of NVA soldiers in the village across the way and we were going to try to force them out. Regardless of how many NVA soldiers were involved, this was not good news. The farmers had recently cut all the rice and the paddies were bare, giving us nothing to hide behind other than the periodic rice paddy dike.

We would be taking off in what was called fire team rushes. The squad leader would blow on a whistle and yell a number; if the number was the number of your fire team, you would get up, run a few yards, and then dive to the ground. The squad leader would do this to change the pattern of the assault. This would keep the enemy on their toes, not knowing who would be getting up next.

Sergeant Lewis came up to me just before the assault began and said that he would be looking for me when it was all over. I hoped in my heart that I would be there for that visit. The assault began.

Team after team leaped forward and we began to make our way towards the village. Our squad was on the far right flank of 2nd Platoon and we were tying in with another element from 3rd Platoon. We were well spread out, a good Marine assault, but there was extreme tension in the air. It was very hot and even without our packs, we were drenched in sweat early in the assault. Somewhere to my right there was someone carrying a communications radio and he was yelling information to his squad leader or platoon leader- it must have been a platoon commander because he called him sir. At one point I heard him say, "Sir, I can see a rifle hanging out of the window of that hooch."

Almost exactly at that moment, the whole world erupted in a huge explosion. Whoever they were, they opened up with tremendous firepower. Fortunately for our fire team, we were lying on the ground, but I couldn't get over the intensity of the gunfire that was going over my head.

I looked around for some cover and saw a huge lump of dried mud just to my right front. I made a decision and crawled as fast as I could to get behind that clump of mud-it wasn't much but it was much better than what I currently had, which was nothing at all. There were a few of us who were relatively safe but there were many others caught in the open when the enemy in the village had opened up on us. Over the din of the battle, I could hear screams and the automatic call of, "Corpsman up."

The intensity of the ground fire stayed at an incredible level- anyone who tried to get up and move didn't make it very far. Every few minutes, you would yell to the Marine to your left and to your right to see if they were still ok. This was much more difficult than you would think, the constant gunfire was very difficult to yell over.

We were stuck, we all knew it and it was going to be a very long day. It was getting close to midday and the sun was beating down on us and we all felt as if we were in an oven roaster. We were in for a long one and we got as comfortable as we could. I took out a canteen, a couple extra magazines, my cigarettes, and my lighter, and I arranged them in front of me behind the clump of mud. At this point, there wasn't much we could do but keep our heads down, and even that wasn't easy.

I knew that there were casualties on my left front and there were problems getting corpsman up there to give them the medical treatment that they needed. I wasn't sure who they were, all I knew for certain was that they were part of our platoon, and that alone was enough to put you in a different mood. At one point during the battle, I heard a grumbling sound and I looked out past my mud clump cover to see what was going on. I saw an Amtrak moving slowly up towards where the wounded were and I was happy that something was being done to get medical help up there.

The tracks had moved into position near where I thought the wounded Marines were and stopped. Activity around me was the same, bullets digging the earth up around me and my clump being slowly diminished. At one point, I heard a boom and a roar and I looked up to see what was going on.
I saw a cloud of smoke coming out of one end of the track and I said to myself, "Get some," meaning that I thought the track was firing on the village. It wasn't until some time later that I realized that it wasn't the track firing on the village, it was the NVA firing an RPG at the track and hitting it. This took quite a bit of steam out of me and I knew that we were in for a much longer fight than anyone had anticipated.

Right from the beginning of the fight, I heard the sounds of our mortars going overhead, and now I could hear the sounds of our distant artillery guns opening fire. It was a welcomed sound and the rounds began to fall within the perimeter of the village. They had their coordinates locked in and the rounds just kept coming but even the artillery didn't slow the ground fire that was going over our heads.

You could hear the high shrill sound of the fighter jets cutting through the air, coming in a steep dive. The sound is made by the wings slicing through the air and it's something that you only hear in a situation like this or on a military base where they practice attack dives. Yells came down the line that we were going to be getting close air support which was fun to watch from a distance, but to be close to was something else. The F-4s came in from behind my position and the first wave scared the hell out of me between the roar of the battle and the roar of their engines- I don't know which was louder. They came wave after wave, one carrying 500-pound high explosive rounds and the next wave would be napalm.

When the HE rounds were being dropped, you wish you had your entrenching tool with you so you could dig deeper.
Between the explosion and the following shrapnel shower, you wanted all the cover you could get. When the napalm was coming down in the long silver containers, everything in the village would stop, even the NVA were trying to get away from the napalm. As soon as the fire from the napalm would begin to diminish, the ground fire would pick up again. After each load was dropped, the jets would climb as fast as possible into the air, banking to the left or right to come around for another run.

Huey Gunships were also called in and in this instance, they were guided by observers on the ground. They would also come in at a diving sweep, straightening out at the last second to unload their rockets at the designated hooches or bunkers. As they flew over the village, they would also climb as fast as possible and bank left or right, in either case the door gunners were hanging out, shooting backwards with their M-60 machine guns- quite a sight to see.

During their banking ascent or descent, their blades would be slapping the air making a very distinctive popping or whopping sound one that anyone there would remember for the rest of their lives. As with the jets, they made pass after pass, trying to dislodge the NVA from their command of the village.

Little by little, we could tell we were making a difference because the ground fire was slacking off. At one point I looked around my clump of mud and saw that much of it had been chipped away by enemy bullets, and I knew that it wouldn't be long before the bullets would start coming right through. The enemy knew I was there and they had been trying desperately to destroy my cover.

I was looking forward trying to determine were to shoot next when I first heard someone coming up behind me, yelling as he ran along. It wasn't unusual for infantry platoons to have backups and in this case, Alpha Company had Delta Company 2nd Platoon as our backup. I couldn't believe what I was hearing, it sounded like a herd of cattle coming up behind us and I really didn't want to look back to see who was making all the ruckus, it definitely wasn't anything that we, Alpha Company, would have done. At one point I heard a Marine's scream very near to my right rear say, "Don't fear, Delta Two is here!" I couldn't believe my ears, I cringed with the thought that any grunt could be so stupid as to say anything like what I just heard.

I looked over my right shoulder and I saw the jerk running up behind me, stripped of his pack as we were. I lay there flat on the ground looking at him and as soon as he had those words out of his mouth, an NVA bullet ripped through his head and he came crashing to the ground a few feet from my right foot. I saw the bullet rip through his head and I saw his lifeless body come crashing to the ground in the wake of a puff of rice paddy dust and he lay there lifeless. I said aloud to myself, "You dumb fuck, you deserved that bullet, you arrogant shit."

I couldn't believe how stupid he was, I sincerely hoped that he was someone new who didn't know what he should be saying and when. I vaguely remember that his fatigues were dirty and worn, telling me that he wasn't someone new, which really surprised me. Anyone that had walked the mud and
jungles of Vietnam as it appeared he had, shouldn't have been talking the way he was, it was something that you just did not do.

Unfortunate as it was, the Marine's death made it quite clear to me that the initiative of the NVA in the village had not slackened- if anything, it had increased. With the jerk's death, I was really beginning to get concerned about the protection that the little clump of mud was providing me. Even after the artillery barrages and the air strikes, the dirt around me was still kicking up and I knew that my time was numbered behind the clump of mud that was currently keeping my butt alive.

I did my best to create a status check- I yelled to my left to see who was there and then I yelled to my right to see if Wright was still alive. After numerous yells, I finally heard Wright's high-pitched voice returning my call. Yelling as loud as I could, I asked him what kind of cover he had. It took numerous responses, but I finally understood that he was hiding behind a rice paddy dike, which was the best cover you could get.

I yelled over to him to make room, that as soon as I could, I was going to make my way over to his position. With that, I began to gather my gear and get ready to move over to Wright's area. I stowed my canteens, cigarettes, lighter and spare magazines, and tried to work up the nerve to get up and run over to Wright's position. I knew that if I stayed where I
was, it would have been a matter of minutes before the enemy bullets would penetrate through what was left of my protection.

I can't remember how long I lay there pondering my predicament but it seemed like an eternity. Finally with a loud scream, I announced that I was on my way.
I jumped up and began my run towards Wright's position. As soon as I was up and moving, I realized that I had much further to go than I had originally realized.

Normally I walked patrol with my M-16 at my hip using an unauthorized jungle sling. This was a strap of rawhide that was tied to my front v-sight, tied to a canvas strap that normally went over my shoulder, to a loop that strapped around the butt of my rifle. When I jumped up from my position, I had no intentions of using my jungle sling- I would use the built-in handle on top of the M-16 as I ran.
Unfortunately I forgot to secure the rawhide loop that extended off the back end of the shoulder strap and it dragged on the ground as I began to run.

I ran in a low crouch as fast as I could toward where Wright was positioned. I could see him up ahead, he was lying on his back watching me as I came towards him. The dirt was kicking up all around me but for some reason I didn't pay much attention to the sprays that were obviously coming from bullets aimed at me. As I ran, the strap that was dragging on the ground began to bounce up and hit my lower legs. The more I ran, the more the strap bounced and it began to wrap around the lower part of my right leg.

I can't remember how fast I was running but I'm sure that it was as fast as I could under the circumstances. The faster I ran the tighter the strap wrapped around my leg as I was getting closer and closer to where Wright was lying. I could see him lying there on his back his eyes as big as saucers watching me running towards him, I'm sure that he never thought that I would make the long journey. With only a few yards left to go, the strap began to wrap around both legs and at the last moment it finally succeeded in tangling both legs together.

When that happened, I lost control of what I was doing and flipped forward towards Wright. I landed on my back on the lower part of his legs and I laid there, thoroughly disgusted. I glanced at Wright, who was lying there with his eyes bug- eyed, later admitting that he thought that I was dead. I immediately sat up and started to gather my gear, attempting to position myself to Wright's right.

What I didn't realize was that I was completely exposed above the rice paddy dike and drawing a lot of attention. I was really pissed at what had happened with my strap and I was kneeling there on my knees, moaning and groaning about what had just taken place. My helmet had flown off during my fall and I bent down to pick it up. As soon as I did, an NVA machine gun strafed the top of the dike that Wright and I were hiding behind- now they knew where two of us were.

As soon as I was somewhat organized, I had a chance to prove to Wright that I was very much alive, which he thought was impossible after seeing the bullets chasing me as I ran towards his position. Obviously in war there are many miracles, and I had just experienced one of my own. We made sure we got in communication with the men on our left and right, and they knew Wright and I were together.

There were more explosions or commotion over by the Amtrak and I rolled back on my side to see if I could figure out what was going on. There were more Marines positioned around the crippled track and there was some serious gunfire going on. From what I could tell, they had set up the backside of the track as a medevac area and the NVA were not happy about that one bit. There seemed to be some attempts on the NVA's part to attack out towards the track and wipe everyone out, but the Marines who were there were holding their own.

Wright and I had our own problems. The NVA directly in front of us didn't like my maneuver at all and were concentrating some heavier gunfire on our position. They were continually strafing our position with machine guns and we were both worried that they would use an RPG or something bigger.

By now it was late in the afternoon and we were still pinned down, the slightest movements were very dangerous and usually fatal. Although we didn't want to get up and do anything, Wright and I were worried that if someone didn't do something soon we would still be lying out there in the middle of the paddy when darkness came, and that would definitely not be a good thing.

Shortly after our personal conversation about getting into the village before nightfall, an officer, I think it was our company CO, stood up with his 45 caliber pistol in his hand and screamed at the top of his lungs, "Let's Go!" As crazy as it sounds, that was all that we needed to hear. With his announcement, Marines in varied parts of the rice paddy got up and began charging the village. Wright and I hastily gathered our gear and I patted him on his helmet and said good luck.

With that, I was up and running. Like everyone else attacking the village, you would get up, run for ten or so feet and then hit the deck, wait an undetermined number of seconds and repeat it all over again. This wasn't the best way of attacking a village but under the circumstances, this is what was needed. After numerous spurts, I finally made it to the edge of the village and I dove into the irrigation ditch that was a standard part of every village. Just before I jumped, I had crawled up to the edge of the ditch and tried to look around to see if there were any dead Marines lying in the shallow depths of the pit.
There were none to be seen which told me that the enemy didn't have an ambush set up in the trench and it was relatively safe to go in. With that, I rolled into the trench at the same time as another Marine jumped in alongside of me.

I took a quick glance to see who had joined me and it was a black Marine that I vaguely recognized. He was definitely not comfortable with what we were doing and I asked him what platoon he belonged to. He said that he was part of the weapons platoon, normally a motorman. Because of the intensity of the fight, everyone was deemed to be an infantryman, even those normally used to dropping mortars on the enemy not carrying an M-16. We were keeping our heads below the edge of the trench and we could hear shouts from other Marines from both sides of us. Down to our right, I heard someone yell my name and I shouted back in recognition. It was my fire team leader checking who of his men had made it to the relative safety of the trench.

He yelled back and asked me if I could see the hooch that was to our right front. I crawled up to the edge of the trench and peeked through some low vegetation to check. Off to our right front, about 50 yards or so, was a thatch hut with the traditional packed clay mud around it like a porch. I didn't see any activity from the hooch but there were plenty of bullets still being sprayed all around us. I yelled back that I could see it, and he instructed me to move forward to begin the search of the hooch. While I was running to get closer, they would lay down cover fire to keep the enemy pinned down until I got close enough to throw hand grenades. I yelled back, "Ok."

I moved back from the front to the back edge of the trench to gain my thoughts. I looked at the Marine next to me and asked him if he was ready and he said yes. I told him that I needed to head towards the hooch and he said that he was going straight into the village- I nodded in agreement.

We both squatted down, made sure we had all our gear, and made one last nod towards each other. We jumped up and forward, enabling ourselves to hit the dirt running. We landed side-by-side, just over the edge of the trench, and at that split second, our lives changed forever. All I remember seeing was a red orange glow and then the next thing I remember was lying there staring up at thick smoke. I had no idea how long I had been lying there but I was on my back on the bottom of the trench that I had tried to jump out of.

Everything seemed confusing. I was definitely not all together and I was trying to figure things out as quickly as possible. It took some time but I eventually picked my head up to try to look around. Straight in front of me was the Marine that tried to leave with me and he was staring at me with very wide
eyes. I couldn't feel any pain but I wasn't sure if that meant anything, the Marine kept staring at me and I still wasn't sure why. Then I saw what he was staring at, I could see a steady stream of smoke curling up from my right leg, just above the knee cap. I looked up at the Marine and I saw his lips move but I couldn't hear what he was saying. I said "what" loud enough for him to hear and he responded back with WP, which made me stop in dead in my thoughts.

WP, short for Willy Peter, which stood for White Phosphorus, was one of the last things you wanted to be hit by. Apparently the red orange glow was a WP artillery round that sent both of us back into the trench. WP is a jelly that will burn as long as it has air until it is totally consumed. There is very little you can do to put it out the only thing that you can temporarily do is smother it with mud. Even putting it under water doesn't work, there is air in water and it will continue to burn.

I felt the other Marine move by me and after a while he came back with a bad look on his face. He had been looking for any moisture in the dirt, anything that he could make some mud with, there was nothing in the trench at all. We were completely out of water and we were so dehydrated that we couldn't even piss to make mud, and my leg continued to burn.

I had propped myself up and moved back against the trench wall. The other Marine moved in front of me and took my trouser leg just above the knee and ripped it apart so we could see what we were up against. Just above my knee you could see a hole the size of a silver dollar, and deeply buried in it was a ball of WP jelly.

Surprisingly I couldn't feel any pain, but that didn't minimize the panic we were in trying to stop the burning. What happened next isn't exactly clear. The little that I can remember was seeing him digging his fingers into my leg, I think to scrape the jelly out with his bare fingers. All I know is that after that, there wasn't any more smoke coming from my leg and he sat back against the opposite wall of the trench.

We sat there for a while trying to work through what had just happened and began to realize that the battle was still raging above the rim of the trench. The sound of some shots directly over our heads woke us up some and he asked me if I was all right. I nodded that I was and he prepared to enter the village again. He took one glance back at me, nodded his head and jumped over the rim of the trench and he was gone.

I started to get my act together to try and re-enter the war, and I got to the kneeling position in preparation of jumping up. At the last second I realized that I didn't have my helmet and I stopped short. I looked around the trench and there was no helmet to be found. I glanced out towards the rice paddy and saw at least one helmet and I was assuming it was mine which must have been blown off when the artillery round initially blew up.

There were still Marines making their way towards the village and I yelled to one of them to grab my helmet on his way in. He threw it to me as he came into the trench. He hesitated for a second and he was on his way, he never stopped to ask any questions. With my helmet secured, I was now ready to get going. I moved to the other side of the trench and listened to see if there were any commands coming from the trench line to my right.

I didn't hear anything but within a few seconds I saw a Marine emerge from the ground cover, running a zig zag pattern towards the hooch that I was originally sent to clear. I recognized him immediately. It was Ralph, one of my closest friends. He was about halfway to the hooch when there was a loud shearing sound of an incoming mortar round. All of us who were watching saw Ralph go from a crouched run to flipping awkwardly through the air.

There was a large cloud of clay dust rising above where the round had hit, and lying there was the lifeless frame of Ralph. I heard commanding shouts coming from my right and I saw a fire team move forward hastily past Ralph, positioning themselves half way between Ralph and the hooch. They began laying down covering fire and other troops began to move out of the trench, all converging on Ralph. When we got to him, he was lying on his stomach and was not moving.

Men started tearing at his jungle fatigues to see how badly hurt he was, I crawled around so I could see his face which was lying on the ground facing towards his left side. I was down on the ground with my face just a few inches from his to see if I could tell if he was breathing or not.

There were slash marks on his face where small pieces of shrapnel had torn pockets of flesh out of his face, like bites from some small animal. Each one had a small trickle of blood seeping down his face. It seemed like forever, but he finally opened his eyes and looked at me.

He whispered something very softly and with all the noise around us I couldn't make out what it was. I inched closer and he said it again, in almost a whisper he mouthed, "Water." I heard it like a lightening bolt. Here was one of my best friends, very badly hurt, his only wish was for some water, and I knew that there wasn't a drop to be had. He didn't move his head, he had his eyes open for a few seconds but after he said the word water his eyes closed slowly. I told everyone what Ralph had said and there was an uneasy silence among us all.

I moved around to the other side of Ralph and straddled his left leg. There was another Marine working on his right leg and had already opened up his jungle fatigues and announced that the leg was a mess. I tugged on the rotted cloth of his fatigues and it tore easily. I was looking down at the backside of his leg just above his knee. Initially I said that everything looked fine but then I tore some more material apart and I stopped in my tracks. His left knee was totally shattered- I was looking at a lump of flesh, bone and blood all mixed together, but not within the skin like it should be.

I mumbled to myself, "Oh shit," which told everyone around me that my findings were just as bad as what they had found. We realized at that point that there wasn't much we could do for him but try to get him to the medevac area on the backside of the Amtrak. We took Ralph's poncho, laid it on the ground and moved him onto it. Four of us grabbed the corners of the poncho and slowly carried it back towards the trench that we had all come out of and eventually out to the Amtrak.

Through all of this, it seemed as if the war had stopped and we were all moving in slow motion. I remember helping to move Ralph onto the poncho, noticing how little he complained, and I know that I was one of the men that helped move him out to the Amtrak but I can't remember how long it took or who provided covering fire while we did it.

A short while after delivering Ralph, I was working my way through the irrigation trench area again and an officer saw my pants leg and my wound inside. He asked me why I wasn't out at the Amtrak being treated, but in all honesty, at that point my leg still didn't hurt. Besides, the men out near the Amtrak needed much more care than I did and the corpsmen were busy enough.

I rejoined what was left of second squad and we began making our way through the village. Dusk was beginning to move in on us and there were still groups caught up in fierce fighting. We joined up with elements of 1st and 3rd squad who were in the midst of a firefight and we moved up on their right flank. It had been a long day with many tragedies and I for one was feeling numb.

Not a numbness of physical pain, but one of a mental or psychological nature. My actions now were somewhat different, less guarded and much chancier. It didn't seem to be just me- men were jumping up, running towards enemy positions, taking the war to them, tired of them being the aggressor. Men were taking incredible chances and getting away with it as if they were invincible. I'm sure the ones who survived Vietnam often think back on what we did, what we got away with and literally shake their heads in amazement that any of us survived; I know I do.

Night was beginning to set in and we knew there were still numerous NVA soldiers held up in different parts of the village, though now darkness was in their favor. We were instructed to string ourselves out to form a complete circle around the village, which was quite a task. By the time they had put us all in place, we were stretched so far that we needed to sit individually about 15 to 20 meters apart.

Our packs were still inside the Amtrack's, so we had no entrenching tools to dig foxholes with. Fortunately for me, I was positioned near a rice paddy dike which gave me good cover. After this long, grueling day we were now faced with the need to stay awake all night, keeping our eyes out for NVA soldiers trying to slip through our positions. Fortunately for us they called Puff out to drop illumination flares which lit up the rice paddy and the village.

We had been out there a few hours when the word was passed from Marine to Marine that Ralph had died, and this hit me very hard. I was mad at the enemy for starting the firefight, I was mad at myself for getting wounded and not personally getting to the objective that Ralph was killed getting to- I was just mad- very, very mad. I passed the word along but I know it really hurt us from 2nd squad the deepest, and I'm sure that the other survivors like me were numb with this word.

Puff was formerly called Puff the Magic Dragon. It was a World War II propeller cargo plane retrofitted with numerous gattling guns. Normally Puff would fly over an area at night and on its first pass, it would drop huge illumination flares, which were extremely bright. It would then circle around and fly above the flares for enemy movement on the ground. If the men onboard spotted anything, they would open up with their gattling guns.

As stated before, every 5th bullet on a machine gun belt was a tracer, which gave off a red orange burning trail, enabling the gunner to see where the rounds were hitting. On a gattling gun, there are numerous barrels and were equipped to fire very fast. For us on the ground, we couldn't actually see the plane in the distance but there were so many tracers coming down from the guns that it looked as if they were pouring molten lava out of the sky. Once we saw the red orange glow, we would listen for the sound of the guns going off which came to us as long buuuuuuuurping sound.

On this night, they were not using any of their gattling guns, they just kept flying over and dropping their flares, enabling us to see any movement. Sometime early in the morning, M- 16s started going off down to my left which startled the hell out of me and forced me to rivet my eyes in the rice paddy between the Marines and the village. Someone nearby said loud enough for many of us to hear that some of the NVA soldiers who were trapped in the village were trying to make it out in small groups. Apparently they were crawling out from the village as far as they could and then at the last minute they would jump up and charge a section of our flimsy perimeter. This news made all of us to sit up a little stiffer, trying to see if we could spot anyone crawling out in front of where we were.

Somewhere in the early morning hours, there was this sense of electricity everywhere. Although I was exhausted, I tried to keep my eyes open and listened to every change of the sounds around us. There was this dead silence that we all hated which told us something was up. Whispers were going from position to position, everyone sensed it and sweat began pouring over my body like I had just taken a shower.

The silence didn't last long- the word came down the line to fix bayonets, terrifying words to all of us. I reached down and snapped my bayonet off of my cartridge belt and slowly slid it forward to the end of my M-16 and attempted to snap it on without making any noise- in this dead silence an almost impossible task. We could all feel it as if it was a script and we all just lay there, waiting for something to erupt. My entire body tingled, seldom have I ever felt fear like this, now I knew how someone could lose control of themselves and shit their
pants, I was very close. Charlie didn't let us down.
Sometime, minutes later, all hell broke loose in front of us.

They had waited for some of Puff's flares to go out and made an attempt to break through our flimsy lines. All we could hear were their screams as they jumped up and came at us, we were heavily outnumbered. Without a word being passed, we all let loose with some controlled rifle fire and we moved up, jumping to our feet and bringing the battle to them. At times like this you let the energy of fear take control, unfortunately this also meant losing control of any morals, self survival is a power that your brain controls and the result is seldom something that you can live with psychologically. If you were smart you would try to match the volume of the other American screams yelling louder until your ears almost burst.

There were muzzle flashes everywhere to our front and to my left and right. The flashes accompanied by the sound of the rifles helped me determine who was the enemy and who wasn't. AK-47s and SKS NVA infantry rifles each had a unique sound, one we all knew too well. The velocity of this attack really surprised me, I thought I had heard some incredible ground action but this made everything else completely insignificant. The muzzle flashes and cracking of bullets going by was incredible and both sides were really opening up.

As I began to move, I concentrated on the NVA rifle sounds, focusing on where they were coming from. No sooner had I jumped up, I got smashed in the head with something on my right side and went tumbling to the ground. As I landed I looked up and briefly saw a silhouette of a man standing over me, coming at me with his rifle at my chest. Somehow I got my M-16 around and let loose with a 3 or 4-round burst, shattering his chest with each of my muzzle flashes showing his face as he flipped backwards, helmet flying off. I was so friggen scared I didn't know what to do. Things were getting worse and I realized that I needed to move again. I jumped up and ran to my left where I heard Vietnamese voices and rifle fire coming from.

I ran forward, firing on semiautomatic at shadows in front of me that didn't have American helmets. There was some light being emanated by the rifle fire alone but also from some distant aerial flares. Again I was hit from my right side and again landed on the ground, the pain was intense but I didn't know if I had been shot or not, adrenaline has this way of taking control of your pain.

Puff had begun to lay down its flares in the distance, which gave us some visibility in this battle; everything was a swaying shadow as the flair drifted slowly to earth. I lay there looking up, feeling as if I had been hit by a truck and saw shadows running around me and their voices were not
American. I knew that if I didn't get up someone would run
by me and shoot me just to make sure I was dead.

Exhausted, with my body screaming in pain and yet scared to death, I got up and again ran towards the non-American voices. Typically one out of three NVA soldiers had AK-47s that could really release some fire, comparable to our M-16s. Fortunately the other two thirds had SKS infantry rifles, which were bolt action and clip fed. In a matter of time, the M-16s began to take the upper hand.

Hand-to-hand fighting was going on directly in front of me and I saw an American helmet out numbered by three NVA pith helmets. I ran into the fray bayonet first and shooting at single shot. The shadows began to go down one by one but yet again I was hit again and downed. Now I was pissed. I
didn't feel as if I had been shot but this getting knocked down
crap was getting old.

I jumped up and heard Smitty's voice in front of me. I yelled, "Smitty is that you?" and a reply came back, "No shit, who the fuck do you think this is?" We teamed up and began to push things back. Standing almost back-to-back. we moved slowly forward raking down the shadows that didn't look like us. At some point the gunfire began to dissipate and within minutes it was silent again. Smitty and I dropped to the ground and laying shoulder-to-shoulder facing the direction of the enemy shadows. Everything was silent, the early morning battle had ended.

Sometime later we heard numerous rifles being fired from the other side of the village and we all assumed that it was other groups of NVA trying to make their way out.
I'm sure that some NVA soldiers did work their way through our lines but many of them didn't make it. I was exhausted and thrilled when I saw the sky begin to lighten with the beginning of dawn; it had been a long 24 hours.

The excitement of the previous day had begun to wear off and my mind began to focus on other things, minimally the pain shooting up from my right leg. With no water to be had, I knew that I was extremely dehydrated and possibly this had some impact as to why my leg was now throbbing.

With daylight on our side, we slowly began to form back together as a squad, if you wanted to call us that, there were only four of us left. With other squads, we did a search of the field around us looking for any NVA survivors, of which we found two. A corpsman was called up who treated the enemy soldiers in place. Our hopes were that once they were interrogated we might find out more about their unit and where they were headed. There were orders to move slowly back into the village looking for any enemy stragglers left.

188

During the first few hours, there were numerous small skirmishes but eventually the village had been searched fairly well and little by little our unit began to make the final sweep of the village. Part of this sweep was to take all dead enemy bodies and drag them out by the disabled Amtrak and pile them up, and of course we had to take the very important body count that the entire war was being based on. Some of the soldiers were female, possibly nurses, and we dragged them by their feet as well and then teamed up to take them by their feet and hands and swing them up on the growing pile. This was how it was done and nobody thought twice about what we were doing and why.

Two Marines dragged a female body back to the pile and said that when they found her she was carrying an AK-47. She was definitely dead but they were both pissed that she was a soldier not a nurse. After they threw her body down, they both swept around, firing a short burst on semi-automatic into her chest and walked away saying, "Take that, bitch." Things
happen that at times are impossible to explain. I wasn't with them when they found her so I really don't know what made them that angry, those actions were not something we took part in. Eventually we all headed back towards the side of the village that we started our assault from.

I began to make my way out of the village, numb with exhaustion and pain from my leg. I remember coming down a trail near the edge of the village and I could see the disabled Amtrak in the rice paddy through the thick bamboo trees that lined the village. As I walked closer, I could see someone standing up on top of the Amtrak watching the Marines straggle out of the village. It was Sergeant Lewis, my friend from Charleston and his eyes lit up when he saw me coming down the trail. He ran over to me sharing how worried he was that he wasn't going to see me walking at all- as a unit we had taken quite a toll during the fight and he thought for sure that I was a casualty.

I told him that I was as well as I could be and that we were all exhausted. He talked briefly about his tractor getting hit and how scared he was when he had to get out and be in the open like us. Sometimes you don't realize how dangerous your job really is until someone compares it to something safer, more controlled. I needed to move on and he went back out to his track and the few corpsmen that were left tending to the less wounded.

Someone started talking about what had taken place the previous day in the heat of the battle around the time I saw Sgt Lewis's Amtrak getting hit with the RPG. As the Amtrak was moving up to be a blocking element against the enemy fire they traveled very close to where Mike Muldovan lay
wounded having been shot numerous times. Bill, Mike's brother, lay next to him, shot only once but unfortunately had been killed. Both Mike and Bill were the most liked Marines within 2nd Platoon and here they were either wounded or dead, this was a great blow to all of us that knew them.

As we began to form up into what was left of 2nd Platoon I could see a Marine unit off in the distance working their way in our direction. I forget what platoon they were, but they were there basically as our replacements. They would continue the search of the village looking for any remaining enemy soldiers as well as hidden weapons or food.

Although this was another Marine element from our company and I'm sure they had seen their share of fierce fighting, many of them had a hard time not looking at us. If 24 hours ago there was anything for any of us to smile about, it was now long gone. That look of emotional numbness was beginning to take over and would be there to help govern our individual activities for the months to come. If you were someone walking by us, you would probably take every precaution to not approach or invoke any activity. I don't think it was an intentional look of hate, but more of an aura of someone that you wouldn't want to mess with, a signal to stay as far away as possible.

Muldovan Twins
Mike on the left Bill on the right
Bill KIA March 7th Phu Tai
Mike WIA March 7th Phu Tai

Buchanan sitting on the left
Ralph Hammel in front of our hooch barefooted
Ralph KIA March 7th Phu Tai

James Banning
KIA March 5th in Dia Do

Battle over, heading for Palace Guard

The other Amtrack's had made their way to where we were and we each searched for our packs and other gear. We eventually formed into a wedge formation and began moving away from Phu Tai in the hot morning sun, and we could barely walk. Our destination was the village of Gia Liem, better known as Palace Guard, our battalion headquarters
while down on the river. It wasn't an R&R or a Stand Down, but we would be there for a few days getting medical treatment and minimized patrols, their best attempt to give us a break.

It was midday by the time we got to the village and they took their time showing us what positions they wanted us to take over. The few remaining members of 2nd squad were assigned two foxholes in front of a hooch, which we took the liberty of throwing all of our gear in. Shortly after getting there, our platoon commander sent the word down the line for me to come up to the platoon command post.

I grabbed my M-16 and cartridge belt and made my way down the village paths to the hooch the command post occupied. I hung around outside the entrance of the hooch, he was on the communications radio and had seen me standing there, and I was just waiting for him to finish. He asked me to come in, which I did. Sergeant Butler, our platoon sergeant, was sitting over in the cool shadows of the room trying to put together a C-ration meal.

Lt Lewy was very straightforward and said that he wanted me to take over as squad leader of 2nd squad. It would be up to me to assign fire team leaders and organize the functionality of the squad. He asked me if I had any problem with that and I said no, we were all still very numb. Unstated in this assignment was a field promotion for me from a Lance Corporal to a Corporal, I had finally made it to be a Non Commissioned Officer (NCO).

As nice as this was, there was still no feeling of excitement, the deep, numbing ache of the last few days was crippling us all. I turned, left, and straggled back to the hooch that we had taken over. As soon as I got back they were asking me what he wanted and when I told them they said, "Cool."

We all sat on the ground with our backs leaning on the side of the hooch going through our packs, pulling together something to eat. While I was working my way towards the bottom of my pack, I pulled out my plastic envelope of writing gear which I started to put down and then stopped. I sat back for a moment and opened the pouch knowing what I was going to find, Ralph and I shared the writing gear. Sometimes he would hump it other times I would, at this time I had it all in my pack. As I started going through it I saw envelopes from home, more specifically from his wife, and then there were the pictures.

This really pushed me back and I remembered the deep feeling of loss that engulfed my gut and I could hardly breathe.
Someone looked at me and asked me what was up, why so glum and I told them. None of us knew what to do with what I had in my hands. Did we burn it, do we bury it, none of us
knew. Sitting here now, I can't remember what we did, I wish
I knew.

Eventually we all got something to eat and we laid back in the shade of the hooch. This small Vietnamese boy came over to our hooch and was looking around. I had just lit a cigarette and he came over to me and asked me for a "took," Vietnamese for cigarette. I shook my head no but he didn't move. He asked me again and I got real pissed. I don't know if it was because of the previous 24 hours' activities, but at that moment he really got on my nerves.

Smitty came over, sat down next to me, took one of my cigarettes, and gave it to the kid- for some reason I was ok with that. The kid squatted down, took my lit cigarette from my hand and lit the cigarette that he had just received from Smitty. With that Doc Bird, our platoon corpsman came walking up and said that I needed to go down to the Battalion CP in about an hour to have my leg taken care of, I nodded in agreement.

Martinez yelled over to Doc to see if he would take our picture. We all looked at him and said, "What?" He just said, "Let's do it," and for some reason it all made sense, who knows who we would lose tomorrow or the next day. Four of us got together on the ground and we dragged an M-60 machine gun in front of us to make it look really official, even the Vietnamese boy joined us. Sound familiar? This is the photo that began this story, the picture that I look at often which enables me to appreciate life.

That afternoon, I went down to the Battalion CP for some medical treatment. They had flown in some doctors from Dong Ha for the day and they were treating us one after another. The doctor was either tired, scared or both but for whatever reason, he had no personality at all. He had me sit next to him and he viewed my wound through the hole in my fatigues.

Initially he took some fluid and let it drip into the wound and all it did was foam up like seltzer water. It created a strange pain, deep within the hole that was created by the burning phosphorus. I'm sure it was the tiny bubbles hitting against raw skin and nerve endings that I was feeling. It wasn't a horrible pain, but something that was very uncomfortable.
When that had stopped bubbling, he poured some more stuff in it, I think he called it saline solution, which didn't seem to be doing anything.

The flies were kind of at a loss. They really wanted to get at the wound but whatever these liquids were kept them at bay, so they simply formed a circle just outside the fluid that was on my skin, kind of waiting for it to go away so they could have a feast.

After the second fluid had sat there for a few minutes, the doctor took out what looked like a small tooth brush and the way he flexed the bristles, I thought they were very soft. Soft my ass. As soon as he put the brush inside my wound, he began to lightly scrub and I wanted to take off like I had a rocket booster tied to my butt, man did it hurt.

I grabbed the side of the stool I was on with both hands and cringed with each stroke. After some time, he stopped and then poured in more of the stuff that bubbled, this time it really hurt and I was afraid that I was going to lose some teeth the way I had them clenched.

He repeated the same process two more times, by the end of the second time, the clear liquid had changed color to a deep red. I almost got the feeling that he hated me and he had been waiting for years to inflict this type of pain on me. Finally he was done with the scrubbing and he put some type of ointment in and around the hole and then put some bandages on top, taping them off around my leg. He told me that he would be coming back in two days and that he wanted to see me again about the same time. As I turned from him and began my hobble back to my area I said to myself there was no way was I going back, my next visit would be with one of our corpsmen. I never did go back.

We all needed to try to deal psychologically with what had taken place in Phu Tai. We lost Ralph and other members of 2nd squad. During the initial blast of the battle, Lt Lewy was hit in the head with a bullet and was thrown backwards to the ground. Everyone running by him assumed him dead on the spot. The twin brothers Bill and Mike had also been caught and they laid there, side-by-side. Mike had seven bullet holes in him but by some miracle was alive, Bill was only a few feet away with one bullet hole in him- unfortunately it was in his head, he was dead.

There are many miracles that take place in battle and Lt Lewy had experienced his first. The enemy bullet had hit his helmet and got lodged between the helmet and the fiberglass helmet liner. It traveled halfway around the helmet between the two layers and went out through the other side of the helmet. The helmet went flying out into the rice paddy as Lewy was thrown to the ground. Many minutes later, he woke up with a splitting headache and eventually rejoined the battle.

There were occasions when doctors and some media came out to the field, but it was only when things were relatively quiet. The media types tried to play John Wayne the most, but I never saw one stick around when we started getting into any shit. There was one operation where we landed in an area with rolling hills, an area known to us then as "Rocket Valley." These names existed before I got there and they all had their own unique meaning, Rocket Valley was no exception.

We were flown in on CH-46 helicopters and the first few waves landed without incident. Our flight was coming in and the choppers made their quick landing, barely giving us time to get out the back. We no sooner got out of the helicopter when all hell broke loose. Rockets and mortars were coming in from everywhere, primarily targeting the area where the choppers were landing

A reporter had come out on one of the prior flights but he was still hanging around the LZ, probably waiting for our commanding officer and his crew. We had fanned out as normal, reinforcing the troops that had already landed and at this point we were still relatively close to the LZ. I lay there, facing outward and the reporter crawled up among us and he was shaking like a leaf.

He was asking a million questions about how often we received incoming like this during one of our landings, what recourse did we have, and how could we get out if need be. We told him that this was pretty standard but normally we got more mortars and artillery than we did rockets. We had no recourse, the enemy hid their artillery and mortar pits very well and we were stuck there, we were on a mission and only when that mission was over would we move on to something else.

A few minutes later, the next wave of helicopters came in and after the Marines had run off, the reporter glanced at us and said, "Fuck this shit, I'm outta here," and he ran on the helicopter. For the most part, that is how they worked with us, never sticking around when things got nasty.

We stayed in Gia Liem a number of days, resting up as best we could. We still had the daily responsibilities of observation posts and running patrols during the day and the ambushes and listening posts at night. Being a squad leader was something that you couldn't prepare for, especially in a combat situation. Up until now, all you really needed to do was to take care of your own butt, but now that had all changed. Being responsible for the lives of a group of men was a challenge at best and most often an emotional challenge as well. These words might not have the same meaning to everyone but for anyone that has this responsibility while in a combat situation, it's a very heavy weight.

You are responsible for these men's lives. The instructions you give, the orders they follow could mean death to one or more of them and you as the squad leader live with the emotional consequences of it all. Today I sit here and periodically relive some battles where good men died doing what I told them to do, some more courageous than others. Regardless of how or why they were killed, I sit here and try to understand how I, 20 years old at the time and not much more experienced than some of them, was qualified enough to be giving orders. I also question my decision making that led to those orders. Believe me, men and women with these kinds of responsibilities carry with them a lot of emotional luggage, memories of wonderful men and you were in control of their individual destinies.

During our stay in Gia Liem, we received some new grunts, what we called FNGs, or Fucking New Guys. I received four men during that round and two of them I will never forget: Ruben and California. They knew each other pretty well, I was assuming that they had gone through staging together.
Ruben was a Mexican from Southern California and California I was assuming came from California- don't always trust nicknames. One of the others I'll remember but for different reasons, his name was Moore. I took these new guys around and introduced them to everyone in 2nd squad and everyone in the platoon. We started doing our patrols and fortunately the first few were quiet, it was a good time for all of them to learn how things were done.

One day we saddled up and we were told that we were moving to another area of villages, still south of the Cua Viet River, but closer to the ocean. We were also warned that most of these villages were not friendly towards Americans. We moved out in a company formation for a very slow hump towards these villages. It was now mid-April and it was extremely hot which made everything much more difficult.

We moved into Le Xuyen, which was the friendliest of all the villages in the area. It was a large village, which gave plenty of room for our entire company to dig in. We began our usual schedule of patrols and the first few days things were nice and quiet.

One day, we were on a platoon patrol in a village called Bo Bang, another relatively large village which was not friendly towards Americans at all. We had been on patrol for a few hours and were well into the village. We were well dispersed and at the time, we were walking in an area that looked to be a vegetable garden or at least an area where they were trying to grow something. We had all the Kit Carson Scouts with us to help interrogate some of the villagers and it was extremely hot, one of those 120 plus degree days. We were moving very slowly through this garden area when all I can remember was the feeling like someone hitting me in the face and chest with a sledgehammer.

The next thing I can remember is opening my eyes and I was lying on my chest on the ground, I couldn't hear anything. My eyes tried to focus on someone waving to me and I can remember watching the hand like it was in slow motion.

Eventually I saw past the hand and I could see the face of Sgt Loc, one of our Kit Carson Scouts, who was also lying on the ground but only so he could get my attention. When he saw that I could see him, he started to motion to me with his hands to stay where I was and not to move at all. Although I couldn't hear, I could tell there was a lot of activity- there was dust flying everywhere like a light, clay-colored fog. I still didn't know what had happened, I was assuming that there had been some kind of explosion and it wasn't long when my body began to ache, though I wasn't sure from what.

Sgt Loc made sure he kept my attention. Eventually, he took out his bayonet and then I began to realize what had happened. We had walked into a minefield and someone in front of me had stepped on one of them, which caused the blast I felt in my face. I was assuming that the other discomfort that I was feeling was from my body being thrown to the ground, but I still wasn't sure of that.

The heat of the sun was also having a major effect on me. Unable to move, I could not get to my canteens for a drink and I knew that I was getting extremely dehydrated. The sun also was baking my jungle fatigues onto my skin. Normally on these very hot days your fatigues didn't bother you because you were always moving. Lying still like I was, the material was getting hot just like it was being ironed. Whenever it came into contact with your skin, it would burn as if it was red hot. Each time I moved my body even in the slightest way, some material touched my skin and it was like being touched by hot irons.

Sgt Loc needed the bayonet to start probing the ground looking for other mines. As he probed in front of him, he slowly started to make his way towards me. This took quite some time, as you needed to probe every few inches to make sure that none of the buried devices were missed. He finally got out to where I was and now needed to continue the tedious process around and under my body. As soon as he got close enough, he put his hand on my head and just patted it, trying to ensure me that everything would be ok.

Eventually he made it all the way around me and came back to me to look at my face. He talked loudly to see if I could hear him and I could barely make out what he was saying. I still wasn't aware of what else was going on around me, I was totally focused on what he was doing. He asked me to see if I could get up on my hands and knees. I can remember how much my body ached when I tried and with a good bit of effort I did.

He then talked to me and used his hands to tell me to follow him out and to put my hands and knees exactly where he did. I wanted to get up and run, I knew that I could run fast enough to run right over any mine before it blew up, at least that is what I thought, I just wanted out of there. The process out was very slow and I tried to follow his every move exactly.

We eventually got out to where he had started from and they pulled me over to an area and laid me on my back to examine my arms, legs and chest for any injuries.

Little by little, my hearing was coming back and I could hear the chaos of men running everywhere. There was some bad news in all of this. As it turned out, I was fine except for the bruises of being thrown to the ground. My good friend Tony Evans wasn't so lucky, he was the one that stepped on the mine. The blast took off his left leg above the knee. The corpsman had moved him off to the side and was treating him for shock while giving him morphine. Tony was another one of the men that came over with me- one by one, they were being taken out either dead or badly wounded and it became obvious to those of us who were left that time was not on our side.

I made it a point to go up to the medevac helicopter when it came in and helped get Tony on. He wasn't in any pain and I can still remember his incredible smile as he looked back at me. After he had been placed on board, one of the corpsman placed his leg, with his boot still on, in his lap. I don't think Tony ever realized what they had done, the morphine had his mind somewhere else. He was gone, never to return and each of us that survived the blast wondered when our time would come.

3rd Squad
John Druen AKA Snake on the left standing
Jay Martinez standing to the right
Sitting Bill Hill, Tony Evans, Prather and Bill MacMyler
Sitting front Mike Duerr

The patrols of the villages in that area were difficult at best. In order to get to one, we usually needed to cross large rice paddies which left us completely open to snipers. Regardless of how well your patrol was organized, individual Marines out in the open fall easy prey to the snipers. You would be walking along looking at the perimeter edges of the villages, trying to determine what was going on in each village.

Normally a village with activity in it was safer than those that appeared quiet, they were usually up to something not in our favor. Every now and then there would be a single loud cracking sound as a bullet would go past, the louder the sound, the closer it was to you. A number of seconds after the crack, you would hear a soft boom somewhere off in the distance, that was the delayed sound of the rifle actually being fired.

The first person that heard the crack would yell, "Sniper!" as loud as they could and everyone would dive for the ground. As soon as you hit the ground, you would begin listening for the boom to try to determine which village it came from. The snipers in the villages were normally Viet Cong and they usually weren't very good aims, but you never knew. The cheapest thing was to lose someone to a sniper, a land mine, or a booby trap, at least give the person a chance to fight.

It would take some time to see if everyone was ok and then we would normally change the course of our patrol to move to where the shot had come from. We would get there and move into the village to find everyone innocent and none of them even heard the rifle being fired. We would search the hooches and our Kit Carson Scouts would interrogate any males that were in the village, but they would all simply say that they
didn't know anything.

You have no idea as to how frustrating this became and it had the tendency to push some units to the edge. If we found that we were being sniped at time and time again as we went past the same village, each time we went in to conduct our search we would be more aggressive in our questioning and more thorough in our searching.

There were times that the sniper had been successful and had either wounded or killed one or more of our unit and our mood would change drastically. Everyone in the U.S. questioned how a unit like Lieutenant Caley's lost control and mowed down innocent villagers, but I knew exactly how they could be pushed to this point, there were times that it was very difficult for us to hold back.

By this time in my tour, most of the men that I had come over with had taken their R&R, but I was holding out for an R&R in Australia. These were very difficult to get and it was very seldom that by the time the list got out to us in the field that Australia was ever on it. Everyone in my unit knew I was holding out for this site and I finally was there long enough to be senior on the list for those who had not taken their R&R yet.

One day we were sitting back within our main perimeter and I was called up to the company command post. I had no idea what was going on and usually a visit to the company CP was not for anything good. The company radio operator saw me coming up the trail and motioned me over. He handed me the R&R list he had just received and Australia was on the top of the list. I can't explain how I felt, finally getting my choice of locations and having the opportunity to dream of a few days away from this hell hole.

I actually began to chuckle as I put my initials next to the line that said Australia. As I started to hand it back, I realized that we were not alone and I turned to see many of the company field people, including some of the officers, standing around watching me sign the sheet. It didn't take much to make troops out in the field feel good and it was something like this that made everyone smile.

Nothing much was said and I walked back down the trail to where my squad was dug in. I had this great feeling inside knowing that in a week or two, I would be in an area much like home, looking at gorgeous round eyes- this was our term for any female that wasn't oriental. It's not good having something that preoccupies your mind and I needed to keep this new excitement in check, I wouldn't be leaving for a few weeks and I needed to stay sharp.

Many of us enjoyed the TV series Mash during the 70s and 80s, and we each remembered a show that had special meaning for one reason or another. One show was about a wacko enemy pilot that would periodically bomb their hospital area but wasn't very good and he would never hit anything.
They had given him the name of Washing Machine Charlie that was one of the shows that I will always remember.

It reminded me of a daily event that took place in our primary village, on my side of the perimeter. Directly in front of where my squad was dug in, there was a stretch of open rice paddy, and a couple of hundred yards out in front was some thick brush and some shallow hilly terrain. Each day, a group of Viet Cong would make their way into that area and almost the same time each day they would open fire on our perimeter. The first couple of times they had done this they caught us off guard and we lost some men, and again we began to take them more seriously. They really weren't that accurate but stupidly they tried to hit us each day at the same time. For a good number of days, we would just wait in our foxholes until they opened fire and we would give return fire. Afterwards, we would send a patrol out to see if we could find anything and there was usually no evidence that anything had taken place.

One day, the company commanding officer said enough is enough. During the early part of the afternoon, we moved numerous machine guns into my squad's positions and also two 106 recoilless rifles were hidden in the surrounding pine trees. These had been equipped with bee hive rounds that would explode at a predetermined distance and when they exploded, they would send out thousands of small metal arrows.

It was getting to be time and everyone spread the word to take cover. I got into my foxhole, which was directly behind my squad's holes and I sat in the bottom of the hole, I was going to get my letter writing gear out and write a letter home. I glanced up and Lieutenant Lewy, my platoon commander, was standing at the edge of my hole. He asked if I had room for one more. Bruce was a large man but somehow we managed to get him into a foxhole that was designed for one along with me.

We were really packed into this tight space and I had no idea why he needed to come visit me, possibly to be near the action of the upcoming counter ambush. We chatted lightly and eventually he said that he had some bad news for me. In Vietnam this could be one of a million things, and I had no idea what to expect.

He said that I had unfortunately been bumped out of my R&R request. I said that I was really surprised, knowing that I could only be bumped by someone senior in rank, most likely an officer, and everyone knew what that request meant to me. He said that unfortunately it had still happened. Now I was in a mental dilemma. I had been there over seven months and well past my time to have some down time and I just lost my requested assignment. I still needed to leave on the next R&R regardless what was left, I was a hair shy of being a basket case.

A short time passed and the VC opened fire from across the rice paddy. As soon as they did, the command was given for our return ambush to open fire. The din of the blast was intense and lasted a total of 45 seconds. It doesn't seem like much, but with the fire power that was being expelled, it was more than enough, then there was silence and the thick layer of the white smoke of gunpowder drifting through the air.

Bruce looked at me and said he wanted me to take 2nd squad across to see what we could find. With that, he got up and stood at the edge of the foxhole peering out towards where the VC had opened fire from. I looked up at him and asked if he would be willing to share with me who bumped me off of the list. He looked down at me and said that he had, and he turned and walked away.

I was speechless. Here was a man that I admired. He had earned his keep in the field by listening to us first and then taking over and we would follow him anywhere. We had a great relationship as platoon commander and squad leader and he more than anyone knew what it meant for me to go to Australia. I was completely dumbfounded and I lost a tremendous amount of respect for him.

To this day, I have no idea why he did what he did, but he has no idea how deeply he hurt me. There were dreams that you tried to keep alive and very guarded, and one of my few was this dream of going to Australia for my R&R. Now with that shattered, I needed to be concerned with the emotional effects, getting bummed out in Vietnam was easy but not good. Here was something else that I needed to suck up into my emotional pouch and not let bother me.

I took my men and conducted the patrol over to the VC ambush site. We didn't find any bodies but there were numerous blood trails going out in varied directions and one boot with some poor souls; foot still in it. Although we didn't find any bodies, they got the message and they never attempted to hit our perimeter again.

A couple of days later we had just returned from a patrol and my men were getting organized, some of them cleaning their weapons. The patrol had only taken a couple of hours and it was midday when we returned to our positions. While we were taking care of business, we could hear a serious firefight unfolding due south of where we were. It was a serious battle that went on and on.

A short time passed and those dreadful words of "Saddle Up" came down the lines and we put our gear together. No packs were needed- just your helmet, flack jacket and fighting gear. Within a matter of minutes, 2nd Platoon was on the way, almost on the double, which was not the way to move around in Vietnam.

One of our companies had walked into a hellacious battle in a village called An Trac and we were the backup platoon. We weren't moving very cautiously which put everyone on edge. The enemy loved troops moving along too fast, not paying attention to their immediate surroundings.

As we got nearer to the village, the intensity of the battle increased. We could see F-4 phantoms and other planes diving in, dropping the loads of high explosive bombs and napalm. Black and gray smoke billowed up through the tall bamboo trees and you could smell the ingredients of intense battle. We were on one side of a flat clearing and a few meters in front of us was a small tree line which began a gradual rise. On the other side of the tree line, there was a sizeable rice paddy and then the beginning border of a village. There were numerous Marines on the safe side of the nearby tree line, at this point observing the intense battle from a safe distance.

We moved across the open area and spread out the length of the tree line. Everything was being poured into the village. 105 and 155 High Explosive howitzer rounds were pouring in, one after the other, intermixed with our 81 mortars. The crumping of the high explosives never seemed to end and they were actually blurring together to become what sounded like one long explosion.

Parts of the company who began this battle were spread out on the far edge of the rice paddy, just a few feet from the last high dike prior to stepping into the village. There were at least 8 men lying there and they were all dead. They had been caught in a sniper's crossfire and at this point we weren't sure if any of the squad had made it across.

With all the HE rounds going off, it was very difficult to sneak peeks at what was going on, shrapnel was flying everywhere and we were simply trying to find a hole or something to hide in. In desperation, they had just called in a Napalm run and the canisters came tumbling down on the far edge of the rice paddy, igniting the edge of the village and the far side of the rice paddy. Unfortunately, the bodies of the eight Marines were in its path and they were just lying there, burning along with everything else.

Word was passed that they were calling air strikes to drop 500-pound HE rounds and for all of us to find cover. Again these rounds were being focused on the far edge of the rice paddy which wasn't all that far from us. During training we were taught to scream when we knew loud explosions were
going to go off, this would prevent your ear drums from being blown in. When you hear some things in training you say, "Yeah... Right," and think you'll never be in a position like that.

Unfortunately here we were, the Phantoms were on their way and we were scrambling for anything to give us better cover. I wound up lying face down just to the edge of the tree line, completely in the open on one side but slightly protected by the tree line and a shallow hill on the other. The screaming of the Phantom's engines was bad enough, they sounded like they were 10 feet above my helmet and I can remember telling myself to scream when the bombs began going off- and scream I did.

I think there were two Phantoms and they made numerous passes, dropping their deadly load, each one sounding louder and closer than the last. There was a very strange feeling that came out of this, not personally physical, but something in the ground. The HEs were called "delayed time fused." That meant they didn't explode when they hit the ground, but they buried themselves into the earth before going off. This was done intentionally to send shock waves through the ground, rattling any NVA's skull that might be hiding in a bunker or a foxhole. As the shock wave went through the ground, it made the earth's surface feel like a very thin piece of paper and it acted like a wave. As the shock waves went under me, each time they gave me the creepy feeling that if I moved the wrong way, I would fall through.

You would think that with all of this, the enemy would be silent- not a chance. No sooner had the jets departed, the ground fire picked right up again. Coming in behind us were some mules with 106 recoilless rifles mounted on top, and I'm sure that someone had a plan as to how to use them and when.

Lt Lewy passed the word on that we would be moving down to the right end of the village, to the far right end of where the major fighting was taking place. We used the cover of the tree line and the shallow hill to make our team rushes down towards that end and eventually 2nd Platoon moved into a Vietnamese gravesite. In most parts of Vietnam, they buried their dead above ground, covered with mounds of sand and grass so this was just a small area full of lumpy ground and we were huddled in among them.

The lieutenant came to me and said that he wanted me to take my squad down the edge of the rice paddy in an attempt to extract the 8 bodies which were out there. In times like this, you do what needs to be done and all the emotions that would normally flood your brain, like panic, hysteria, whatever are pushed aside because there is simply no time for that. I moved among my squad members, telling them what we needed to do and how we were going to do it.

Nacamura was going to take point, followed by Smitty, then Dave Winslow, then myself followed by Oklahoma, my radio operator, who was followed by Ray, our grenadier. The remainder of my squad would trail behind Ray and it was critical that we kept a good distance apart. We needed to crawl the full length of the rice paddy at least out to the last body- Nacamura would need to count to 8 and he would be at the last one. One by one, we crawled out of the gravesite, dropping down the foot or two into the dry rice paddy. Slowly and painfully we crawled forward, keeping the rice paddy dike directly to our right.

In training, you were taught how to do the low crawl. At one point during this training, you went through a course where they were actually firing machine guns over your head and you were scared to death. This low crawl was completely different. You moved extremely slow, trying not to be a noticeable moving target and you literally hugged the ground. We dragged our weapons alongside of us by their forearm strap, trying to keep as low a profile as possible. Oklahoma had to drag our PRC 25 communications radio alongside him, which was very hard to do.

The battle was still raging but being so close to the ground, it seemed some distance from us. In actuality, it was only inches above our heads. Getting by the bodies was difficult. They were all burning and the smell was enough to make you throw up. You tried not to look at them as you went by. Although they were burnt beyond recognition, you were afraid you would recognize one of them by either a helmet marking or some type of unique feature.

Just after crawling past one of the burning bodies, I yelled forward to Dave to stop and freeze in place. From where I was, I could see that both legs of his jungle fatigues were saturated in blood. This stopped everyone's forward progress. With everyone stopped, I slowly crawled ahead until I was even with him and we laid there side-by-side, our faces only inches apart. I asked him to slowly reach down, first with one hand and then the other to check his body for a wound that he didn't feel. He said that he couldn't find anything that hurt. I said ok and began to crawl back a few feet to get a closer
look- that's when I saw what had happened.

Just behind Dave was this huge pool of blood that had drained out of the body we had just passed and Dave, like a good Marine, had crawled right through it. I looked forward to him and said that he was ok and for him to pass the word to Smitty and Nacamura to continue on out. We began to hear bullets passing closer and closer to us and we assumed that at least one sniper had spotted our slow move along the dike. I yelled forward and then to the men behind us that they were on to us and to move like snails, making it difficult for them to tell if we were dead or not.

Our progress forward was going very slowly. The battle in front of us and to our right inside the village had reached a new intensity. Down at our level, there was a strange kind of quiet. We were crawling forward inch-by-inch and one side of your head was always pressed into the ground. If we had it our way, we all wished we could have crawled up inside of our helmets and just hidden there until it was all over- but that option wasn't in the cards this day.

After much struggle, we had made it out past the 6th body. Lt Lewy was calling up periodically on the squad radio, asking for a situation report and I would have Oklahoma tell him which body we had passed as some type of a progress barometer.

heard a noise up ahead and I couldn't figure out what it was. It was the sound of something hitting combined with a verbal expression, but it happened so fast I couldn't figure out what it was. A few seconds later, Smitty passed the word back to Dave and Dave to me that Nacamura had been hit. It didn't seem to be life threatening, somewhere in the lower leg or shin. There was no way of giving any medical assistance, so he had to lie there and rough it out. I had Oklahoma share that with Lt Lewy and the only response was for us to continue moving forward until we got to the end of the bodies.

There was a great deal of conversation on the radio and I asked Oklahoma what was going on. He said that some officers who were positioned to our left on the other side of the rice paddy had the 106 recoilless rifles set up in the tree line and they wanted to open fire with beehive rounds. This was their master plan to nail down the remaining NVA, including the elusive snipers.

They weren't joking, the conversation on the radio was full steam ahead and they were moments away from giving the order to open fire. I took the handset and barked as loud as I dared, "Break, break, break," which was the radio protocol to stop all other conversation and listen to whomever just gave that command. I informed them that we were directly out in front, exactly where they wanted to unleash the beehive rounds and we would all be killed instantly.

The whole time, we were still doing our snail crawl forward, trying to get to that last body. One of the officers involved with the 106 mess said that we needed to silence the sniper; he was taking out too many men. I told him I knew that, I already had one Marine hit but from where we were, we couldn't tell the direction from where the sniper might have been firing.

I told him where my position was based on the visible burning bodies, so he knew where I was in relation to where they thought the sniper was. According to them, he was just ahead of us, dug in somewhere to our right just over the rice paddy dike.

I called up to Dave and told him that he would need to throw some hand grenades over the top of the dike in an attempt to get the sniper. He very slowly rolled over on his back and lay there for a few minutes, staring straight up to the sky. I got back on the radio and informed the Lt with the 106s what we were going to do and he said he would tell us where the grenades were landing and if we needed to aim for another area.

While I was talking to him, Dave was very slowly reaching down and taking an M-26 grenade off of his cartridge belt. He took the grenade and moved it up to his chest and with his left hand, he pulled the pin. He then slowly extended his right hand and arm out until it was lying on the ground, like you would if you were lying in snow and trying to make a snow angel. With one quick motion he rolled quickly to his left, launching the grenade as his arm swung through the air. After throwing the grenade, he was perfectly still, basically lying on his left side.

The grenade went off just over the edge of the dike, sending down globs of dirt, dust and the heavy smoke from burnt gunpowder. The radio woke up in my hand and the Lt said they needed to go a little further past the dike, a little further ahead of us. As he was talking to me, Dave was very slowly rolling onto his back to begin his process all over. I whispered up to him what he needed to try to do and he nodded back.

He worked the other grenade off of his belt and went through the same motions, getting ready to throw the grenade. He determined when and again he rolled quickly to his left and launched the second grenade. Again more dirt and more dust came raining down on us. The Lt said that the last shot was deep enough, but needed to go a little further ahead than the last one.

I looked up at Dave who was in the process of getting back onto his back and when he had finished, I gave him the corrections. He put his hands down by his cartridge belt indicating that he had no more grenades. I slowly moved my left hand back towards my side and worked one of my grenades off of my belt and slowly moved my hand forward. I rolled the grenade forward to Dave who had to reach out to get it and pulled it into his side. Again he began the process. It took him a few seconds to straighten out the pin that I normally bent to ensure it wouldn't pull out accidentally and he pulled the ring with his left hand. He extended his right arm out and took his time planning his roll. As in the past he quickly rolled to his left.

At that same split second, there was a crashing sound just above my head. We had our faces pressed into the ground waiting for the grenade to go off but the seconds ticked by and there was nothing. I slowly looked up and saw Dave curled up in the fetal position, unlike his previous attempts. I moved forward a little, extending my left hand out towards his right boot and I was quickly grabbed by Oklahoma. I turned my head to look at him and his eyes were wide with panic and fear, Dave had not thrown the grenade. As Dave had made his last roll, the sniper had timed his shot and caught him as he rolled over, hitting him just prior to releasing the grenade. Now we were all lying there waiting for the grenade to go off, precious seconds passed and still nothing.

Smitty had turned slightly and was whispering back to Dave but there was no response and no movement at all. We waited and waited for all of us to be blown to kingdom come but nothing. The radio was squawking with chatter and everyone was screaming, trying to find out why we hadn't thrown the grenade yet. I broke into the conversation telling them what had happened and we feared that we had a K.I.A. with a grenade locked in a death grip. Now the body count in front of the dike was up to 9 and our mood was in a horrible

tailspin. The fact that Dave was dead didn't stop the chaos- if anything it escalated.

I heard some different voices on the radio and it was another team of officers and men who were setting up a line of machine guns at the end of the rice paddy back towards where we had started from. Their idea was to line up all the machine guns and simply open fire and shoot everything. Again, I had to break into the magical plan to let them know that we were still out there and we were in more trouble than before. I

couldn't believe my ears, between them and the bozos with the 106s, they had no clue we were out there, all of this just made me madder and madder. My yelling paid off and they gave up on that attempt as well. All of us who were close to Dave whispered back and forth and we all agreed that he must be

dead and we also agreed that we couldn't move him at all with concern of dislodging the grenade.

At the very end of this, Oklahoma was gently tugging on my right arm. I turned to look at him and he moved his eyes in such a way telling me to look behind us. Ray, our grenadier, had moved back considerably doing a reversed low crawl and everyone behind him was doing the same. He eventually looked in my direction and I looked into his eyes asking where the hell he thought he was going. Somehow he indicated to me that the word had been passed up to pull back.

If I could have turned and shot him at that second I would have. The son of a bitch got the word to move back but never passed the word to Oklahoma or myself. He was simply moving back and he had to know that we had not moved one bit. I got on the radio to Lt Lewy and asked what was going on and he said to pull back. This was no time for an argument but I was truly pissed that he didn't radio out to us with those instructions.

The remaining four of us took our time as we slowly and painfully turned to begin our long crawl back. I can remember looking at Dave for the last time as I began my turn. Smitty and Nacamura had to turn and then crawl past Dave, and I can't imagine what was going through their minds. We made it back to where we had crawled into the rice paddy and made our way out.

Elements of 2nd Platoon were scattered about, mostly in defensive positions trying to keep out of sight of the snipers. There was very little that was said. Those of us from 2nd squad were quiet, especially those of us who had been up
front. We had lost one of our own and we didn't even have a way of fighting back. Worse was the fact that we had left Dave out there with no way of bringing him in under the circumstances. Marines don't leave their dead behind- that's all that was going through my head at the moment.

Even more personal was the fact that Dave died doing what I had told him to do. Any confidence that I had in myself as a squad leader was gone, I let one of my men die. The word was passed that we were moving back to the area we hid behind during the initial air strikes. We were going to set in there for the night and hopefully finish off this battle the next day. For a short period, the activities of moving 2nd Platoon back over to that area and setting in kept my mind busy, but as the activities settled down, all I could do was think about Dave.

He had only been with us 3 weeks and he seemed like he had a lot of promise. He learned quickly and was never out of line. Three weeks and gone- boy did that suck. There were many of us who would prefer to have it that way. If I'm going to die in Vietnam, please make it early in my tour so I don't have to go through too many months of hell. I tried to put him out of my mind but it was impossible, nightfall was coming and we needed to get ready for a long night.

Charlie wasn't done with us yet. The night was full of skirmishes and was never quiet. I kept hearing an American voice moaning out there somewhere and all I could do was think that it was Dave who miraculously was alive but now lying there with the enemy all around him. Purposely they would let him moan and cry out all night knowing how it would mentally torment us.

Sometime during the night, Smitty came crawling over to where I was and asked if I would help man the lines. The NVA were probing us constantly and everyone was completely exhausted, he was actually pleading with me to
help. I still can't believe that I did this, but I refused him and reluctantly he crawled back to his foxhole. I know that he was really pissed that night and he really deserved to be- I had
really let him and the others down. I'll guarantee that what I said to him that night is with him today, just like it is for me. I was numb that night, I had no self-respect, I felt like a complete failure and all I wanted to do was to take my mind somewhere else, somewhere away from all of this.

There were skirmishes all night but 2nd Platoon didn't take any more K.I.A.s or W.I.A.s. Nakamura had been medevaced out later in the afternoon on the day he got hit, he had been shot through the ankle. The next morning, things were considerably quieter; it was obvious to us that Charlie had slipped away during the early morning hours.

2nd Platoon moved back over to the graves where we had been the previous day. Lenny Tuckett took his squad out on their crawl past the bodies. Without incident they got to Dave and gently rolled him over, trying to get at his hand and the live grenade. Fortunately the way Dave was holding the grenade, the holes for the pin were exposed and they slipped another in place. His body had not been tampered with which gave me somewhat of a peaceful feeling. This gave me some confidence that he really was dead when we crawled away from him the previous afternoon. Charlie had fled, which made it somewhat easier to get the remaining bodies out of the village. Medevac choppers were called in and we loaded the charred bodies on for their flight to some triage area.

We eventually made our way over to Le Xuyen and resumed our patrols of the river and village area, the mood within our squad had changed.

Standing: Nakamura on the left Smitty on the right
Quang Tri Combat Base
January 1968

Sweeping to the DMZ - June 1968

A short time later, we received the word that we would be taking part in a Battalion-sized sweep of the area north of us called Leatherneck Square. We had received a couple of new replacements and we went about our business of getting ready for another operation. The NVA had been spotted moving down in force and this sweep was intended to break up their southerly progress.

Early one morning we were picked up and flown north on CH- 53s, better known as Jolly Green Giants. These are much larger than the CH-34s and we could carry many more men on each trip. There was never a good feeling on these rides.

Each time we got into helicopters, we were on our way to another mission and we never knew what would be waiting for us. There was very little conversation, everyone was in their own little world of thoughts. Some were saying prayers while others would be going through a mental list of loved ones, saying a goodbye to each. Knowing that potential death was at the hatch of the helicopter was a very sobering thought and we all dealt with it in our own ways.

The helicopters began their descent and I glanced out the hatch to see what was going on. I could see numerous choppers already either on the ground or closer than we were and periodic bursts of incoming enemy artillery. I was assuming there would be small arms fire as well even though we hadn't heard any hit our chopper yet.

Before we realized what was happening, the door gunner was yelling to get ready and the rear ramp of the helicopter started going down. As the heat of the Vietnam day rushed into the helicopter, we ran out and began our normal landing procedures. Before we got into our initial hasty perimeter, the helicopter was gone. We could hear some small arms fire coming from the North as well as the periodic crumping of incoming artillery.

We slowly began to fan out in somewhat of a straight line, keeping men both to your left and to your right in sight. This was going to be an online sweep, meaning that we would walk side-by-side in a line, keeping together as we advanced. We were sufficiently spread out and eventually we were all tied in with units on our left and right. Once everyone was in place, we began to move forward very slowly, taking cover behind anything that would protect us from a sniper.

I was positioned a short distance behind my squad and Oklahoma, my radio operator, was a little behind me. We began to take on some fire coming from directly ahead of us and everyone quickly took cover. We were positioned on the upside of a knoll, giving us the advantage of being able to look down into a gully that was just in front of us. There were numerous NVA fighting positions dug into the side of the gully, which was where the rifle shots were coming from.

NVA fighting positions were different than our foxholes, and they basically had two different types. The first type would be a hole that they would dig into the side of a hill or something with a little elevation.

They would dig a small tunnel straight into the mound and then they would turn to either the left or the right, dig in, and make a bigger chamber. Once dug, they would get in by crawling into the small tunnel and then crawl into the bigger chamber. When fighting, they would crawl out just enough to be able to see out the end of the tunnel and shoot from there. If the enemy came to close, meaning us, they would crawl back into the larger chamber for safety. Outside the tunnel was usually well-camouflaged, which made it difficult to see where they were shooting from.

If we did spot their position, it was very difficult to get them out. Their little complex was dug in such a way that you couldn't shoot into the chamber from the beginning of the tunnel and crawling in would be suicide. Even if you threw a hand grenade in, they were usually safe. There was no way to throw the grenade into the chamber and it would land at the end of the tunnel. They would simply pick it up and throw it back, the four second fuse is plenty of time for that.

The other type of position was called a spider trap. This was a round cylinder-type hole dug straight down, just wide enough so they could squat down in the hole and be completely out of sight. When standing in the hole, the only thing that would be exposed would be from the top of their shoulders on up.
Again, the top of the hole would be well-camouflaged, making it very difficult to see them.

The NVA that we were currently fighting were in the chamber type and they were well protected. Smitty's grenade merely forced the NVA soldier to move back to the protection of his chamber. My men were laying down protecting fire that was keeping the NVA soldiers inside their chambers, allowing other Marines to move forward to take cover closer to the actual enemy positions. Everyone needed to be very careful.

Just like us, the enemy dug their positions in such a way that they could defend each other if need be. While the first group of Marines were moving forward, other enemy positions began firing at the Marines in the open in front of them. Our front lines needed to continually find these positions and concentrate small arms fire on them to make them move back into their chambers. Each time the enemy holes went silent, more of our Marines would work their way forward, closer to the openings.

Smitty and Ray had worked forward and were close to the opening of one hole, and Ruben and California had moved in on another. This was Ruben's and California's first up close and personal firefight and they were a wreck. It's hard enough to worry about stepping on land mines or booby traps, enemy snipers and the incoming artillery, mortars and rockets, but now it's up close and personal with bullets cracking by your ears. At first, each one of them was on different sides of the hole and they were periodically leaning forward, firing short bursts of gunfire into the opening. After a few repetitions of this, I guess they thought they might have wounded or killed the soldier but they decided to make sure by throwing in a hand grenade.

No sooner had the hand grenade gone in the hole, it came flying out. Both Ruben and California dove for cover and somehow escaped being blown up or injured. They scrambled back into position and talked back and forth in front of the hole, trying to decide their next move. They decided that one of them would get ready with the grenade the other with his rifle. The Marine with the rifle would fire some short bursts into the hole at the same time the grenade was being tossed in.

They worked out the timing and they started. Ruben rolled in close and fired bursts into the hole and California rolled over and threw the grenade in. Much to their dismay, it came flying right back out again, and again they needed to dive for cover. They scrambled back to their safe positions but now they were really perplexed. They glanced back to where I was watching all of this and gave me a look like, "Now what?"

I held up my hand as if I had a grenade in it and simulated pulling the pin with my other hand. With the pin pulled I opened my right hand letting the spoon of the grenade to fly off activating the 4 second fuse. I nodded my head like I was counting one, two and then I simulated tossing the grenade. California nodded that he understood. They were going to go through the same routine as last time, but this time, California was going to count to two before tossing the grenade in.

Ruben rolled and started shooting, and then California rolled, waited a couple of seconds, tossed the grenade, and then they both rolled back. From where I was sitting, I could see into the tunnel and the arm groping for the grenade. This all disappeared with a huge explosion inside the tunnel, with California and Ruben lying there while dirt and debris came down on them. By the time they had finished with their hole, most of the others had been silenced as well and it was time to check everything out.

I worked my way over to where California and Ruben were and they were obviously shaken. Neither one of them had ever killed a human before and just because that man was the enemy it didn't make it any easier, not this time anyway. I talked to them for a bit, simply trying to get their minds off of what had just taken place and they seemed to be doing a little bit better.

Unfortunately there was more dirty work to be done. Now they needed to get into the NVA's chamber and pull the body out as well as any other gear. This was never a nice job and they went through the paces, moving everything outside. One of them got stomach sick after trying numerous times to grab hold of the body that had been smashed by the explosion.

Everyone was moving around, checking out every possible hiding place to ensure we didn't leave any NVA alive in their bunkers. I had moved from down in the gully back up to where I had been when I was watching Ruben and California. Further to my right, there was a larger enemy bunker which had been dug much more like one of our fighting positions- a big square open hole. A small group of Marines were moving away from it and I decided to check it out.

I approached the bunker cautiously, making my way up to the edge and then peered down and I immediately jumped back, my heart in my throat. I was staring down the barrel of an NVA machine gun that was leaning up against the wall of the hole. I moved around to one of the corners and approached the hole from a different angle, seeing easily that the hole was empty. You could see small tunnels in each corner, implying that there were enemy chambers inside.

I went back to where our packs were, got some rope off of my pack and came back up to the bunker. I made a loop at one end of the rope and tossed it down over part of the machine gun. I moved back from the hole and gently pulled on the rope. Little by little the loop closed, snagging part of the gun and then I pulled it gently up. I was waiting for an explosion; this would have been a perfect war souvenir to booby trap.

With no explosion, I pulled the gun all the way out of the hole and dragged it until it was well clear of the opening. Although the hole was empty, I didn't have a good feeling looking down into it. I carried the gun down to a staging area where we were stacking all the equipment that was captured. I showed the gun to Ruben and California who had never seen one before, it was the NVA equivalent to our M-60 machine gun.

I had only been away from the enemy bunker for a few minutes and I was still talking to Ruben and California when we heard shooting and a small ruckus going on behind me. The three of us crouched down, took cover, and began watching the action. After I left the bunker, one of our tracked vehicles had pulled up alongside it. Two of the crew were on top manning a machine gun, providing cover for some of the Marines as they moved forward.

All of a sudden, one of the crewmembers spun around, grabbed a 45 pistol, and began firing down into the enemy bunker. It seems that the bunker had never been officially cleared and he had spotted an NVA soldier inside one of the tunnels. They backed the track vehicle up a bit and then began throwing hand grenades in each of the tunnels. Once the smoke had cleared, two Marines jumped down and began checking and clearing each tunnel hide out.

Sure enough, they found a dead NVA soldier in one of the tunnels and just the thought of that put a knot in my stomach. What if he had been behind that machine gun when I first peeked over the side? Many of us believed in fate and at this point, that's all I had to go on, that was not my time.

Although the action had slowed where we were, other areas were quite hot. The enemy unit was well spread out and the numerous Marine units trying to move forward were running into resistance. With everything under control in our area, the word finally came down to saddle up. We grabbed our gear, resumed our positions online and began to inch our way forward again.

Sure enough, they found a dead NVA soldier in one of the tunnels and just the thought of that put a knot in my stomach. What if he had been behind that machine gun when I first peeked over the side? Many of us believed in fate and at this point, that's all I had to go on, that was not my time.

Although the action had slowed where we were, other areas were quite hot. The enemy unit was well spread out and the numerous Marine units trying to move forward were running into resistance. With everything under control in our area, the word finally came down to saddle up. We grabbed our gear, resumed our positions online and began to inch our way forward again.

You could never assume that just because you had cleared one area that Charlie wasn't waiting patiently just ahead. We had just come down a small knoll and we were walking on what appeared to be an old rice paddy, more sand now than soil.
Up front to our left front were some Vietnamese graves with a good bit vegetation around them, not jungle-like, just good ground cover. Smitty was just in front of me to my left and we both saw it at the same time.

An NVA soldier poked his head up out of his spider trap not realizing that we were that close to his position. As soon as he popped up and saw us, he must have said to himself, "Oh shit," and tried to get back down without being seen. Smitty took off up to the grave area and ran up to the edge of the spider trap. He hesitated for a moment and then leaned forward with his M-16 pointing down into the hole and pulled the trigger. The sound of "click" made us all cringe, his weapon had misfired and was now jammed.

As soon as that happened, the NVA soldier tried to take advantage of the situation and began to rise out of his hole. You could see him beginning to come up with his SKS assault rifle raised. Smitty didn't wait for him to have the chance to either bayonet him or shoot him. He threw his M-16 down and grabbed the soldier by his fatigue shirt. He jerked him out of the hole and the two of them came tumbling down the side of the gravesite.

The enemy lost his rifle and wound up with Smitty straddling him with both knees on the ground on either side of him, basically sitting on his chest. At this point it was obvious to us who were standing there with our rifles trained on him that he was scared to death and wasn't resisting at all. Just as we realized that, Staff Sergeant Jones came running over, pushed Smitty aside, put a 45 caliber pistol to the enemy's head and announced that he had it all under control. Jones was a jerk and was always on an ego trip. His actions here really pissed us off- Smitty had everything under control, we didn't need Jones's help at all.

Our Kit Carson scouts came over and took the soldier off to the side and began to interrogate him. Although the enemy didn't give too much of a struggle it was still enough to put all of us on edge, especially Smitty who was a bit shaken and really pissed that his rifle had misfired. It was beginning to become late into the day and we knew that before long we would begin to set in for the night.

We had gone through the exercise of setting the lines and everyone was going through the process of digging in for the night. There was a unit just slightly ahead of us to our right that had been engaged with the enemy most of the afternoon and it became obvious that the enemy was fighting from a mix of spider traps and regular bunkers. It's hard to try to set in your positions when you're still fighting and eventually they called up some of our M-60 tanks to help.

I can remember sitting there taking a break from digging my foxhole and watching the tanks moving slowly ahead. It wasn't quite dark yet and every now and then, you would see the tank stop, its barrel slowly being pointed down and then the loud explosion of the cannon going off. It was aimed only a few feet in front of the tank and when it went off, it sent enemy bodies and gear flying through the air.

One hole down, let's move to the next. Point the barrel down and shoot the cannon, more bodies and gear flying. This went on for quite a while, actually until it got too dark to see anymore and then the tanks returned to our perimeter. By then, they had silenced many of the enemy that had been causing trouble all afternoon.

2nd squad had an easy night- we stayed in our own foxholes, which was better than an ambush or a listening post. Others weren't as lucky and there was quite a bit of action that night. Although we had it somewhat easier, very few of us slept at all, we knew that the enemy was everywhere and the numerous skirmishes proved it. When morning came,
everything was relatively quiet, at least there wasn't any
fighting.

When everyone was ready, we saddled up and began our slow march north, determined to eliminate everyone in our path.
We had moved for an hour or so and we were now in an area of relatively soft sand- hard for digging, running, just about everything, and yet everything was still relatively quiet. Far off in the distance we heard a boom and everyone yelled,
"Incoming!" at the same time and dove for cover. You could tell by the sound and the scream of the shell coming through the air that it was going to be close.

The shell landed, sending a large cloud of sand into the air, followed by the hundreds of pieces of shrapnel flying every which way. We let the dust settle on that one before anyone moved a muscle and there was this fake pause where most of us almost began to get up. Incoming was the call again and we all settled back down where we had originally landed. The loud crump told us all that it wasn't far away and then the whooshing sound of the molten shrapnel whipping through the air.

Now the guns fired at will, one round coming in after another and none of us had a place to hide except for the slight ability to wiggle lower and lower into the sand. With each exploding round came the horrible sound of the shrapnel and each one of us cringed, waiting for the hot pieces to come whipping through our bodies. There was almost a comfort if you heard the artillery round explode- that meant it had missed you, but the shrapnel, on the other hand, was following close behind. I wasn't religious by any means, but my grandmother had sent me a serviceman's cross when I was in boot camp. It was a small pocket cross that never got into the way.

On this day I remember reaching into my pocket and grabbing that cross, squeezing it as hard as I could. Prayers for me were very rare, but I prayed that day. With each exploding artillery round, we would force our bodies closer and closer to the ground, praying for the shrapnel to miss and land harmless somewhere out in the sand.

The barrage went on and on, and periodically you could hear more and more men screaming in pain as they were hit. As quickly as it started, it ended, but none of us moved for quite some time, leery that they would begin shooting again.
Apparently they had shot their wad in more ways than one. There were no more artillery barrages and after that, there was very little enemy contact. It seemed that they had pulled back to regroup for another day.

Eventually when our leaders felt that we had met our objectives, we all resumed other missions. We were heli-lifted back to the river area where we resumed patrols in and around the villages. We were positioned between the village of Gia Liem and the river in an area that was relatively flat except for the trails and the occasional Vietnamese cemetery plots.

The next morning I was called up to the Platoon CP to talk to Lt Lewy about a daytime patrol. This was to be a reinforced squad patrol which would include a machine gun team in an area that would begin to the south of our current position, being that of a marketplace. A marketplace was nothing more than a large village where villagers from the surrounding area would bring their goods for sale. From that village, we were to move north to the Cua Viet River and once there, move left along the southern bank through numerous small villages and then eventually a southern tack back to the position we started from.

Patrols like this were not uncommon, basically part of a normal day's activity. From the varied activities during the past weeks, everyone was tired and basically worn out, and no one was looking forward to today's mission. I went back to the squad area, having first gone by Gosa and his machine gun team to let them know that we would be moving out shortly. Once back to our area, I briefed my two fire team leaders on what would be going on and also contacted Cow, one of our Kit Carson Scouts, letting him know that he would be going as well.

Without much fanfare, we straggled out of our perimeter and quickly got into a wedge formation for our approach to the first village, the marketplace. When approaching the village, Cow noticed that there were Popular Force troops already in the village. In a brief discussion, we learned that they had been there for a few days and planned on staying there for a number of days more.

With this information, Cow and I had a chat on what options we had for the day. One was to do something very bad but also something that was definitely needed by the men of 2nd squad. What we ultimately chose to do was to have the Popular Force troops set up some positions around the village, basically giving us some down time.

I called everyone together and told them we would be staying in the village all day in an attempt to give them a very illegal R&R day. This was eagerly greeted and everyone went about doing nothing, some just sitting in the shade with a soda purchased from one of the village booths. Just knowing that they had no responsibilities was a tremendous relief, hard for anyone that never had their day-to-day responsibilities to understand. The extreme down side to this was that for each position that we were supposed to move through during the day, I needed to call into the Platoon CP with a situation report, basically giving them an update with the patrol's progress and more importantly, letting them know exactly where we were.

Sounds simple but if another unit spotted troops out in the open, they would quickly get up on their radios asking if there were any friendlies in the area. Our Platoon CP might get involved and say, "Oh yes, we have a squad patrolling in that area." Obviously if we were not really there, those troops could be the enemy and some American forces could be walking into something, thinking everything was ok.

Early in the afternoon, Cow took me to a small hooch, which was a Vietnamese village version of a restaurant. The crowded interior had at least one small table, possibly two, with a few stools along the wall.

Cow wanted to treat me to a nice meal and he quickly chatted with the cook. What came out was some ham and Vietnamese pasta made out of rice, which was actually quite good. Along with the meal they also brought out 3 small bowls filled with sauce, each one hotter than the other.

Over my few months there, I had already been introduced to these and some were outrageously hot. Playing it safe, I found the mildest one and used that to dip the ham into, making it quite tasty. All of this was quite a novelty to some of the villagers who had surrounded our small table, trying to coax me into trying the hotter sauce, saying, "G.I., this one number one," and I would quickly reply, "Oh no, number 10," which would quickly get a laugh out of them.

After our snack, Cow and I were sitting outside, leaning back against one of the hooches enjoying the shade and the much needed down time. I glanced across the courtyard to see Bobby Briscoll, one member of the machine gun team, sitting on a small stool getting a haircut. At the same time, he was enjoying a cold bottle of Tiger Piss, a local Vietnamese beer, much better than anything that was provided to us through normal supplies.

Periodically, I would go over to where our squad radio was and call in a fake situation report, cringing with each one and hoping nothing bad was going to happen. Eventually all of this needed to come to an end and we needed to sneak to an area up by the river so that our approach to our platoon's lines would be coming from the right direction. We pulled it off and it's not something I tell with a lot of pride- things could have gone very badly but on that day, we were extremely lucky.

One evening, I needed to take out an ambush and in the early evening, we began the ritual of getting our gear ready. It was a warm, dry night so we needed very little except for our weapons and ammunition. We had a machine gun team with us and we slowly made our way well out into the cemetery area where a major trail wound its way through. Our responsibility was to ambush anyone or anything that came down the path. Although ambushes were very dangerous, they were also an opportunity to get plenty of sleep.

Just like on the lines when we first set into position, everyone was on 100% alert. Eventually that shifted to one man at a time on watch. We would divide the number of hours that we needed to be out there by the number of men on the mission and that would determine how long each one of us had to stand watch. The radio would be passed to the far end of the ambush and each man would take their turn standing watch, waking their replacement, and passing the communications radio down. Just like on a listening post, there were frequent situation reports that would be called out and you would respond by pressing the key on the handset accordingly.

During the middle of this night, I woke up from my position somewhere in the middle of the ambush and I just knew that something was wrong. I lay there for quite some time before I realized what it was. I slowly crawled backwards and then began to crawl behind the men as they lay there, looking for the person with the radio.

I spotted the square box alongside the man's leg and now I just lay there, waiting to see what was going to happen. After a few minutes, I heard the soft sound of the squelch of the radio and the radio operator from our Platoon CP was asking for a situation report. I kept hearing the squelch, telling me that my man was not responding to the call, obviously asleep. I slowly crawled up behind him and saw him with the handset placed close to his right ear, sound asleep.

Without rising, I took my helmet off, gripped it by the edge, and swung it forward clocking the man on the back of the head, sending out an audible clunk. I realized later that I should never have done that because of the noise, but I was just reacting the way I needed. After I clunked him on the head, I moved forward and grabbed him by the neck. I said, "Mother fucker, I'm turning 21 tomorrow and you're not
going to prevent that from happening." There was no movement on his part except for the glaring whites of his eyes as he looked at me in fear, in pain, and in anger.

Early the next morning, we cautiously moved back to our perimeter and got there just after daybreak. As we came in single file through 2nd squad's fighting positions, a couple of the men softly asked me if I heard a clunking sound in the middle of the night. I ignored them and went to the lieutenant to talk about what had happened. The Marine was mumbling that I acted out of order but it was a moot point. He had a minor concussion and needed to be medevaced, we never saw him again after that.

Later that morning, word came down the line that the squad leaders were to report to the Platoon CP. I grabbed my helmet, rifle, cartridge belt, and M-16, and headed up the
village path to Lt Lewy's position. 2nd Platoon would be moving out again on foot this time, heading west towards Phu Tai for a sweep and then on to the village of An Gia, which was slightly north of Phu Tai on the Cua Viet River.

It took us the remainder of the morning to get packed up and ready to move out. We traveled in a large wedge formation until we came near Phu Tai. In the distance, we could see villagers walking the paths of the village, going about their daily business. We all came up online and moved forward slowly making our way through the village, this time without incident. Once out of the village, we turned slightly north and resumed our wedge formation for our move towards An Gia.

The village was as busy as Phu Tai and the occupants were not concerned with our presence. Just like the village with the Catholic Church, there was a main path that worked its way close to the river with the bulk of the village on the other side. There was a masonry building that at one time was a schoolhouse, but the tides of war had removed its roof and the walls were scarred with the pockmarks of shrapnel and stray bullets.

This wasn't just a sweep; the word was that we were going to be here for a number of days, preventing any enemy movement on the main trail and the river. It took the remainder of the afternoon to set the lines and everyone began to dig in.

We had no sooner begun to dig in when we heard the beginning of a fight directly across the river from where we were. I took out my squad map and determined that the action was taking place in Dai Do, the same village where we captured the 75 recoilless and where James had gotten killed.

There was a steady increase in the intensity of the fight and before long, the artillery and air support began. For us it was one of those times to sit back and witness another group deal with the agonies of war, but this didn't go without emotions. With one breath, you felt bad for the Marines who were crawling around on the other side of the river, obviously locked in a fierce battle. There were those subconscious thoughts that we could be called up as reserves and none of us wanted that at all.

The battle raged on and on and with darkness approaching, it didn't show any signs of slacking off. The squad leaders were called up to the CP and none of us had any good feelings about what we were going to be told. Lt Lewy waited for all four of us to be there before he gave his report. The unit across the river was a company from 2nd Battalion 4th Marines and their backup was Bravo Company from our unit, 1st Battalion 3rd Marines. They had walked into an NVA regiment ambush and the enemy was well dug in and supplied.

I was to take 2nd squad down the main trail and set up an ambush of an area designated on our maps as a river crossing. The other squads got their orders for listening posts and regular perimeter watch. There was a good chance that some enemy soldier would be attempting to come across the river and we would be there to stop them. It would be a normal squad ambush being reinforced with an M-60 machine gun team.

During the early evening hours, we were listening to our communications radios and we could listen in on the chatter that was taking place across the river. 2/4 was in a real bind and the NVA were making mince meat of them. We could hear squad leaders screaming on the radio and then being cut off abruptly, giving us the indication that they had just been wiped out. Our bombardment of the village was being stepped up and the Phantoms and the Huey Gunships were constantly diving into the village, releasing their deadly loads.

The South Vietnamese Air Force was involved as well, and they were always a treat for us to watch in action. They didn't fly jets-they were equipped with old World War II fighter planes, retrofitted with Gattling guns. They all thought they were John Wayne and when diving in for their bombing and strafing runs, they would come screaming straight down,
coming out of the sun so they couldn't be seen. We would watch them dive lower and lower with their Gattling guns blaring and eventually disappear in the tree line of the village, and we would be taking bets to see if they pulled out in time or not.

A few seconds later, you would hear the distinctive roar of their engines as they were pulling up and banking, working their way around for another pass. During all my months there, I never saw one of them shot down or even put out of commission. From where we were, it looked as if the entire village was on fire, thick black smoke was curling skyward from all parts of the village. Still the battle raged on.

A CH-46 Sea Knight helicopter was involved and it had taken numerous hits. Most if not all of the crew, except for the pilot, were either dead or severely wounded. From what I can remember, he had a chance to fly the chopper to a safer location before landing or crashing, but other things were on his mind.

Below him, he saw a Marine squad that was pinned down and would soon be flanked by an enemy squad that was sneaking around to their right. Instead of flying his craft to safety, he chose to crash it between the Marines and the flanking NVA soldiers, giving the Marines a chance to move to a safer location.

We all sat there with blank stares on our faces, listening to the communications on the radio, we couldn't believe our ears. At the same time, we felt the pain of what was taking place across the river. As we sat there, we were getting our gear ready for our nightly assignment, which none of us were overly thrilled about, especially tonight.

As darkness approached, the squad gathered by the main path of the village, the one that ran parallel to the river. I had gone over our approach plan with my fire team leaders and as soon as the gun team arrived, I filled them in as to what we were going to do. We would be leaving the village center, traveling the down stream direction of the path. It was very important that we kept well dispersed, leaving enough space to be safe but at the same time enabling each other to see the person in front in the quickly fading light.

A few hundred yards down the path there would be a break in the foliage on the river side of the trail, when we reached that point we would stop on the side of the trail and wait for total darkness. With the arrival of darkness, I instructed the lead elements to move out cautiously, mostly crawling their way to our objective which was a rice paddy dike very near the bank of the river. Slowly the reinforced squad moved out, each man crawling after the one in front of him. When we arrived at the dike, each man positioned himself slightly to the right of the man in front of him. Eventually we were all in position and now it was just a matter of waiting.

The big difference for us on this night was the raging battle that was taking place directly across the river from us.

Everyone knew that this was the narrowest part of the river in this area and our position was designated as a popular river crossing. I'm sure this was on everyone's mind- I know for a fact it was on mine. It was still relatively early in the evening time-wise and we were still on 100% alert.

I don't know who heard it first, but I began to hear a deep mechanical rumbling sound. I moved back and crawled behind our ambush line to where the machine gun team was positioned. I found their team leader and crawled up to him, asking if he had any idea of what we were listening to. He was as mystified as I was, we were all clueless.

I carefully crawled back to my position next to my radio operator and continued waiting like everyone else. There were times where the sound seemed closer to us than others, and at times it almost seemed to be coming from underneath us, we were all completely baffled.

Just before we were to begin our rotational shifts, my radio operator elbowed me and whispered to me that I needed to talk to someone on the radio. This was very rarely done and I didn't like the sounds of it right from the beginning. I took the handset and said, "This is Alpha Two Bravo," which was radio talk for Alpha Company, Second Platoon, Second Squad. The person on the other end was our platoon radio operator, Corporal Hearns, someone that few of us had any use for.

He asked if he was talking to Corporal Janicki and I said, "That's an affirmative." He then went on to ask if I heard any strange sounds coming from out in front of our position, something like a rumbling sound. I was very surprised by his question and responded back in an inquisitive way, surprised that he could hear it from where he was. Well that wasn't really the case at all, Corporal Hearns was much too far away to hear any of this. I asked him if he knew what the hell it was and he said he most definitely did.

Alpha Company had received a radio call from the captain of a river patrol boat that had been sent up the river to help in the battle of Dai Do. These were very large boats similar to the PT boats of World War II and they were heavily armed with Gattling guns, automatic grenade launchers and Starlight scopes to enable them to see at night. Somehow one of their crewmembers had spotted someone in our ambush moving and they were double-checking before they opened fire. They knew that friendlies had been deployed in numerous ambushes on our side of the river and they were being very careful, thank God for being careful.

Corporal Hearns went on and on, indicating that I must have done a shitty job of setting my men in, obviously exposing ourselves to the gun boat. I was really pissed, not so much at my men or myself but at Hearns. We had taken all our normal precautions on setting in and we were more than careful this night, knowing that the enemy was directly across from us. If it wasn't for the high tech Starlight scope, they never would have seen us so my anger went back to Hearns and his insinuations.

I ended the conversation with Hearns and passed the word down the ambush line, informing everyone as to what we were listening to. I waited until the next morning to fill them in on the other details but gave them enough info to understand what was out in front of us. As mysteriously as it came, it went and none of us had a chance to see the patrol boat that had spotted us.

245

Fortunately the night went without incident and daylight came. We cautiously moved back from the dike and moved back down the trail to our regular positions. While my men went about their early morning chores of cooking breakfast and cleaning their weapons, I continued on up the path to where our platoon command post was set up. I came to the hooch and Hearns was sitting out in front, having had a rather peaceful night of radio watch. Lt Lewy and Sergeant Hall were sitting around, each trying to get some C-rations heated. Hearns saw me coming but didn't really think anything of it. I came up and stood directly in front of him, my boots just inches from his. He was messing around with the frequency knobs of the radio and I waited for him to look up. Finally he finished whatever he was doing and looked up to see what I wanted. I looked him squarely in the eye and let my tongue loose.

I said, "You low life peace of shit, don't you ever contact me on the radio and criticize what I do and how I manage my men. Night after night, you sit here on your dumb ass and all you do is take turns on radio watch sitting here behind the safety of the men in our squads.

Every now and then you are required to go out on platoon- sized ambushes and I hope you are scared shitless because that's what we have to deal with every night. The next time you talk to me the way you did last night, I'll track you down and shove that radio handset of yours so far up your ass, you'll need a reinforced squad to help you pull it out."

I then looked at Lewy and Hall and said quite clearly, "Keep this piece of shit away from my men and better yet, all the men of the other squads as well." With that, I turned and walked back to my foxhole and tried to find something halfway decent to eat for breakfast. Before I turned, I glanced over at Sgt Hall and he had this pleasant smirk on his face, I think he was thankful for me tying into Hearns, he really was a jerk.

246

I guess when I made my delivery, many men who were scattered around the area heard what I had to say to Hearns. Little by little during the course of the day, men would walk by my area, they would somehow get my attention, and then give me a thumbs up, one of our simple ways of saying "good job." It was so hard doing what we did day in and day out, and it was almost impossible to keep our moral up, we didn't need our own people dumping on us-that just made things worse.

The battle of Dai Do finally came to an end but at a tremendous Marine loss, little did we know then that it would go in the history books as one of the worse battles of the war.

Around this time I was having a problem with one of my upper teeth and for days on end, I suffered a horrible toothache. One day, one of our corpsman was walking by and I asked him what could be done, he had been giving me regular doses of Darvon to subdue the pain. He began to indicate that he thought I might be sandbagging and I quickly tied into him, letting him know in no uncertain terms that I was not messing around. I had a good track record for not taking advantage of the system and he finally made arrangements for me to go up to Dong Ha where they had a dentist.

It took a day or two for all of this to work but finally a small boat came down the river to pick me up. These were like little Boston Whalers but they were painted green and they were our quick taxicabs on the river. When he got to me, the boat was empty but he told me that he had a couple of more picks to make before we could head towards Dong Ha. I didn't really care to be riding in this small open boat regardless of how fast it was. From the time we left the riverbank in front of my foxhole, he had the engine wide open as we raced down the river for his next customer.

I positioned myself in the bow of the boat, keeping as low a profile as possible. Having grown up on the water and in boats, I knew that sitting up front would enable him to get the boat up on plane quickly which would get our speed up faster. As we screamed along, he yelled forward to me and said that we would be picking some Major up at our next stop. Time went by quickly and it was actually fun to be on a boat like this again, it reminded me of home and how I grew up.

Every now and then, you could remove yourself from the fact that you were in the middle of a war and in a very dangerous place. Being on this boat skimming along on the water was one of those moments. The river was quite wide at parts and the greens of the rice paddies on either side and the occasional fishing village was truly beautiful. Looking at everything
from this angle, you couldn't see the devastation that you did when flying in a helicopter looking down. Everything here looked tranquil and beautiful- moments like this didn't come often and even while you were trying to enjoy them, there was a part of you that was on guard.

Eventually the boat slowed and began making its way towards shore. The driver positioned the boat about 30 or so feet from shore and yelled into the village saying that he was here to pick up Major so-and-so. As we sat there waiting, I was looking at the village and there was something about it that was much too familiar, but I couldn't pin point what it was.
As we sat there, the current of the river was dragging us downstream slowly, giving us a slow motion view of the village. The village was completely blown to hell, definitely one or more major battles had taken place to create the damage I was looking at.

Finally some things came into view that really hit home. I began to make out what was left of a rather large church that was on the edge of the main trail. I then quickly looked to its left to see if there was a footbridge and there was one, not the one that I remembered but something that had been recently constructed. I looked directly in front of the church to see if I could make out the shape of an old foxhole, sure enough it was there.

This was the village that we had come to after our beach assault, where Mike Muldovan and I had tried our fishing skills with the little boy. I was really taken back by what I was looking at and I felt bad for the villagers, most of whom were most likely dead. Eventually the Major came down the village trail and worked his way towards the river bank. The driver moved in closer and our second passenger climbed in. During our boat ride north, I learned that the village had acquired the Marine name of Camp Big John, in honor of a Marine that took part in one of the significant battles in the village.

The ride to Dong Ha was a quiet one. I was enjoying the views of the river and the villages the entire trip and I think the Major might have been enjoying it as well. Every now and then, you would get a chill and realize that you should really be more observant of what was going on around you other than just sightseeing. So for a moment, you would focus your attention, looking for any activity on the river banks.

Arriving at the dock at Dong Ha was like coming out of a cave into New York City. Not that it was glamorous or anything- far from it- but there was a tremendous amount of activity.

From the river bank, you needed to climb up a small hill which brought you to the edge of the road. Highway 1 went by you from left to right and somewhere nearby, there was an intersection for Highway 9 which took you out past Cam Lo, heading west towards Camp Evans, the Rock Pile, LZ Vandergriff aka LZ Stud, the infamous Khe Sahn, and if you followed it long enough, Laos and Cambodia.

There was a constant stream of military traffic, mostly tractor-trailers and 6-bys, and the clay dust was like a fog everywhere near the road. Both highways were red clay roads with no pavement and the dry clay dust went all over. Somehow through all the chaos, I made it across the road and began working my way through the big base camp of Dong Ha.

With numerous questions being asked, I found my way to where the dental clinics were set up and informed someone that I was there. Eventually I was shown into a room that looked just like a dental office back in the States and it was actually air-conditioned. A dentist came in and began a quick examination of my mouth, focusing on where I was experiencing the pain. After a bit he had determined what the problem was and wanted to set up a schedule with me to have it fixed.

I asked him what he meant by a schedule and he said that numerous things needed to be done and it would take a period of days to do it all. Feeling guilty about being out of the field, I asked him what other options there were. He said the only other option there was would be to pull the tooth. I tried to
explain to him how I felt about being somewhat out of harm's way while my men were still out there doing all the crap that they needed to do each and every day- it felt weird not being out there with them.

He was frustrated with me to a point because he really didn't want to pull the tooth, he really wanted to save it for me. I told him it would be easier for me to go on without a tooth instead of living with the guilt that was building by not being with my men. With all that said, he went about his business and pulled the tooth. He had numbed me up pretty well and gave me some pills to take for the next few days to ward off the pain I was going to experience from what he had just done.

I left there and began to make my way out of the Dong Ha base, trying to find a way to get to our base camp which was a few miles away in Quang Tri base. I hitched a ride on a military convoy and eventually made it to our Battalion compound with its layers of clay dust and hot squad-sized tents that were used for the troops in transit.

There were a few Marines hanging around, either going to or coming back from R&R, and one new guy that had been there a day or two who was scared shitless. He was asking everyone a million questions and everyone was trying to ignore him, which I think made him even more uncomfortable.

Sometime shortly after dinner, a gunny sergeant came into the tent and was pointing to each person, telling them they had line watch that night which was pretty standard in the transit tent. He pointed to me and I said no way, that I had just come from the dentist and that I felt like shit. He said, "Don't give me any of that crap, just get out there." With that, I took and spit a good sized puddle of blood on the red clay dust floor and he just stood there, looking down at it. He looked up at me and told me to take it easy. I was actually surprised to find that he had any compassion in him at all, and I just said,

"Thanks."

After breakfast the next morning, I began making my way back down Highway 1 towards Dong Ha and to the riverbank. Eventually, one of the little transit skiffs came by and I climbed aboard. The trip down river went quickly and without incident, and before I knew it, the skiff was pulling in to the riverbank area for An Gia. I came ashore without fanfare and walked back down to my squad area and it was as if I had never left, the beat went on. Sometime later the corpsman came by- he saw me there and made a snide remark about me sandbagging for a couple of days. I went up to him, opened my mouth showing him the freshly dug hole- he just looked at me and said, "Oh," and that was that.

For the next week or so, we ran patrols in the villages to the north and south of our position on the river. Many of the villagers were quite edgy with all the fighting that had been taking place in the recent weeks and months. Most of them were not big fans of the NVA, but they were always caught in a difficult situation. If they helped us, the NVA would eventually come in and punish them. If they were NVA
sympathizers, we weren't all that nice, not an easy life.

252

One day, we were running a platoon patrol through one of the villages that was directly on the river and there were numerous small fishing boats. These were all handmade boats, nothing fancy but functional for the work they were made for. One of the things we always looked for were weapons and ammunition hidden under the thatch flooring of the boats. It was seldom that we found any, but we had to search all the boats anyway.

On this day, we moved into the village without incident and shortly afterwards, began the tedious job of searching the boats. At one point someone yelled out, "Where the hell does he think he's going?" and everyone looked out at the river. One of the small fishing boats was being quickly paddled away from the village. The person doing the paddling was crouched down in the bow and you could barely make out that there was someone actually in the boat.

Our Kit Carson Scout began yelling at the boat in Vietnamese, telling him to return to the village, but the boat just kept going. No one else in the village seemed overly concerned with what was going on and they were simply going about their business as usual. Someone yelled for guns up, and our machine gun teams came forward. They had their guns set up on the side of the trail with a clear view of the fishing boat.

They first put a burst of rounds across the bow of the boat, sending a light spray down on the paddler. That didn't change anything and they did it again, still no change. With that, the Lt said, "That son of a bitch," waited a few seconds and said, "Light em up." With that, all three guns came to life, each strafing the boat. Instantly the paddler went limp and slumped forward, and slowly the boat began to sink and eventually went out of sight. There was a little sign of interest from the villagers but it was clear to most of us that whomever it was, they were not a local, not from this village anyway.

Time for R&R - Late July 1968

My time had finally come. I said goodbye to everyone and left for my long overdue R&R, which I was very much looking forward to even though it wasn't going to be Sydney. I hitched another ride with one of the river skiffs out to a large Navy barge that was going up the river, and I climbed on board that for my ride to Dong Ha. I quickly made my way back to Quang Tri, checked all my gear in except for the essentials: M-16, flack jacket, helmet, and a few magazines of M-16 ammo. The next morning, I got on a convoy out of Quang Tri to Dong Ha and then waited for a C-130 to come in that could take me to Da Nang. Within hours, I was on my way with a nice, cool ride on the C-130. This time, I chose to sit in one of the strap seats and not look out at the countryside.

Time was becoming to be a big part of my day-to-day thoughts. I had made it through 9 months of my 13-month tour. In everyone's minds, the DEROS clock was always ticking and I was definitely on the down hill side of the count. Unfortunately this is something that you didn't want to do consciously- you needed to keep it way back in your thoughts. If you let it, the short timer's clock would work against you and become your worst enemy. You needed to continue to be sharp and to continue the immediate action behavior that allowed you to get this far. Letting the clock take over made your mind think about it too often, keeping your mind pre- occupied.

Even sitting there on the plane heading to Da Nang, I purposely chose to sit in a sling chair, not in the back like I would normally, thinking that somehow sitting away from the open door was somehow safer. Completely far from the truth, if the men in the back were somehow killed, it would not stop there, the plane was going down and we would all be lost.

254

Eventually we made it to Da Nang and I made my way to the transit area which had gone through a major transformation since I was here last, which was when I first got to Vietnam. The building, which had multiple floors, was still made out of wood but had somewhat of a modern look to it, definitely nothing like the hard backs and tents that were common in most bases.

I checked in and began to look around for anyone who looked familiar, hoping to find someone to go on R&R with. I was told there was something that was called the R&R pool, where if you didn't like the destination that you had acquired, you could put it in the pool and hope that you found something that was more appealing. I didn't waste any time and I put my R&R in immediately.

I finally spotted someone that I vaguely recognized, I knew he was from our unit but I didn't really know his name. I approached him anyway and told him who I was and what unit I was from. He was from my unit, a machine gunner from one of the other platoons and we began to hang around together.

There were a couple of others from our unit as well and they were all going to Taipei for their R&R. I went to the pool to see what was available and there was one for Taipei and I put my name on it immediately. Feeling somewhat better about where I was going, I began to relax and to enjoy the relative safety of Da Nang.

The R&R center was at the base of the hill, almost exactly where the transit tents were that we stayed in, and the airstrip was only a short distance away. That afternoon, I walked down to the airstrip and stood in the transit hut watching a new batch of Marines scurrying out of their C-130's to get into formation just as we had. As they stood there at attention, their eyes were scouring the area getting as much input as possible, trying to allow their minds to start answering the millions of questions they had about Vietnam, and now was their first chance on trying to get some answers. One of the new men looked somewhat familiar and I kept looking at him, hoping to catch his eyes. Eventually we did lock eyes and it was obvious that he recognized me as well.

His name was David Magher, also someone who served as an MP in Charleston with us and when he came up to me, it was obvious that he was happy to see me, had a million questions but didn't know where to begin. He had a million questions about Vietnam, what unit I was with, did I know where Tom England was and how he was doing. He wanted to know if I knew that others had died and were they also part of my unit.

Unlike other conversation with someone I hadn't seen for some time for this one I stayed very reserved. I barely answered any of his questions to his satisfaction, and for good reason. Vietnam was something that you needed to learn on your own, nothing anyone else told you was going to make any sense unless you had already experienced it or you had been there long enough to realize that nothing was so crazy that it couldn't happen, not in Vietnam.

He said that he had been assigned to the 3rd Marines and did I know where they were, and I said yes. I told him that most of the Marines I knew of from Charleston were in the 3rd Marines and we were all up in the I Corp area. He asked a million questions about being in the bush, being in combat and more- for the most part I didn't answer, again you have to go through it for yourself. I know he left me much more discouraged than when he approached me, and I never saw him again. I have never checked to see if his name is on our wall in Washington, maybe some day I will.

Being in Da Nang alone was an experience filled with numerous emotions. Da Nang itself was relatively safe, 100 times safer than where I had come from but relatively safe in general. At night you could hear the war far outside its perimeter through the low rumbling of artillery and mortars and also the periodic skipping of machine gun tracers reflecting off into the sky. This alone was enough to make you sit back and realize how safe you were in Da Nang and what that unit was going through at that moment, night battles were always the scariest.

The Marine billet for R&R was at the base of the hill, relatively close to the airstrip. Day and night, you could stand on one of the balconies and watch F4 Phantoms taking off and returning from missions somewhere out there in Injun country. There was always the whooping sound of helicopter blades slapping the air, with their crews running missions of re- supply and medevac extractions. This was like being in the central nervous system of the war- it was like being in the center of all activity coming and going. It had its own pulse and simple daily jobs for those who were wrapped up in its process.

The bulk of Da Nang was like a small industrial town, each building or section with its own purpose and people with what appeared to be normal daily jobs. One big downside of being in the rear was that everyone was expected to be squared away- polished boots, clean and pressed utilities- just like stateside, they even needed to salute an officer when one passed by. For each of us who came from the field, there was a subtle pride in the fact that we were Marine grunts and everyone around us had a million questions of us, but they would never be asked.

We were what the Marine Corp was all about. It was hard to realize then, but we were becoming a big part of Marine Corp history, one that would be used in military teachings and as political refresher courses for years to come. The underlying theme....don't ever let this happen again.

All the time you were walking around, you couldn't let the relatively safe environment fake you out. Whenever you heard a noise that you knew had trouble associated with it, you immediately took precautionary steps to make sure that everything was ok. Even here in the rear, you couldn't let your guard down completely. That internal instinct was always at work and you really needed to listen to it.

During your early months in Vietnam, you listen to the stories from your close friends as they went to and came back from R&R. I think the most popular among Marines was Bangkok, Thailand. They would talk about going to wonderful bars and they would be escorted into special rooms with one wall being a two-way mirror, allowing them to see out into a much larger cocktail lounge.

The cocktail lounge was filled with beautiful Tai young ladies and each had a number assigned to them. When you found one that you liked, you would tell your waiter and he would escort her back to you. You would then sit for a while to see if she was someone you really wanted to spend some time with or see if she did things that would really irritate you. If you found one that you liked, you would be escorted to
another lounge to have fun; if you weren't satisfied yet, you would scan the room through the mirror until you could pick another.

Regardless of where these men went on R&R I really don't remember hearing any bad stories just loud conversation about their escapades while they were gone.

In the R&R world, there was one word that the girls really wanted to get your feelings on and that was "butterfly." There is an Asian knife called a butterfly knife, which when folded looked like a normal knife but usually quite elegant. On a butterfly knife, the handle is split down the middle. When you take each side of the handle and fold them back, the blade is exposed.

The Asian men and ladies had a way of flipping the knife in their hands in such a way that the blade was quickly exposed, much faster than any switch blade I had ever seen. They made a similar motion to close the knife each time you could hear the metal parts being worked.

This however is not the butterfly I'm referring to. Butterfly in the R&R sense was when you wouldn't stay with one girl the entire week, like butterflying from one to another. The Asian girls liked it much better if you would stick with one, it made everyone's life much simpler. So that would be their first
question, "You no butterfly me?" and they would hope for the answer, "No."

Another suggestion that came back from the others was to take all the money you took on R&R and give it to the girl you were with to manage. Initially this sounded absolutely absurd, but I heard it from more than one Marine, so it stuck with me as a safe thing to do. The girl you were with would manage what you spent on what and would step in and negotiate to make sure you got the best price possible. In the end, they would hope that you would be a nice guy and give them a big tip from the money that was left at the end of your stay.

Those were the two main rules that I carried with me as I prepared to go and try to relax for 5 days. Hopefully Taipei would be a nice place, I would find a nice girl to be with and I would have some fun.

Finally the morning came and our civilian plane destined for Taipei arrived and we scurried on board. During our day or so in Da Nang, we tried to get as clean as possible, but when we got close to the stewardess and crew of the plane, we realized that we had a lot more work to do in the hygiene area. This was a very strange feeling, being on this plane with American civilians as the crew, you really liked the feeling but you couldn't let your mind enjoy it too much, after R&R we would all be going back to our individual hells and we hadn't earned the right to feel free, not yet anyway. There was some apprehension as we waited on the runway to take off, but eventually the pilot hit the throttles and we were on our way.

The flight to Taipei was very relaxing- for the first time, you could really put the war away for a few minutes and enjoy the down time. Up forward in the plane, just behind the door that led to where the pilot and navigator were, there was a small round table. You were free to walk around the plane and at one point, I sat at the table and thought it was pretty cool.

Towards the end of the flight, the stewardesses had some spare time and they would sit there and ask some basic questions, mostly about where you were from, how long you had been there, that kind of stuff.

It was obvious that they had a million more questions and every now and then, one of them would ask a real question, one they really wanted to know the answer to.

Regardless of what the question was, they were very difficult to answer, some bordered on personal and others touched on emotions, and when you asked yourself how you really felt, you realized that you had become quite a cold individual- things that would have upset you 6, 8, 10 months ago were no longer an issue. So here we were, trying to answer, realizing that their mindset and ours were completely different. They weren't frustrated with our lack of response, we were sure that they had received the same hesitations from other Marines going on R&R.

Eventually the plane landed at an airport and we filed off of the plane onto a military bus that was there to take us to the R&R center. We sat there for a few minutes and this Air Force sergeant came on board, who was actually our greeting party. He gave us some basic info, starting with the currency exchange rate, which at the time was 40 New Taiwanese dollars or NT to one American dollar. This gave you great buying power, but sometimes calculating what you actually owed was difficult. He continued to say that there were lists of hotels at the center that had been pre approved by the US government and we needed to stay in one of those. He gave us the time we needed to be back at the center on the day of our return, one item none of us wanted to think about too much.

His final topic was the girls and the VD rate on the island. He said that the girls were beautiful but the VD rate at the time was 80%. I can't remember what anybody else said but I do remember thinking to myself, "Hot damn." The worst that could happen is that I really have a good time, find a beautiful girl, and in the end come down with the clap. Minimally, when I returned to my unit in Vietnam, I would be kept out of the field for medical reasons until I was cured. There were times that your mind would allow anything to happen to you to keep you from going out into the field, being a little sick was definitely better than being dead.

Listings of hotels were approved to stay in and we got together to pick one for our small group, I believe we picked Hotel Taipei as our first choice. Somehow we found our way to the hotel and checked in, my room wound up being somewhere on either the 4th or 5th floor, and my friends were just down the hall. It seemed as if I had no sooner thrown my travel bag down on the bed when there was a knock on the door.
Standing there was a Chinese man asking if I wanted to go out and meet some girls. I walked down the hall with him and knocked on the doors of my friends to determine their schedules- needless to say we were all in the mood to go.

We left the hotel and walked down the street just a short way to the London Bar, where we made ourselves comfortable for a few hours. We immediately ordered some drinks and began soaking in the surroundings, one beautiful girl after another. The drink of the day was a Singapore Sling and I think we all had the same thing. The Chinese guy gave us some time to look around and then he asked us to go into a side room which had a large table and chairs to sit. We made ourselves comfortable and ordered another round of drinks.

A short time later, the Chinese guy came back with 4 girls who made themselves comfortable in the chairs that weren't occupied. Once they were situated, the Chinese guy left us alone. They were all quite cute and we each struck up a conversation with one of them. Every now and then, the Chinese guy would come back to see how everything was going and we would basically take a vote- if we didn't like one or more of the girls for some reason, they were taken away and replaced by others.

Eventually everyone was happy with one of the girls except for me, and I had the chance to meet two more girls. The last one was called Mary and she was very pretty. We chatted for a while and had some more drinks and at that point, we were all comfortable with our female companion choices.

We all made our way back to the hotel for our first night with our heads on a pillow, completely out of harm's way and it was a wonderful feeling. Early in the evening, I went through the process of calling home to my father's house. I had heard from him once since I went to Vietnam and that was a miracle in itself. He had addressed the envelope to me but he had put down the wrong unit name. Fortunately someone in that mailroom knew me, again someone from Charleston, and they re-directed the letter to me.

I had left home at 16 for more than one reason, but my father was the biggest one. Over the years, there were times when he tried to be the father he never was, but too much damage had been done. But here I was, my first call stateside to be made and it was to him.

I knew he had been notified that I had been wounded and I wanted to reassure him that it was minor and I was ok.
Through some magic, the call went through and it felt strange to hear voices that you really recognized- up until now, everyone outside of Vietnam was a myth, possibly something that wasn't real.

There were times when you would sit in your foxhole at night in a frenzy to keep your mind busy, in an attempt to keep the heavy eyelids of sleep away. I would sit there and talk to my sister or brother or other close friend, telling them what was going on and as hard as I would try, I couldn't put a face to the person I was talking to- not even someone as close as my sister. Many times I would unpack my wallet from its plastic bag and pull out the picture of my sister and brother that had been taken at Loring Studio in New Haven, then and only then could I put a face to the person I was trying to talk to.

During the conversation, my father was almost comical. I thought later that he was probably experiencing many emotions and the comical part was mostly to cover up his
nervousness. Although we didn't have much of a relationship, I knew deep down he was very proud of me but didn't have a clue as to how to show it. Another feeling that had to be close was based on my chances of surviving long enough to get out of that hell hole. Every night, the American public sat there in front of the TV, listening to the daily body counts and the atrocities the American servicemen were inflicting on the
Vietnamese. I'm sure he was worried that I might not make it home, something no father wants to have going through his mind.

I knew that back in March when I had gotten wounded, they had been notified, so even without communications via mail they knew that I didn't have a desk job. It's hard to put yourself in the position of a parent that has someone serving in a combat area and all the emotions that take place; simply with not knowing what is taking place and is their family member safe and out of harm's way? We were obviously on the other side of those concerns, our focus was on minimizing what we shared, trying not to give them anything to worry about.

Through that, very few of them got any real insight as to exactly how bad it was where we were and how helpless we felt at times, with friends dying on almost a daily basis.

My conversation with my father was relatively brief. I basically needed to tell them that I was ok and that for the next few days, I would be out of harm's way. I needed for him to share the word back in Connecticut with other family members and friends.

Mary and I enjoyed our first night together and I had a million questions for her, as she did of me. One of her first questions for me was one that I expected; she wanted to know if I was going to "butterfly." I told her that I had no plans to. With the basic ground rules established, she asked me if I needed to stay at the hotel or could I move in with her at her apartment.

Before I answered her, I needed to know if she would help me spend my money wisely and not get ripped off by the local vendors. She was more than happy to take on this role and described how she could save me money. The rules said that I needed to stay at the hotel but I wasn't overly worried about following all the rules. Early on the second day, we decided to move to her apartment a few blocks away. It was obvious that with Mary, managing my money and staying at her place would save me hotel charges- her chance on getting a good tip would be good.

While on R&R, I wanted to get a suit made and also wanted to have something made for my sister, Judy, and a good friend, Bonnie. One of our early conversations was on having a suit made. Early on the morning of the second day, before we checked out to her apartment, a man knocked on my hotel room door- he said he was a tailor. Before letting him in, I turned to check with Mary, she whispered that he made good suits.

He went about his business of measuring my arms, legs, shoulders, and then I sat down to discuss the color and material type. Of course I wanted a silk suit and it was going to be a dark green. During this conversation, I sat in the easy chair in the room and Mary sat on my lap, holding my hand.

We discussed a white shirt to go along with the suit, a tie and even a belt, and he took notes on what was decided. He asked me what style shoes I wanted and before I could answer, Mary bent my thumb back, causing me some intended pain but definitely got my attention. She leaned closer to me and said that his shoes were number ten, very bad. With that, I told him that I was going to another vendor for the shoes.

A little later that morning we moved to her apartment, which was quite a surprise. It was a tiny place in what seemed to be some type of hotel and most of the units were occupied by the local prostitutes. The room was tiny and she had very few decorative items to make it homier, it was simply a place to
stay when she wasn't staying in a hotel with a serviceman. There was definitely a feeling of home to the place for her, and the other girls that were there were very vocal about their support. For the most part I was in the dark, I had no idea as to what they were saying but I did know that they were having fun with the fact that I had chosen to stay there with Mary.

In conversations, Mary told me that her being a prostitute was not a disgrace for her family. Most, if not all the money she made through her prostitution went back to her family, helping them to keep food on the table one month at a time. The survival culture in Third World nations are much different than what we are accustomed to and unfortunately, many American servicemen made fun of their lifestyle. I felt differently, I respected their need to support each other and how tight their family unit was.

I told her that I wanted to have two silk bo dia's made, one for my sister and the other for my friend, Bonnie. She thought this was very funny but knew it was something that I really wanted to do. We left her room and began walking through the old China side of town; dirt roads, bamboo buildings with thatch roofs, I'm sure similar to where they lived back in China. She took me to a tailor and talked to them in Chinese about showing me some different colors and styles of silk. I picked out two colors; one was a pale yellow with a flower
pattern, but I can't remember what the other was like. The
yellow one was for my sister.

After choosing the colors, she let me try to explain the measurements with the tailor on my own. They really had a good time with me, making me use my hands to identify what part of the body the different measurements were for, really laughing when I held my hands over my chest and the measurements that I had written down. They must have thought that my measurements were wrong but minimally, Bonnie had a large chest, something they were not used to in this part of Taipei. They eventually got everything they needed and it was obvious that Mary wanted me to wait outside for a bit, so I went to the front door of the small shop and sat on the sill.

Across the street was a traveling theatre that was preparing for their nightly performance. This was completely made of bamboo with a stage deck, a back stage area and bamboo stairs which allowed the actors to exit behind the structure.

This was also your typical Chinese theatre with all the actors being males, some being heavily made up to look like females. I was sitting at an angle to the stage so I actually saw more of what was going on behind the scenes than on the performance area. It was very interesting to watch and I sat there, waiting for Mary to finish her business inside and to go on with our nightly plans.

Throughout my five days in Taipei, we traveled quite a bit and saw as much of the island as possible. She showed me parts of the city that most servicemen didn't see and I was very grateful for a chance to see the backside of their lifestyle. My time was running short and it was obvious that Mary wasn't happy that I was leaving. Their lives were so different from anything I had known. Their work, which would have been a family disgrace here in the US, was the main family's stream of income and food, and Mary's sacrifice was understood by her family.

One evening, we were back at the Taipei hotel where my friends were staying. We had been out for a few drinks and were just lounging around the hotel lobby, getting ready to go out to some nightclubs. That day was some type of Chinese holiday and people were partying up and down the streets.

We saw some of the big Chinese dragons and other large figures parading up and down, and everyone was throwing firecrackers. Somewhere in the middle of all of this, someone out in the street lit numerous long rows of them.

From inside where we were sitting, it sounded like a firefight unfolding and we were all a little on edge. Unfortunately one of the men I was with was an M-60 machine gunner and the overwhelming sounds from outside got the best of him and he really began to freak out. We were pretty confident that all the booze we were consuming helped this along, but it took us quite a while to put him at ease. Needless to say, some of the other people that were staying in the hotel and the hotel staff were not all that impressed, but at that point we really didn't care what they thought- what did they know anyway?

Eventually the time came when I had to get back to the R&R center, and back to Vietnam. We drove to the center together in a cab and I went in to see what the rules were. There would be a main bus taking most of the G.I.s out to the air base, but I asked if we go by ourselves in cabs and they said, "Sure." I went back outside, got in the cab and told her what to tell the driver. We were to follow the bus to the air base and into the transit area, which would be as far as she would go. Within a short period of time, the bus pulled out and we along with the other cabs, followed in a long line.

On the way, I thanked Mary for showing me a wonderful time, more than I had ever expected from five days on R&R. She sat there in silence for a bit and eventually reached into her pocketbook, pulled out an envelope and handed it to me.
Somewhat confused, I sat there for a few minutes before actually opening it up. Inside were hundreds of dollars that we had not spent, mostly due to her bargaining during our time together. I remembered what my friends had said and I took half the money and I gave it to her as a show of appreciation for our time together. Before we knew it, we were passing through the sentry gate at the air base and the bus and the chain of cabs pulled off to the side.

There was only a minute or two for good-byes, but I can still remember looking back at her, standing outside the cab as we all moved onto the bus for the final short trip to the waiting plane. On the bus there was no humor, none at all. For everyone, the fun and excitement of R&R was quickly slipping away, being replaced by the fears of what we were going back to. Everyone had varied jobs back in the Nam, but for us grunts, we all knew that we were going back to that shitty uncertainty of not knowing where you would be from one second to the other. I was not in a good mood, I knew what I was going back to and there was nothing to feel good about, nothing at all.

The plane ride back was very quiet, everyone was in their own little world of distance. We arrived at Da Nang Air Base and moved quickly to the R&R tent for a few hours' sleep before heading back to our units. In the morning, the few of us that were going to Dong Ha got on a C-130 and headed north.
Once in Dong Ha, the few of us that were continuing on to Quang Tri caught a convoy that would eventually get us there. All this was only a few hours in duration, but by the time we walked into our Company headquarters, we looked as dirty as the day we left-welcome back. We checked in and we were
quickly told that we wouldn't be going anywhere and to check into the R&R tent.

During the last couple of days of R&R, the lower part of my left ear was getting sore and I took the time to go to the battalion aid station to have one of the corpsman look it over.

I was fortunate to get corpsman J. Johnson, better known as JJ. He had me lay down on a gurney and took some antiseptic cleaners and wiped the ear clean. He took his time, looking it over and eventually said that I had a cyst growing in the lower lobe and it needed a few more days before it was mature. He gave me a light duty chit, which allowed me to stay away from heavy duty work details, basically taking it easy. I was to report back in a few days to have it re-examined.

A few days later, I went back and JJ looked me over again. He said that it had matured and it was time to have it removed.

He had me lay down on the gurney again and took his time cleaning the ear. He gave me a shot in the lower lobe to numb the area that he was going to cut. He was talking to me while he was working, asking how things were back out in the bush, it had been a number of weeks since he had left.

He said that if he was successful, he would be able to remove the puss sack without making a mess of things. He was talking very calmly, cutting away when all of a sudden he said, "Shit," in not so happy a way. During his cutting, he nicked the sack and the puss oozed out everywhere so he began to clean it up. After everything was cleaned up, he wrapped the lobe with white gauze, something that really stood out in Nam.

He gave me another light duty chit, which would enable me to escape some of the dirtier work details, but didn't get me out of everything. Every night, the gunny would come through the R&R tent to see who was available to stand line watch. As bad as this was, it was nowhere near as difficult as standing line watch out in the bush, but you were still up most of the night. The first night, the gunny asked me to stand watch and I had him look at my ear all wrapped in white, quite a nice target in the dark. Regardless of how much I said it was ridiculous for me to go on watch, he said that I was needed and that I had to go.

Returning from R&R - July 1968

When the time came, I fell in with the other transients and climbed into the 6-by truck and rode out to one of the outer perimeters of the base. When we got there, we all climbed off and went over to the command post and waited for our bunker assignments. Eventually, someone came out and divided us up among the defensive bunkers and we all took our time moving over to check out our turf for the night.

There was a rail line that ran through Quang Tri and my fighting position for the night was just down from where the tracks cut through our perimeter. There was a very large bunker that had been built on top of the tracks that was heavily sandbagged. Once I got my gear put away, I began to check the area out a bit, mostly what was out in front of our position. It was always good to study your area in the daylight to identify the bush or knoll that could be come a probing VC during the night when you were overly tired and your mind began to play games with you.

Once I had everything relatively under control, I visited the troops in the bunker to my left and then the one to our right, which was the one built on the railroad tracks. This bunker was being manned by a few Air Force troops from a unit called Red Pony, a little-known group in the Quang Tri area that ran B-52 tracking systems for the bombing runs over Hanoi. I went up and introduced myself as part of the crew that would be in the bunker to their left.

Off to the side were these M-16s resting on bipods, models that I had never seen before. I asked if I could take a look at one and they said, "Sure," and handed me one. This was a completely new model that was for the most part just like the one that I carried. But, they had placed an M-79 grenade launching barrel under the normal barrel, so you could fire
grenades as well as your M-16. Along with that, each of these new weapons had a Starlight scope attached on top for night sighting of enemy movement. Here these guys were every so often standing perimeter watch and they had all this high- powered technology, and somewhere out in front of us was my unit. Every single Marine would give anything to have a weapon like this, sometimes there was no justice.

Within a matter of days, my ear had healed enough to allow me to return to the field and I began getting my gear ready. Jimmy Smith was in the rear for some reason, I can't remember why, but the two of us prepared for the trip from Quang Tri base to the supply point down on the Cua Viet River. Early one morning, we headed out to catch a convoy
from Quang Tri base to Dong Ha, where we started searching for a boat that would be heading down the river.

Finally we found a Navy supply boat that was heading down towards Cua Viet Base. We hitched a ride sitting in the relative security of its long, forward storage area surrounded by pallets of C-rations heading somewhere. Eventually we neared the 3rd Marines Supply point at the bend of the river and a small skiff came out to bring us ashore.

Smitty and I had no sooner gotten out of the skiff and this gunny came up to us asking us what the hell we were doing coming down the river to his site. Smitty and I were somewhat confused and basically said that we were there to rejoin 2nd Platoon, wherever they were. The gunny pointed across the river to the north and said that they had been over there for a number of days, locked in a very nasty battle with an NVA unit, and there was no way in hell that we would be able to get to them.

With those words said, Smitty and I were stuck there, not knowing what to do. Somewhere around midday, a big Navy supply boat was coming up the river, loaded down with telephone poles and Smitty and I jumped back into the skiff and headed out for a ride north to Dong Ha. They slowed down long enough for us to come aboard and we took off.

This was a much larger vessel with crew's quarters, and everything was in the stern area of the ship. The sailors had no idea what we were doing, but minimally they all assumed that Smitty and I had been out in the field for a long time and told us to help ourselves to anything that we could find of interest in the galley.

Smitty and I went below and found fresh pies, a Norris machine with cold milk, the works. We sat there, eating pies and drinking milk until we both thought we would throw up. Eventually we got to Dong Ha without incident and caught another convoy back to Quang Tri where we were forced to spend the next few nights on the perimeter, which was fortunately uneventful.

Finally we were given the word that Alpha Company had returned to the river villages and 2nd Platoon was currently in the village named An Gia. Smitty and I had a little extra time to prepare for this trip and we used that time to acquire anything and everything that we could afford and personally transport to the village. We managed to purchase a few cases of soda, some cigarettes and some chewing tobacco, and then tried to figure out how we were going to get all this stuff first to Dong Ha and then eventually down the river to An Gia.

We asked around and finally found someone with a vehicle who was willing to take us, and our stuff, to Dong Ha. Once there, we waited on the riverbank for one of the small river boats to come by and asked if they had time to take us down. All of this worked out fairly well and we eventually got underway heading down the Cua Viet River towards An Gia.

Being on the river always gave me the creeps. Although you were traveling down an absolutely beautiful river with villages staggered on either side, there was always a tremendous risk that Charlie would make target practice out of you.
Fortunately on this day, we had an uneventful ride and eventually began to pull into the small river beach at An Gia.

Some of the men spotted us coming down the river and walked out into the water to greet us. It's hard to put into words the feelings each of us had for each other during those difficult times. We all held each other in such high esteem, especially the squad leaders and those who had been in country for quite some time, they were gods of sorts.
As they helped walk the small boat to shore, they were all quite thrilled with the goodies Smitty and I had acquired.

When we got ashore, Smitty and I followed the men from 2nd squad back to their section of perimeter, eventually getting to the command area for 2nd Platoon. Someone said that this other Marine named Ray had filled in for me while I was gone and he had not been relieved as squad leader. With that piece of info, I quickly said hi to everyone and then made my way up to the platoon command post, eventually finding Lt Lewy and quickly asked him what he wanted me to do. He said that he had been comfortable with Ray in charge of 2nd squad and wasn't sure what he wanted to do with me.

With that, I sat back, opened some C-rations and began cooking myself something to eat, in Vietnam you learned quickly to go with the flow and this was no exception. A short time later, the two fire team leaders from 2nd squad came up to the CP, asking if they could talk to Lt Lewy. Basically they said that while they were on the last operation, which turned out to be a very nasty one, Ray showed little if no leadership. Basically he was always behind them, yelling at the rest of the squad to keep moving forward. After laying all of that out, they then said that if he was to remain their squad leader, they would basically take matters into their own hands to get Ray out of the picture. The Lt got the picture. He turned to me and asked me to rejoin 2nd squad and to send Ray up to the CP.

The three of us straggled back down the path to 2nd squads location where Ray waited with a bit of an attitude. I threw my gear off to the side and said to him that the Lt wanted him back up at the CP and I was being reassigned to 2nd squad. He took great offense to this but packed up and went back up the trail. Ray and I got to Vietnam at the same time and he always had his nose out of joint that I was given 2nd squad after Phu Tai, he thought for sure that he should have become squad leader.

Supplies were being brought in, which was a definite sign that we were going to be involved in something. It was no surprise when all the squad leaders were called up to the platoon CP for the initial briefing. All of Alpha Company as well as other elements of 1/3 were to move northwest in the Hayride Valley area as a blocking force, with the hopes of stopping or slowing the NVA troop movement into the south.

Just prior to Smitty and I rejoining the platoon, a new replacement for Lt Lewy had joined the unit- his name was 2nd Lt Bovine. As soon as I met him, the chemistry turned the wrong way, most likely my fault. The new lieutenant was considerably shorter than Lt Lewy and his helmet seemed to wobble on his head. On top of that, he loved wearing sunglasses and immediately he gained the nickname Lt Hollywood.

There was definitely an attitude shared by him and me and it was pretty obvious that he didn't care for me much. That was ok with me- I didn't care for him much either, he had a cocky, arrogant, attitude that didn't go well out in the bush. This next operation would be his first with us and it was going to be interesting to see how everyone accepted him. I for one was not looking forward to it.

We were to be heli-lifted to a mountainous area somewhere outside of Khe Sanh to run search and destroy patrols in an attempt to flush out the NVA units expected to be moving through the area. Prior to our landing, the entire area was heavily bombed, which was both good and bad. The good part of it was if there were any enemy units in the exact area, they would be heavily battered and scattered. The bad part was that the NVA knew all too well how we operated and if they saw an area being bombarded, they would know that the troops were soon to follow and they could easily set up devastating cross fire of the landing zone. Fortunately for us, either they were too far away from the intended zone or didn't care, our landing was relatively quiet.

For this assault, we flew in on CH-46s, which were the largest choppers available and they had loading ramps off the back. I remember running out of the chopper that day into a hillside covered in smoke from fires that the bombardment had started. We set up a hasty perimeter around the zone and I remember seeing a terrified small deer standing there in the smoke with all of this activity going on around it. Very seldom did we see animals like this, and this was the first and last deer I saw during my 13 months.

The company eventually moved up the hillside to an area overlooking a wide expanse of a mountain valley. If it were another time, I'm sure this view would be beautiful. Much of the area was still on fire and the smoke was thick, fortunately for us Charlie chose not to oppose us this day and our movements went relatively without incident.

The daytime activities were relatively quiet with minimal, if any, contact. The nights however were extremely eerie.
While you were sitting in your foxhole looking out at the mountains in the distance, you could see NVA troop movement carrying torches as they went. This was quite a distance from where we were and none of us could understand why no one was calling in air strikes on them. Night after night it was like this, yet no air strikes, none that I can remember anyway. Each day, smaller units would run patrols down the mountainside into the varied valleys in search of the enemy we saw moving each night, and again, with minimal or no contact.

Our platoon went out one day and we initially started in a wedge formation going down the mountainside. When we reached the valley floor, we came into a gorge with a ridgeline to the left, a pretty wide stream and then an open flat area that ran the length of the valley. Lt Bovine told me to take my squad across the stream and to give the rest of the platoon flanking security while they moved along the ridgeline.

I'm positive he thought he was giving me and my squad a shit detail, minimally making us wade through the stream. The reality of it though was he did us a tremendous favor. We moved across the stream and took cover in the small bushes that filled the valley floor. Our movements were very simple compared to the battle they were having, traversing the ledges on their side. It seemed to take them forever to move a few hundred feet while we would cover the same ground in just a few minutes with very little effort.

The icing on the cake for me was at one point, the Lt was trying to walk around the corner on a very narrow ledge. He lost his balance and fell straight down into the river. At that point, the river was deep enough for him to go under. His helmet was the first thing to pop up in the water and then his head with his sunglasses drooped sideways on his face.
Everyone was laughing, but the only laughing he really heard was from me, coming out of a bush on the other side of the river. Needless to say, that didn't help with the rift that was already building between us.

We spent a week or so up on those mountains, running patrols with minimal contact and I still can't figure out with all the activity we saw each evening, why was the NVA avoiding contact? It was definitely not their style.

We were eventually heli-lifted off of the mountains, landing just south of the Cam Lo firebase, which was just outside of the actual village of Cam Lo. We moved into the firebase, relieving the Marines that had been standing perimeter watch. This was a well-fortified base with well-built fighting positions and underground squad-sized bunkers.

The artillery used there were self-propelled 155 howitzers, which roared when they went off. Each night, you would stand watch on the perimeter and you could never be prepared for the blast when it came. They were positioned well inside the perimeter so you couldn't hear them loading or preparing to fire. All of a sudden, there would be a huge flash of light as the cannon went off and then the roar of charge, each time all of us would jump right out of our skins.

Soon after getting to the firebase, I was called up to the CP bunker to see the Lt. He made it short and sweet, but basically told me that he was relieving me as squad leader and replacing me with Oklahoma, my radio man, who had just come back from Okinawa and NCO school. Quite honestly, this did not bother me and Oklahoma was quite upset. He really didn't think he was up to the task, I was more than sure that he was. Being a regular squad member again was easy to take, minimally there was much less pressure and far fewer decisions for you to make.

One night shortly after I was relieved as squad leader, our squad was to go out on a squad-sized ambush of a riverbed somewhere outside of the firebase. This was Oklahoma's first ambush and we went over the task well before going out. The position we were told to take really sucked, one of the worst positions we had ever been put in. There was no dry ground, the best we could do was find a spot where the water was only a few inches deep.

Getting into position took forever, each one us of needed to crawl through varied parts of the stream to get to our ambush site, but we all eventually got in place. Most ambushes allow you to get some extra sleep, with the radio being passed from one man to the next as they took their turn on watch. This night was different; no one could go to sleep.

We were all so cold from lying in the water all night and none of us could get comfortable. If you lay still long enough you could get the water immediately around your body warm and you were ok for a few seconds, but with the slightest move, the warm water was disturbed and you were cold again. The only good thing was that there was no contact that night and as the next day began, we crawled out the same way we crawled in.

A number of days later, we went out for a platoon-sized patrol of the area north of the firebase. We set out early in the morning in a wedge formation, initially heading east towards the coast. From what I could tell we were going back and forth in a zigzag pattern, first to the east then to the west, each time heading at a slight angle to the north. I couldn't tell for sure because I no longer had the squad map that was with Oklahoma, I just had a feeling that was what we were doing.

During the latter part of the day, we had taken position in a series of gullies with numerous bushes for cover, quite nice actually. We sat there for the longest time, each of us facing outward watching for movement but all was quiet. At one point, I crawled over to Oklahoma and asked why we were staying there so long and he had no idea. More time passed and I got his attention again and still, no idea why we were staying put.

Finally I asked Oklahoma if it was ok for me to talk to Sgt Hall, our platoon sergeant, and he said ok. I crawled down the gully to where Sgt Hall was and asked him what was up. He said that the patrol had gone better than expected and Lt was holding us up before going back into our perimeter, which was just over the hill. I looked at him with disbelief and asked him what he was talking about. He restated that we were merely waiting for a little longer before going over the next hill back to the Cam Lo firebase.

I asked him to crawl forward with me a bit so we could see the layout of the land, which he did. We crawled forward a bit until we could see the beginning of the perimeter out in the distance. He said, "See, just what I was telling you." I said, "Don't you see anything missing?" Initially he said no but then looking a little closer he became very uneasy.

Out in the distance there truly was a perimeter, but it wasn't Cam Lo; it was that of Charlie 2, an observation post that was just north of the Cam Lo base. What was so obvious to me was that there were no observation towers in Charlie 2 as there are within the Cam Lo base. Unfortunately it was now quite late in the day and we had a long way to hump to get back to our perimeter.

Although the first part of the patrol went smoothly, now we had to move more quickly than usual, opening ourselves up to a quick enemy ambush- fortunately none came. By the time we got back to our perimeter, it was dark and the Lt needed to do some serious convincing that we were out in front of the perimeter and the men in the fighting positions needed to be told not to shoot at us coming in. This was nuts and extremely dangerous, enemy infiltrators had been know to follow returning patrols coming back in the dark, easily passing by the outer perimeter. From what I know, it didn't happen that night, but you never knew.

While at the Cam Lo base I began feeling somewhat ill, mostly due to sinus problems or more simply put, trouble breathing through my nose. One day we were coming back from a patrol and we were walking by an aid station so I stopped in to be checked out.

After waiting for a bit, a corpsman came up and asked me what was going on, and I told him that my nose seemed to be stuffed up but no signs of having a cold. He took that little examination tool that has a light at the end of it and looked up my nose. In my left nostril, he found a large pimple that was causing the blockage. He didn't want to open it himself but said that it was fairly mature and should burst soon on its own. With that info, I went on my way feeling, somewhat better with what was going on.

A couple of days later, we went on another platoon-sized sweep, heading further north going past the Charlie 2 base camp. The area that we were in was known as Leatherneck Square and we frequently would go through this area in an attempt to keep enemy movement to a minimum. Most of these areas were also known as free fire zones, basically meaning that any Vietnamese we came across in this area were assumed to be bad guys and we need not wait to take action. On this patrol we stumbled onto what seemed to be a Vietnamese family, 3 kids of varied age with an older man and woman. What they were doing there I don't know and they were lucky that whomever first spotted them did not open fire.

Our scouts interpreted for them but never understood how or why they were in that area of the DMZ. We needed to take them with us and it was going to be a long trek back to our compound. To make matters worse, none of the kids had anything on their feet and this was extremely rough going, hiking wise.

In any situation like this where we needed to bring Vietnamese people into our camps, we would need to blindfold them so they wouldn't know the exact way through the perimeter. I chose to take one of the girls and the rest were guided by other members of the platoon. We started out on our way back but quickly learned that without shoes, their feet would be a bloody mess if we didn't do something. I had our scout tell the girl who I was guiding that I was going to carry her on my back in piggyback fashion. Being blindfolded made this even more difficult, but we tried it anyway.

I squatted down and the scout took her hands, put them over my shoulders, and then tried to tell her how to wrap her legs around my waste. She didn't care too much for any of this and was freaking out a bit. Eventually we got everything set and we went on our way making much better time than earlier. Periodically we would stop for a break- even though they were small, the extra weight wore on you quickly. Each time we needed to move out again, all I would need to do was to squat down in front of where she was sitting, take one of her hands, put it on my shoulder, and she would climb on up, it was actually going quite well. Somehow we had taken longer on the patrol than expected and as we were approaching the perimeter, it was getting dark.

Again we needed to have the word passed through all the fighting positions, letting them know that they had friendlies out in front of them. As we were making our way through the maze of concertina wire, someone in front of me tripped a ground flare, startling everyone. Fortunately no one on the perimeter overreacted and no shots were fired. With the flash of the flare, I fell backwards, falling on the poor young girl.

To make matters worse she fell on a thorn bush, the kind that had thorns up to 4 and 5 inches long, and she let out a yelp in pain. We quickly looked her over and found a huge thorn in one of her feet and she was crying with the pain of the thorn as well as just being plain scared. We began to move out and again she was on my back as we entered the perimeter.

There were numerous Marines waiting as we came in to talk to these people some more, one of them being a corpsman. I got his attention and told him what had happened to the little girl. He went to help me get her down and she didn't like the idea of someone else being involved. She had begun to accept what I was doing as safe, she wasn't too sure of this new person. I told her that this was a boxie, which in Vietnamese meant doctor. With that, she reacted much better and let the corpsman inspect her feet and hands. Eventually they took them all away to a tent to be more thoroughly interrogated and we never saw them again. I can only hope that they were treated properly and that the little girl was ok.

Sometime the next day, Oklahoma and I were called up to the platoon command bunker where the Lt and Sgt Hall were waiting for us. In a very strange change of attitude, the Lt informed Oklahoma that he was reinstating me to squad leader. No surprise to me, Oklahoma was more than comfortable with this. I guess it was a compliment coming from the Lt like that, but here I was, back to the same old shit and responsibility of being a squad leader again.

Although our stay at Cam Lo was a very loud one with the big guns going off all the time, our week or so there went without any major events taking place. Rumors were going around that we were heading out again going further north- when supplies started coming in, it made it all too real. The word was that we were joining other units and creating another very large sweep, leaving no stone unturned as we made our way north.

Creating a blocking force for Khe Sahn - August 1968

Two days later, we began moving out heading north on Highway 9 to join up with other units waiting just outside the Charlie 2 camp. We linked up and began our sweep online, side-by-side, leaving very little room for Charlie to slip by unnoticed. Fighting broke out to our far left and the tension grew quickly. The further we moved, the denser the terrain got, and before long it almost seemed like we were in the jungles again.

As we moved forward, there were constant air strikes being launched in front of us to hopefully soften the aggressiveness of the NVA before we got there. There was the constant smell of napalm and the distant rumbling of the heavy 500-pound bombs that were being dropped. As the afternoon came to an end, we began making contact to my immediate left.

We all took cover and began making our way forward in fire team rushes which became more and more difficult in the thickening terrain. As quickly as it started, it ended- most likely, the NVA chose to regroup and try it again later. The smells of combat were thick in the still air and it became very eerie, and every one of us had the hair standing up on the backs of our necks.

We slowly moved into an area where the smoke and smells of combat were hanging in the air, like a light fog, and everyone was moving with extreme caution. It was very obvious that a significant battle had taken place here recently. I was moving through some short underbrush when I saw a Marine helmet lying on the ground, not a good sign. Foolishly I went to it and slowly kicked it over with my foot.

As soon as I did that I was screaming inside, what a stupid move. I was expecting the explosion of a booby trap but none came, and I just stood there dripping with nervous sweat. I was looking down at the helmet and gagged at what I saw.
Inside the helmet was the hair and partial scull of the Marine that had formerly worn it, most definitely a K.I.A. Something really bad had taken place here and we slowly began to make out how bad it was.

Someone to my right called for Sgt Hall and the Lt, apparently they had found some tunnels under some bushes which needed to be investigated. It took some time to find members of our platoon small enough to go into the tunnels, but eventually they came forward and started on their way down. Fortunately after what seemed to be an eternity they came back up, flabbergasted at what they had seen. With this, other members of the platoon went below to investigate.

What they found was a complete underground complex of barracks, mess halls, even a medical center, carved out from the dirt below. From what we could determine, the exhaust from the cooking area of the mess hall went out through numerous small tunnels, allowing the smoke to escape from numerous bushes scattered in the landscape.

Above all, this was an amazing find and a few of us had the opportunity to crawl and walk through it. Before leaving however, the engineers came in with the plastic explosive and set charges to destroy the entire complex.

The word was passed to move out and around 30 minutes later, the word was passed for "Fire in the hole," indicating that the underground complex was about to blow. It did so with a tremendous rumble in the ground below our feet. We continued our path northwest and fortunately had little contact.

Somewhere during this operation, we came across another very small Marine outpost that had a small PX where we could purchase items that were not normally supplied. This PX was so small it was in a small Conex box, or storage container.

We asked around and found someone who had access to the Conex box and we finally got in. At this point in my tour, I was getting extremely short, with 30 days or so to go before making it long enough to go home. Many troops in rear areas had short timer calendars, but for us out in the bush, this was not something we could do and I was looking for an alternative.

We went into the Conex box and put aside the cigarettes and other items we knew we wanted. When I was getting ready to pay for my share of the loot, I noticed a small plastic bottle of 30-day vitamins, what a neat way to count down your calendar. I picked it up as well and tried to figure out exactly when I needed to start taking them for the vitamins to become my calendar.

While leaving the Conex box, I noticed another small medical aid tent and with my nose still bothering me, I went over for a visit. Just like before when the corpsman looked up my nose, he said that there was a large pimple in the left nostril that he felt would soon take care of itself. I told him that periodically a trickle of blood would come out of that nostril but eventually would stop, how could that be related to a pimple? With that he had no answers but ensured me that the pimple would soon take care of itself and my breathing would be back to normal. Somewhat frustrated, I accepted what he had to say and went back to my squad and platoon.

Within a few days, the operation was coming to an end and we were finishing up at the Rock Pile, a base camp on the DMZ to the west of Camp Carroll, slightly north of the LZ Vandergriff, also known as LZ Stud, and slightly east of Khe Sahn. We had been here numerous times and it was never a comfortable spot. We were in easy range of the NVA artillery and rockets, which came in daily. It was a rough compound with most of the bunkers dug underground, built well to survive even the strongest artillery barrage. The monsoons had begun and the compound was no more than thick, muddy clay, which made it almost impossible to walk in.

I had teamed up with Andy, the current machine gun squad leader, and we had created a great hooch that for the most part kept us dry. We had a daily objective of creating enough coffee each morning to supply both his men and those in 2nd squad with all the coffee they needed. In order to do this, we needed to become extremely resourceful and we stole a lot of coffee from various units.

Directly behind our hooch, there was a 6-foot deep trench covered by a very thick sheet of sheet metal and numerous sandbags, which was then buried under numerous inches of thick clay soil. This was our bomb shelter for when we got incoming. All we would need to do is hear the incoming coming in, turn around, and dive into the trench, which we had to practice much too often.

The rain started and became worse each day, which made our lives extremely uncomfortable. Between being soaking wet and the lower temperatures, we were all very cold and miserable. Somewhere along the line, I had acquired a broken military cot that was ok, except that the canvas support was split down the middle. You could still sleep on it, but it took practice not to fall through the tear.

One early morning I got up to go check the lines and it was extremely miserable out, the rain was coming down so hard you could hardly see two or three feet ahead. I started down the lines, coming up slowly behind each fighting position to see how things were going and as usual, they were all making the best out of a horrible situation. At one point, I took my watch out of my pocket to check the time. It still worked, but both sides of the metal strap were gone so all that was left was the watch itself. It glowed at night so it was always in demand to find out the time.

I took the watch out of my pocket and for whatever reason, I dropped it. I'm sure it was either due to my hands being so cold or it was so water-soaked that I couldn't keep a grip on it. The watch fell right next to my boot and I reached down to get it back with no luck. My hand groped this side and that side but to no avail, my watch was history. This was sad because that watch came back with me from R&R and it was all I had left of those great memories.

I completed the check of the lines, made my way back to the hooch that Andy and I had created, and attempted to get back into my cot. I was completely drenched and covered with thick, clay mud and my poncho liner which was being used as a blanket was quite wet as well.

Regardless of all that, I curled up on my side, pulled the poncho liner up over me, and tried my best to close my eyes and go to sleep. The heat of my body under the poncho liner began to heat things up and as wet as I was, I was getting warmer. I lay there for some time in the pitch black of night, feeling somewhat thankful that I at least had this broken cot to keep me off the wet, muddy ground.

As I lay there, my nose began to run, which was nothing unusual, especially during the monsoon season. I took my right hand and reached up to wipe my nose and did so but with a minor shock. When my hand rubbed against my nose, there was something there-not just snot, but something else. I put my hand just below my chin on my chest and waited for my nose to begin running again, which came only moments later. I waited patiently and then quickly reached up with my fingers to my nostrils to find something, not sure what, but something other than snot. I remember saying, "Oh shit!" I had something in my nose, but I had no idea what that meant.

Exhaustion took over and I finally fell asleep and stayed that way most of the night. Early the next morning I woke up, as did Andy, and we set out with our normal early morning task of making coffee for everyone. We didn't have a coffee pot like you might think- we had nothing other than our small cook stoves, using trioxane tablets, or heat tabs, to boil the water with. This was no easy task and everyone on the line really appreciated what Andy and I went through to get them hot coffee each morning.

I was sitting on my cot working with Andy, trying to get the coffee in progress when I felt my nose begin to run. A few days before, Lt Bovine gave me a care package of tissues because my nose was always running, which was on the cot to my right. I turned and reached for some tissues to wipe my nose and the angle of my eyes looking over the tip of my nose caught something that shocked me. There in front of my eyes was something sticking out of my nose, like a small tentacle of an octopus, I had no idea what was going on. In that brief moment, I remembered the early morning hours when I felt something on my nose, and now it was all coming full circle.

I snapped my head straightforward towards Andy and said, "Andy, do me a big favor and look at my nose." With the sudden jerk of my head, whatever it was disappeared and Andy just sat there like I was nuts, and maybe I was. As I sat there, I felt an itchy sensation inside my nostril and I asked him to continue to stare at my nose and with a little more sensation, I announced to Andy, "Here it comes". Andy's eyes widened and he just stared at me with his mouth wide open. He said that he had never experienced leeches, but he was more than sure that I had a leech sticking out of my nose.

This was all interrupted quickly with the sound of NVA rockets slamming into the ground not too far from our hooch. With nothing needing to be said, we both turned and dove for our trench, which was directly behind us. I was in mid-air, diving into the trench when a rocket, obviously very close to our position, went off and my body was slammed into the side of the trench, which really hurt. Dirt rained down on each of us as we lay there, waiting for the most current onslaught to end. Eventually it did and we both emerged to analyze the damage to our hooch and the troops on the line. Fortunately we had no casualties or injuries on our side and our men began making their way towards our hooch for their morning coffee.

I was back sitting on my cot and I said to Andy, "It's starting again, please call for the corpsman." Andy passed the word up the line for a corpsman and eventually Doc Daily, our most senior corpsman, came down to our hooch. Andy was now all familiar with the activities of my nose and gave Doc a cup of coffee and asked him to sit there and watch my nose.
Obviously Doc thought he was nuts but watched my nose all the same.

I sat there motionless and eventually said, "Here it comes." Whatever was in my nose began to come out again and Doc almost fell off the end of the cot, saying, "Holy shit, you've got to come with me." I followed him out of our little hooch, across most of the main Rock Pile base camp, to an underground medical bunker, which was struggling to come back to life. The recent rocket attack had wiped out their
power source and they were running around, lighting candles.

They had me stand in the middle of the underground bunker and they held a candle up in front of my face. While we were going through this, Doc was telling them what he saw and they were all shaking their heads. One corpsman was in front of me, Doc Daily was to my left holding my left forearm, and another corpsman was behind me, looking over my shoulder at the candle.

As in the past, I said, "Here it comes," and Doc Daily squeezed my arm just a bit. As it came out, there was nervous tension in the air. The corpsman behind me reached forward with a pair of forceps and clamped onto the tip that was exposed. The corpsman in front took the candle and began cooking the captured tip in an effort to kill it. The candle burnt the tip for some time and the corpsman stepped back while the corpsman in back began to tug with the forceps.

I immediately dropped to my knees in extreme pain. He was tugging on this thing and it was connected somewhere within my head and was by no means letting go. Seeing my pain, they stood me back up and started over again, this time burning the tip much longer. This time they tugged very gently when trying to pull it out and it began to slide. I had a gagging, horrible feeling that almost made me throw up.

Whatever it was, it was quite long. As it was being pulled through my nasal passages, I felt an extremely unique sensation, one I never want to experience again. It was in fact a leech that had been in my sinus for quite some time, most likely from that night during the ambush in Cam Lo when we were lying in water all night.

With no exaggeration, it was as big around as my index finger and no less than 8 to 10 inches long. The only reason it was trying to come out was that there was no more room in my sinus cavity, it had grown too big. Everyone was beside themselves with all of this. The corpsman put the leech in a Dixie cup for me to keep- what a trophy.

We made our way back to the coffee hooch to share the news. The first person we called down was Doc Bird, who had dealt with my nose issues over the past few weeks. Doc came down, we made him a cup of coffee, and we just sat there, chatting. I started to remind Doc of all the issues with my nose and if he was curious to find out exactly what was causing them. Of course he said sure, and with that, I held up the Dixie cup with the dead leech rolled up at the bottom. At first he just sat there and stared at the cup, trying to absorb what I was telling him. Then he just lost it and ran out of the hooch, shaking his head in disbelief. From then on, my nick name was none other than Leech.

The word traveled quickly up and down the line and everyone came to visit and to see the leech for themselves.

Entertainment out in the bush came in small doses and my leech incident was the entertainment of the week. Before nightfall set in, I put the cup under my broken cot and the next morning it had been tipped over on its side, and the leech was gone. Our only guess was that one of the hundreds of rats that lived with us had a nice breakfast that morning.

Assault on Mutters Ridge - September 1968

Unfortunately our stay there was going to be short-lived, there was a big operation being planned for Mutter's Ridge which we would become a part of. Khe Sahn was being heavily hit and they needed Marines to go in as a blocking force to slow down the NVA troops heading to Khe Sahn from the north- we were to be that force. We were to be heli-lifted from the Rock Pile to an area known as Rocket Valley, and from there we were to fight our way up onto the ridge and reek havoc on the NVA activities.

A few days later, we found ourselves on the Rock Pile LZ waiting for our CH-46 transports up to the ridge. A few of us that were extremely short went to our Lt and asked that we stay behind, a few of us had less than 30 days left to go in country, way too short to go on an operation like this. He basically said tough shit, he needed every experienced body up on the ridge, and things were going to be bad enough as it was. We gathered at the LZ and prepared the best we could for the assault, none of us being in a good mood at all.

We were going in on the big CH-46 choppers, the ones with twin blades and the loading ramp on the back, they carried the most men by far. The first wave of choppers came in and the first group of Marines climbed aboard. Our platoon was to be part of the second wave to go in. As they flew north, we listened to our squad radios that had been tuned in to the same frequency as those of the helicopters.

As they approached the prepped LZ, they were hit with extremely heavy ground fire and the first chopper came crashing to the ground, shot right out of the sky. Fortunately when it went down, it was close enough to the ground where most of the men on board were not injured. They rushed out the back, created a hasty perimeter around the chopper, and began giving suppressive fire back to the NVA.

The other choppers flew around in a panic, not wanting to get shot down yet not wanting to leave those troops on the ground by themselves. They flew around for what seemed to be an eternity, especially for those on the ground, before they started their way down again. Meanwhile back at the Rock Pile, we were listening to all of this on the radio as well as the carnage that was taking place down at the LZ. Needless to say we were not happy, more precisely we were beyond words, and not a word was being said. The initial wave of choppers had made their deposit and now they were on their way back to get us, I just wanted to run away. I was terrified beyond belief.

Ironically, there were some media people with us who wanted to see Marines in action and they were heading out with the second wave. All of 2nd squad got on one chopper with numerous others, including at least one reporter. As we took off there was not a sound, everyone was in their own personal world of saying goodbye. Some were saying prayers, others were in deep thought, saying goodbye the only way we could. It was not a happy moment for any of us, each of us was sure that we would never make it through this. The choppers made their way back up to Rocket Valley to deliver us and to bring us into one of the most horrible segments of fighting that I experienced.

As the choppers descended on the LZ, we began receiving heavy fire from enemy machine gun emplacements. From what I remember, no one got hit while we were on the chopper, which is very hard to believe. As we were coming in, you could hear the bullets slamming into the sides and undercarriage of the chopper, more often than not coming through into the cargo area, yet no one got hit. The pilots were having a very hard time getting down to the ground to let us out. It wasn't unusual for them to hover a few feet above the ground, forcing us to jump, but we weren't getting close to the ground at all. Even jumping a few feet with full combat gear was really taking a chance on breaking a leg, an arm, whatever.

I don't know about the other chopper pilots but ours wanted to get out of the cross fire as quickly as possible. Without getting any closer, he dropped the back loading ramp and began lifting the bow of the chopper up, forcing us to fall or slide out the back of the chopper, landing in a huge heap on the ground. I know a lot of men got hurt badly and one for sure died having fallen on someone else's M-16, which pierced his chest, what a mess. On top of this, mortars, artillery, rockets, and tremendous small arms fire were raining down on the entire LZ, and everyone was scrambling for whatever cover they could find. We were in the rolling hills just prior to going into the semi jungle area further up, better known as Rocket Valley, and there was very little cover to be had.

We were trying to get our squads together so we could move further away from the center of the LZ but communications were tough, the din of the battle drowned out the loudest screams. The reporter that was on our chopper was lying next to me, literally shitting in his pants, he was so scared he could barely talk or look around. As we were getting our act together to move further away from the LZ, the next wave of choppers were coming in and one actually came close to the ground. The reporter that was next to me looked at me and said this is fucking crazy, I'm out of here. With that he got up and ran on the chopper as it began its ascent- never saw that jerk again.

We spread out and moved forward away from the center and linked up with the other Marines who had landed prior to us. The intensity of the fire dimmed somewhat but there was still dirt and crap flying everywhere from the bullets hitting all around us. Why we didn't take more casualties during that landing, I don't know. I'm sure there were many more than I can remember. Thoughts are a simple blur during action like that, I'm surprised I can remember any of it at all.

298

Eventually the majority of the force was on the ground and we began making our way up the slopes, which was mind- boggling. Every time you would get up for a fire team rush, you would hear this roar of gunfire and I was always amazed that when I dove back to the ground, I had not been hit. The enemy lay ahead in the thick underbrush of the semi jungle and the closer we got to that area, the more intense the fighting.

Elements to our left were the first to go into the semi jungle terrain and I know they were having a rough time. We continued to move forward and began our task of pushing the enemy back or killing them outright, it was a long hard fight and eventually the NVA began to thin out while retreating to fight another day.

It was beginning to get dark and we needed to set in our lines for the night. Everyone was completely wiped, yet we all needed to dig a foxhole and stand watch for their own half of the extremely dark and long night, from sunset to sunrise. I set my men into 4 foxhole positions and they began digging in. Andy, the machine gun squad leader, set his two teams; one just to the right of my men and the other up the other side of the gully to our right. This was not triple canopy jungle but it was still very dense and with that we had limited visibility of anything that would be probing our lines during the night, and Charlie was out there and very hungry.

Andy and I began to dig a hole directly behind my men, which would allow us to keep tabs on everyone without moving. With the limited visibility, the foxholes were placed fairly close together so all 4 holes of 2nd squad were very close to where Andy and I were digging our hole. We were all in the process of digging in with others on watch for enemy movement when a stream of Marines came walking down the path, each pair carrying a dead Marine- there were quite a few of them.

I can remember them stopping to catch their breath, putting the bodies in the ponchos right in front of us. One man I definitely knew, he was from 2nd Platoon but I can't remember his name. I just remember lying there, resting up against the hole I had begun, looking at his face and it really bummed all of us out. They eventually moved on but there was not a word said on our side of the lines, everyone knew that they could have been any of us and that could happen to us tonight, tomorrow or the next day- morale was in the toilet.

We heard more people coming down the path and I looked up to see the Captain standing there, checking out the positions of the foxholes. At one point he looked down and saw me and said, "Janicki, what the hell are you doing here? You should be back in the rear." I told him that I had had a discussion with Lt Bovine prior to coming up on the ridge and what he had said. I told him that there was at least 4 men who had less than 30 days left that were ordered to go. He was really pissed, but it didn't do us any good- we were stuck there.

We heard some choppers coming in, assumingly with re- supplies, and all hell began to break loose. The enemy had machine gunners with 50 cals somewhere high up and they were pounding the hell out of the choppers on their way in. They did manage to drop the supplies which were badly needed, we had gone through a lot of ammunition fighting our way up from the LZ. At least we felt somewhat better that we could engage in a good-sized battle and have enough to get us through it all, that was somewhat of a consolation.

Although Lt Bovine had ordered us all to go up on the ridge with the initial assault, he did not join us. He was the pay officer of the month back at Quang Tri base and needed to get that done prior to coming out. Apparently he had been on one of the choppers with the re-supplies and he was badly wounded.

300

From what we were told, at least one or two 50 caliber rounds had come up through the bottom of the chopper, slamming into the bottom of one of his knees while he sat there, blowing off the top of his knee and a few of the fingers from one of his hands. He had gone back on the same chopper and we never heard from him again and to this day, I'm not sure if he survived. In his absence, Sgt Connelly took over the platoon and initially I thought that would be ok, though my feelings changed in the next few days.

Everyone on the line was getting ready for the upcoming grueling night. They were taking turns cleaning their weapons and choking down some C-rations before the dark of night set in, daybreak couldn't come fast enough. The word came down the perimeter to fix bayonets, which traveled from hole to hole with fear dripping off each word. For a Marine grunt, this was the worst set of words to hear. Hand-to-hand combat was the horrible depth of war that no one wanted to experience, and it was that time again.

This wasn't the first time that I heard it, but with only a few more days left in the Nam, this wasn't what I wanted. There was no conversation other than passing the word from hole to hole, these words struck deep into your soul. It's hard to describe the thoughts that go through your mind when you're at this level of survival. We no sooner started settling down for the night and the NVA began probing our lines, and grenades were being thrown by both sides. Grenades are quite loud in the daytime but when it's dark and relatively quiet, they sound like a 500-pound bomb going off. Our grenades were much more reliable than the ones used by the NVA, more often than not their fuse would stop before the grenade went off, lucky for us anyway.

Periodically, exchanges of rifle fire followed a grenade going off, in an attempt to get the NVA while they were on the run. It was so dark it was hard to tell what if anything was getting done. Someone had called in for aerial flares to be dropped which helped some, but for the most part, they just created wavering shadows which made it look like everything in front of us was on the move. Fortunately after a short while, the enemy stopped their probes and the lines became quiet again.

Andy and I had dug a reasonably deep foxhole and then we made a camouflaged cover out of vines and tree branches to go over the top of it. From 3 or 4 feet away, it was hard to tell our hole from the surrounding ground cover, blending in was very important and we were both pleased with our hard work. We took turns standing watch just like the men in the foxholes out in front of us and during each watch, we would crawl the lines behind our men, ensuring that everything was ok and that at least one of them was awake.

Sometime in the early morning hours, guessing around 3 or 4 A.M., all hell began to break loose. The NVA were coming up the hill over towards Andy's second machine gun position and everything turned into chaos. Andy and I lay in our foxhole, facing within the perimeter. My men were behind us in their foxholes but at the moment, we were more concerned with what was going on behind us.

Our machine gun tracers were a yellow-orange and the NVA's were almost lavender in color. Again on a machine gun, every 5th round was a tracer enabling the gunner to see where his rounds were hitting. Lavender tracers were everywhere and every now and then, our own tracers were being aimed within the perimeter. Andy and I couldn't make any sense of this but when we heard Vietnamese voices running by us, firing as they ran, we realized that at least one part of our lines had been overrun and now they were both in front of us as well as behind us.

Andy and I made the assumption that any Marine would be hunkered down in their fighting positions and wouldn't be running around in the open. From our camouflaged foxhole, we had the lower part of a large gully out in front of us. With all of the Marine positions located on higher ground, we knew anything we shot at in the gully would be the bad guys.

Sometime in the early morning hours, guessing around 3 or 4 A.M., all hell began to break loose. The NVA were coming up the hill over towards Andy's second machine gun position and everything turned into chaos. Andy and I lay in our foxhole, facing within the perimeter. My men were behind us in their foxholes but at the moment, we were more concerned with what was going on behind us.

Our machine gun tracers were a yellow-orange and the NVA's were almost lavender in color. Again on a machine gun, every 5th round was a tracer enabling the gunner to see where his rounds were hitting. Lavender tracers were everywhere and every now and then, our own tracers were being aimed within the perimeter. Andy and I couldn't make any sense of this but when we heard Vietnamese voices running by us, firing as they ran, we realized that at least one part of our lines had been overrun and now they were both in front of us as well as behind us.

Andy and I made the assumption that any Marine would be hunkered down in their fighting positions and wouldn't be running around in the open. From our camouflaged foxhole, we had the lower part of a large gully out in front of us. With all of the Marine positions located on higher ground, we knew anything we shot at in the gully would be the bad guys.

I crawled to the back of our foxhole and told my men to concentrate on what was taking place out in front of their holes, and that Andy and I were going to be opening up on the traffic inside the perimeter. I moved back up, lay alongside Andy, and checked the location of all my magazines, grenades and extra ammo.

We both knew that Charlie had not and most likely never would spot us where we were, but as soon as we opened fire, all that would change quickly. We took a couple of deep breaths in an attempt to relax, and decided to begin our intervention into this growing mess with each of us tossing a grenade out in front of our position, making sure they were deep in the gully.

With the pins pulled on the grenades, we took a three count and let them fly. I can still hear the sounds of the spoons flying as soon as we let go of them and the distant thud as the grenades hit the ground. Almost simultaneously, the grenades went off sending out two large flashes of light, showing us where some of the NVA were for that split second. Screams began immediately and we both knew that the grenades had done their work on some of them, and we opened fire where our eyes last saw enemy movement. With the battle going on all around us, there were periodic flashes of light coming from hand grenades or distant illumination flares which were to our benefit. Frequently we would get glimpses of movement and continued to open fire.

The NVA didn't let us down- as soon as they saw our muzzle flashes, they turned their attention on suppressing our fire. We were well dug in and protected by the edges of the foxhole while they were out in the open, even though there was some cover. Now it became a tag team shootout. When we would see their muzzle flashes, we would concentrate our fire on those exact locations and in turn, they would be shooting at ours. This seemingly kept up for hours and periodically, either Andy or I would need to move around in our hole to catch an NVA trying to sneak up on either side. It truly was a cat and mouse battle.

Things were getting worse and we knew there were Marines out in front of us as well as the NVA, so Andy and I needed to change our tactics. Andy realized this at the same time I did and said, "Fuck I hate this shit." I replied, "Roger that." We had both come to the realization that we needed to leave our cover and head down into the gully for some up close combat.

There are all levels of being terrified, but knowing that you are about to be close enough to the enemy to smell their sweat with hand-to-hand combat being imminent. This is where fear can take you one of two ways. If you let it, you will crawl into a corner or under a rock and hide. The other way was to use the extreme power of fear to your advantage, unfortunately that turns you into a person that no one can imagine. The way we were taught to get this switch going in the positive way was to let out a blood-curdling scream and at that moment, jump forward, committing yourself to the battle. It's a terrifying thought what fear can enable you to do. At this point, all your mind is worried about is to keep the hunk of flesh that it survives in alive and it will let you do anything to do that.

With that, Andy said, "Are you ready?" I swallowed very hard and said, "Yes," it was time to put our bayonets to use.

Andy said, "On the count of three," and began the count. On one, we both leaped out of the hole, screaming at the top of our lungs and ran into the chaos in the gully. It's hard to explain what or how your mindset can change in situations like this. Fear is a powerful force if you can get it going in the right direction, we were riding the high of adrenaline.

The adrenaline kept us going and by some miracle, neither one of us got wounded through it all. Time was on our side and their attempts to root us out had slowed. Ever so slowly, the sky was beginning to lighten, with sunrise on its way. We all knew they would not stick around much longer. We were already able to see them better and could be much more accurate with our shots. As the day began, the enemy that survived slithered away back down the hillside to wait for another opportunity either later in the day or even again the following night.

As the fighting waned, we each had to absorb what had just taken place. I sat on the ground, leaning against a shattered tree and just stared at the blood and bodies out in front of me. Some were enemies or Marines laying by themselves, others were NVA and Marine locked in a knot on the ground, we would never know how they all died.

Sometime during the last few hours, something smashed into my helmet and sent me flying. My only thought was that I got hit with a rifle butt and when I fell, whomever had hit me couldn't find me to finish me off. My head was pounding and I took my helmet off to be sure it didn't have a crease in it from a bullet, no crease found. Andy was nowhere to be seen, but my thoughts were in a deep dark cloud. I was at a complete loss of words, more precisely none of us wanted to talk to anyone. These were moments where you talked to yourself, numb and lost in thought.

Our focus now was to try to determine the damage that was done to our troops and boy, what a mess we had on our hands. We had numerous K.I.A.s scattered up and down the line, but the biggest tragedy was up on the top of the slope where Andy had positioned his second gun team.

From what we could determine, there was a Marine on watch with the other 3 lying off to the side of the gun position, trying to get some sleep as they normally would, one was even curled up under a bush. When the Marine realized that the NVA had crawled right up to their hole, he freaked out and ran leaving the other 3 asleep on the ground. An NVA soldier picked up our machine gun and poured bullets into the three sleeping men.

When the morning haze was beginning to clear and it was light enough, we had men crawling from hole to hole checking things out. When someone got to the former gun position, they let out a yell for "Corpsman up!" and Doc Bird was on his way. They quickly crawled around from man to man, and Dewater and Glegg were definitely dead. When they found Clarkson under the bush, Doc rolled him over, he was still alive. Alive long enough to look Doc in the face and to say, "Fuck it," that was it, he was dead.

**Jenkins standing on the left, Dewater in the middle,
Clarkson on the right and Glegg sitting.
June 1968**

A quick search started for the other Marine that was in the hole, PFC Moore. They found him a good distance behind the lines on the ground, out cold. The best we could determine was that he was running fast and his head hit the lower limb of a tree and that's what knocked him out, because other than that, he had no wounds. Clarkson was originally in 2nd squad with me but he always wanted to be with the gun boys and a number of weeks prior to this operation he was moved over to Andy and his two teams.

We were all in a state of shock from the nightlong battle, but this news of the machine gun position really had everyone pissed. 2nd squad had been decimated, in the early morning hours I found that there were only 4 squad members left.

Three bodies were found some distance down the hill, locked in a death grip with an NVA soldier.

I sat at the edge of the shelter that Andy and I had built in disbelief, not able to look any of my dead men in the face. It was even overwhelming to turn and look at the ones who survived to display any kind of leadership, saying, "Trust me, I'll get you out of this." I was completely at my end; I had no self respect, no confidence as a leader and felt accountable of what took place on my side of the lines. In an attempt to get away from the overwhelming pain I got from my squad, I began trying to track Andy down.

I found him on the other side of the gully where we had been fighting all night and he was involved in a group conversation with Sgt Connelly and PFC Moore, who was shitting in his pants. I still find it a miracle that no one pulled out a 45 and shot him in his head, we had no time for that kind of crap out where we were. The mood on our side of the perimeter was really in the toilet.

I think our side caught the worse of the night's activities and we had dead NVA soldiers everywhere. Andy and I were scoping out the damage we rained down out in front of our position and we both hoped that any of the surviving NVA soldiers never got a good look at our fighting position as daylight was coming.

We didn't realize it in the heat of the battle, but four of the NVA soldiers had made it within feet of our position before they were killed, they all lay in shattered piles of blood just outside the edge of our foxhole. For the most part, Andy and I were still not talking, we were each dealing with our actions through the night and swallowing hard with the loss of some of our men.

In true Marine Corps fashion, we launched a mini offensive almost immediately. 2nd Platoon was ordered down the hillside where all the bad guys had come from the night before in an attempt to make contact. The word was passed up the line that no short timers were allowed to go out on any patrol and that eliminated Andy and I, as well as a few others from 2nd Platoon.

Although we were relieved that we wouldn't be going, we had lumps in our throats for those that were because this was nothing short of a suicide mission. It's hard to describe the different levels of fear that go on at a time like this. We were all terrified each day and night but at least we had one another to try to keep us all alive. We also had our foxholes for protection, knowing that there were Marines on either side of you. Yet you were still terrified, we were in a very bad situation.

The Marines in 2nd Platoon were given the word to saddle up with just their combat gear for the counter attack. For them, the fear was even deeper for they had to get up, leave the relative security of our perimeter, as little as there was, and head down a path where they knew the NVA were waiting for them. Coming face to face with an enemy soldier or worse, looking down their rifle barrel, rips your soul right out of your body. This is when grunts rise to the top. Time and time again, they are given orders like this and time and time again, they conduct them without question. How many times can someone go through this level of emotions and still be the same person?

Within a few hours of daybreak, they were beginning their trek down the side of the hill towards more dense jungle. I expected them to get hit immediately and was surprised with how long it took for them to make contact. What surprised me was they actually did catch the enemy off guard, I guess they were assuming that no one in their right mind would be coming after them.

Although this fight began with us having the upper hand. it quickly turned the other way. 2nd Platoon was heavily outnumbered and quickly began pulling back up the hill to our perimeter. That was the end of the patrols for the day. We

needed supplies and were hoping for choppers to come in with everything, which they did but again, they were heavily shot up on their way.

We needed some replacements but we knew they wouldn't be coming. We couldn't even get the wounded and dead out, the choppers couldn't land under the intense fire so the LZ was littered with blowing ponchos covering the bodies of our men. Supplies came in and were quickly distributed and the rest of the day, we tried to reposition our foxholes so they could be manned with fewer men.

We purposely moved the machine gun emplacements around so they wouldn't know where they were at first anyway. Their initial probes each night were an attempt to get our machine guns involved so they could pinpoint their positions. When nighttime came and they began probing again, we didn't let that happen and suppressed their activity with small arms fire instead.

At least tonight when they would make a more formidable move at us, they wouldn't know where the guns were and we could inflict some immediate damage right up front.

The fighting began early but never got to the fever pitch as the night before, this time we managed to keep them outside our perimeter and I really think we did a lot of damage at the same time.

Shortly after midnight, they backed off and all was quiet for a while other than an occasional grenade or two. Just before daybreak, they came at us again and again, we were ready. As soon as they started, we threw volley after volley of grenades down on them, which for the most part broke their spirit and it wasn't long before they went quiet again for the rest of the night.

Apparently the captain and the other high-ranking officers were in a thither about this ongoing action. Again on the second day, 2nd Platoon was sent down the hill, I guess the Marines need to be consistent at all costs. This time, they met resistance much earlier and again broke off and came back up the hill.

Most of the remainder of that day stayed quiet, leaving us time to clean our weapons and again time to reposition parts of our lines. The third night, it began all over again but if anything, we were getting more tenacious and again we held our own.
As exhausted as we were, we lasted another night and we were not looking forward to the following day.

Shortly after sun up, we conducted a thorough inspection of our lines and yet again made needed adjustments. There was a period of quiet which we took advantage of by having some chow and cleaning our weapons. The word came down the line for everyone to move up the hill towards the CP. The word said to leave everything in position except for weapons and ammunition. We were all very confused; we had never done anything like this before. As we came up the hill, we were told to move up as far as we could and to try to take cover anywhere.

They had arranged for a bombardment from the 175 and 8- inch howitzers from Dong Ha base and were hoping to catch the enemy out in the open. They had a spotter somewhere down the side of the hill who watched as the NVA made their way up, moving right past our fighting positions, quite cocky in their movements. The order was given and the distant guns began to fire, pouring the huge shells down on the unprotected NVA troops.

That part of the plan was working quite well, but shrapnel flies in all directions and we had very little cover. I had found the base of a tree to get behind but even then, part of my body was exposed. These were the biggest shells that could be fired by land-based guns and they were tearing apart the countryside. Eventually the bombardment ended and we were put online to move back down the hill to our positions, being very leery of wounded or trapped NVA soldiers. There were bodies and body parts everywhere the carnage was unbelievable, we had quite a mess to clean up and our hopes were that this would really take the wind out of the NVA.

The morning went on and we kept dragging the NVA bodies over to the edge of our perimeter and rolling them down the hill, trying to send the message home.

Quite by surprise, early in the afternoon we got word that we would be pulling back to another LZ closer to LZ Mac where the Battalion CP was set up. By no means were we going to complain. We quickly policed up our areas, making sure not to leave any munitions behind and began the move further up the finger to begin establishing another perimeter.

We set about our business of setting in, each of us in our own little world of thought. We had just gone through three days of horrific fighting, losing many good friends along the way. It's hard to describe where your mind goes at times like this. On its own, it's trying to deal with the emotions of the last few days and even more the psychological impact on what you had done to stay alive. There is almost a sense of numbness unplugging you from the normal emotions someone who had not been through events like this would freak out with. You were alive, you had made it, everything was going to be ok.

We set in and prepared ourselves for a night like those we encountered over the past few days. Fortunately we had a quiet night, almost surreal and it was almost a let down. Our senses were at such a fever pitch all night, and when nothing happened, it was hard to recover from. Most of us moved in total silence, our minds were mush with our own internal thoughts.

We stayed at that LZ for a couple of days and again we were told to saddle up, this time we were actually moving up onto LZ Mac. We made our way up the finger up to Mac and Sgt Connelly began setting in 2nd Platoon. Smitty, Tuckett, LCpl Rickard, and I were told that we would not be going out on the line. Instead we were told to dig in right alongside the main trail and to make ourselves at home. We would be living in this foxhole until they could get a helicopter to land so we could get on. As good as this was, the battle was only a few feet away so we always needed to be ready. The four of us got to Vietnam at the same time and it was almost too good to be true that we just might make it out of that hellhole.

LZ Mac
September 68

Day after day all, we did was dig deeper and deeper until we had this tremendously safe bunker to hide and sleep in.

Supplies were coming in as was the mail, they were all being dropped from external loads on the choppers. Every so often I would get a care package from my brother that was extremely special: beer. Not just beer, extremely powerful beer called Pale Ale India, made in Puerto Rico.

Our battalion commander was a real jerk with a twisted mind. His idea of punishing someone was for that person to order and to pay for a case of military beer, usually Falstaff. They would then be instructed to open each can and pour it into the dirt. He didn't think any of his Marines should be drinking this foul stuff called alcohol. Our battalion supply sergeant was a gunnery sergeant who loved his beer but obviously with the jerk we had for a skipper, he had not had a beer in a long time.

Mail had come in and this load included packages. Eventually we saw a small group of men from 2nd Platoon coming down the path with the mail that belonged to us and with it was this beautiful, small box from my brother.

We all slipped below into the safety of our bunker and we opened the box. As in previous deliveries, it was filled with small cans, each one of them filled with extremely powerful beer. We each had one and went on about our business. With my time running short out in the bush, I needed to get the biggest bang for my buck, using the beer as a negotiating chip.

The next day I caught the battalion supply sergeant as he went walking up the path towards the LZ and asked him to stop by on his return. Sometime later he came straggling back down the trail and stopped to ask me what I wanted. I told him that it might be in his best interest to come down below, I had something that I wanted to show him. He reluctantly followed me below and the lack of expression on his face quickly turned to a smile. I gave him a beer and although it was quite warm, he enjoyed every ounce of it. I told him that the men in 2nd Platoon needed boot socks very badly and many of them
didn't have any poncho liners. If he was interested in helping with that, the rest of the beer was his. Done deal.

As soon as they could after the bad incident at our first LZ where the machine gun position got overrun, they got PFC Moore out of the field and sent him back for psychological evaluation. At some point Moore had rejoined the outfit but nobody wanted anything to do with him. We had also received a new platoon commander and a 2nd Lt that had done some service further south of our normal AO and everyone had some confidence in him. One evening they were having mail call as well as pay call, and the new Lt asked all the squad leaders to come up to the CP to oversee the pay distribution. Even though Tuckett and I were former squad leaders, we were included in the invite.

For the most part we just lay back in the dirt, watching each man come up, sign the pay roster and get their money in return, no big deal. Towards the end of pay call, PFC Moore approached the Lt and asked if he could talk to him in private. The Lt said that he would talk but not necessarily in private, all the squad leaders would also be in attendance.

Moore began by giving his interpretation of what happened the night the NVA over ran our lines and just to hear him say what he did made me sick, he basically painted himself as being innocent. The Lt listened to what he had to say and at the end, Moore had said that he felt like there was a price on his head and he feared for his life.

The Lt thought for a few minutes, looked at us for a second, and then turned back to Moore. He said that Moore was right, he should be afraid for his life, and with that turned and walked back to the CP. We all sat there amused with what the Lt had said and we all loved it, he didn't buy any of Moore's bullshit and left him to fend for himself.

Eventually we made our way back to our bunker and went below for a long evening of talking. The next day went without incident for us until the latter part of the afternoon, when the supply sergeant came running up the trail and said for us to grab our gear and to head to the LZ. There was a chopper coming in and he said that he would land long enough for us to get on, but we really needed to hustle.

Although we had been waiting days for this we were all shocked with the news and we were running around with no plan. We quickly grabbed what gear we had left and began the run up the trail to the LZ. There was no one around to yell goodbye to, they were all busy with their daily chores and much lower on the hill than we were. The chopper was an old CH-34 and it was just coming in to the LZ as we got there, he set his wheels down for a second and the four of us dove on. I lay on my stomach for a few seconds while the chopper took off, getting up just in time to look down for my last view of 2nd Platoon and the hellhole known as Mutter's Ridge.

Janicki on the left Ruben Valdez on the right
Mutters Ridge
September 68

We made it, time to go home - October 1968

We all sat back from the open hatch and prayed that we didn't start to receive ground fire. As we flew, none came and we each tried to begin to relax and to realize exactly what was going on. We were going home, and none of us ever thought we would ever make it to this point. Periodically I would glance out the hatch to look at the scar-torn surface of Vietnam- what a mess, bomb craters everywhere.

The chopper began to descend and I could make out the LZ at Quang Tri base, the next step to getting home. We landed without incident and I had a nice surprise- Tom England, my best friend from Charleston, was there to greet me. He had lucked out and before we all left for Mutter's Ridge, his Lt had told him to stay back. He had been checking each day at my company headquarters for when I would be coming back. He wanted to be there for me, and it was a wonderful treat having him there.

We walked together up to my company compound and I needed to check in at the main office. This was quickly done and we strolled down to the transit tent where I bumped into the sergeant who was in charge of all transit activity. He told me to get over to the mess hall before it closed and to get something to eat. There were few men in the transit tent and they would need me to stand the lines that night. I couldn't believe what I was hearing and all Tom could do was laugh.

We got to the mess hall and had a wonderful meal, it was very seldom that we got meals like this and I enjoyed each bite.

After chow, Tom began heading towards his company area and I returned to the transit tent. The few of us that were there gathered and waited to see what was up. Most of them were relatively new in-country and they kept me at a distance, realizing that I had made it through my tour, a very strange feeling. The sergeant finally came in and told us that a transit truck would be coming by in a few minutes to pick us up and bring us to one of the perimeters to stand watch. I was really in no mood for this and I finally realized that one of the men was a corpsman from our company, so at least I had someone to talk to.

The 6-by eventually came and we loaded on the back and headed down the dusty road to somewhere on one of the perimeters. Within a relatively short ride, the truck stopped and the driver pointed to where we had to report. We straggled off the back of the truck and made our way to the command post to get our next set of instructions. A sergeant came to the doorway of the bunker to look over his fill-ins for the night. Somehow he recognized the corpsman and said, "Doc, we will be needing you on radio watch here in the bunker." After that, he began pointing at some men and saying, "Ok, you two go to bunker 22, you two bunker 27," and so on. He finally pointed to me and said you and you go to such-and-such a bunker. I said, "Sarge, no offense but fuck you, I'm not going anywhere." He came back at me by saying that there was no time for my crap just for me to grab my gear and go to the bunker he had assigned me to.

I again said, "Sarge, no offense I can't do that, I'm not going anywhere." For a short few seconds, he just stood there with no response and I had a chance to say that I had just gotten back from Mutter's Ridge within the hour, I was going home tomorrow and I had no interest in standing bunker watch again. This he understood completely and said for me to join the Doc in the command bunker and I would help stand radio watch.

This by far was one of the easiest watches I stood my entire time in Vietnam. There were about six of us in the bunker, which required each of us to stand a 2-hour watch, it was a cakewalk. Dawn came and we all moved back outside, waiting for the 6-by to come pick us up. We eventually saw it coming in the distance and knew that it would stop up on the ridge where it had dropped us off. The Doc had walked out in front of me a bit and I was taking my time getting there, my mouth was watering for a nice breakfast. When I looked up, the Doc was a good way ahead of me and he stopped and held something up in his hand. I recognized it immediately, it was a round tear gas grenade and he began to laugh. He pulled the pin on it, leaned back and threw it as far as he could in the air and eventually there was a soft, popping sound and a soft yellow cloud that just hung there in the still morning air.

Not thinking too much about it, I began my trek up to where the truck was and then I began to feel it, beginning with a tingling on my lips and the immediate sensation of my nose running. I began to laugh and run at the same time but by the time I got up to the truck, the corpsman and I both had snot running down our face and we had tears as well, he thought it was hysterical. The truck got us back to our company area and the Doc and I went in for breakfast. After I got out of there, I went into the company office for my paperwork, which was ready for me. I grabbed it and walked out heading over to S2 where I had some captured equipment that was being saved under my name, namely 2 SKS rifles, an NVA flag, an officer's belt buckle, and some Ho Chi Minh sandals, they all meant quite a bit to me.

I bumped into Tom as he was coming out of the mess hall and he said he was all set to go, we needed to catch a ride over to Dong Ha to catch a flight to Da Nang. I asked him what his next duty assignment was to be and he said Camp LeJuene in North Carolina. I told him I was pissed, my next duty station was 29 Palms, way out on the West Coast. We got back over to my company area and I told him that I needed to go in and try to have my next duty assignment changed. He said no problem, we still needed to turn in our weapons and he would begin sourcing a ride.

I walked into the company office to be faced by this pucky- looking office clerk with an attitude. I asked if there was any way to get my next duty station changed from the West Coast to the East Coast, I was an East Coast kid. He said flatly not, they had to stay the way they were. Now I was even madder and I was getting ready to leave when I turned and asked if the Top Sergeant was in. The clerk was clearly irritated and he said yes, but that I couldn't see him. I said, "We'll see about that," and continued to walk right past the clerk towards the Top's office.

The Top had heard some of what was going on and was on his way out to check it out for himself, and we met in the small hallway. He recognized me immediately and asked me what was up. I told him that I was going home and that I had just picked up my orders and they said 29 Palms.

He asked if there was something wrong with that and I told him that I was from the East Coast and I was hoping for Camp LeJuene. He said that was no problem at all and turned to the clerk and said very clearly for him to make the necessary changes.

I thanked him tremendously, his intervention really made my day. Now I needed to find Tom, turn in our weapons and get our butts over to Dong Ha for our first flight to Da Nang.
Tom was right outside waiting for me and we quickly went over and turned in our weapons and 782 gear. That was it, we were done.

Tom, being overly creative, said that he had acquired a ride for us and as we walked around one of the tents, we were looking at a jeep. We loaded our gear into the back and I asked where the driver was, he just looked at me and got behind the wheel- we both began to laugh, this was our ride. Off we went, making our way slowly through Quang Tri base eventually getting down to Highway 9. Once on Highway 9, we drove quickly to Dong Ha and found a place to hide the jeep. We moved our gear to the terminal area and asked around for the timing of the next flight to Da Nang. Apparently, there were frequent flights and we just sat back and waited.

Someone yelled out that the C-130 out on the tarmac was the next plane to leave and for anyone going to Da Nang to get on board. Tom and I straggled out with our gear and climbed on board. There were no extras on a C-130 flight, we just threw our gear in the corner and sat in the strap seats that were on both sides of the fuselage. Fortunately Dong Ha was nice and quiet, they definitely got there share of incoming but good news for us, it was nice and quiet that day. Not too much time had passed and the plane made its way out to the runway and quickly took off. From there, it was a short flight to Da Nang.

We got into Da Nang and made our way over to the transit area, checked in and stowed our gear. Our flight to Okinawa wasn't leaving until the next day. We went into the barracks area and headed for the showers to try to get the multiple layers of scum off of our skin.

We washed until our skin was raw, but still knowing that we were relatively filthy. We dressed and went out to see what Da Nang had to offer. It was happening so fast; one day we are on a mountain under siege, the next back in a relatively safe area, and now, we are one day away from going home, just hours but it seemed like seconds.

We set out for the area known as Freedom Hill which was straight up the hill from the transit area, quite near the MP area I visited my first day in Nam, looking for Doug. We couldn't believe it, it was like being in an American town except for the dirt roads and rough construction. We found the PX area which had a slop shoot, also known as a beer hall. We grabbed a couple of beers and went to sit out on the patio that over looked much of Da Nang base, it was a very strange feeling.

We were really enjoying ourselves sitting there, sipping on some good beer and everything was going great until two other Marines sat at the table next to us. These pukes were definitely not grunts they wore starched utilities, polished brass and polished boots, definitely office P.O.G.s. They no sooner sat down and they started complaining about how warm the beer was, they went on and on over this.

There are times when I have very little patience and other times when Tom has even less, and at the moment, we had both just run out. Tom took a sip of his beer as did I, he gave me a nod and we both got up slowly, simply turned to the two jerks sitting next to us and began punching the daylights out of each of them. We knew when we made our point when we heard the whistles of the MPs off in the distance and we took off in a run. We ran and ran, laughing all the way and eventually we were completely lost, moving around some butler buildings that looked like huge storage facilities. There were signs on them and Tom pointed to me to go into one, which turned out to be a beautiful indoor theatre. I can't remember what they had as far as refreshments, but I do remember watching a James Bond movie or the last 20 or so minutes of it anyway.

We staggered out with the rest of the movie goers expecting the MPs to be waiting for us, but they were nowhere to be seen. We avoided going by the PX on our way down the hill and at that point, we were just looking around. Somewhere down towards the bottom of the hill there were some tents one saying the Red Cross. We took a few minutes and went in.
There was punch set up, coffee, donuts and numerous other American-type snacks and we were enjoying all of it. I was standing there, sipping on some lemonade and I was listening to a conversation behind me.

When I turned, I almost dropped my cup on the floor, I'm sure that was where my chin was. There standing in front of me was an American female, I was completely floored. I stood there gaping at her, she was the first American female I had seen since getting there and it really threw me off balance.

I couldn't help but stand there and look at her, I felt like a little kid in a candy store, 13 months of being torn away from the only world I really knew had really had an impact on me.

Tom and I stayed there for a little bit, but we had also heard that the Air Force PX down by China Beach was the best place to do any last-minute shopping, so off we went to find the PX. I can't remember how we got there, but eventually we did. We were both looking for this relatively new thing called a 35 millimeter single reflex camera and they had plenty of them to choose from. We had no idea what we were looking at but we both settled on a package deal that included the camera body, three different lenses and a nice carrying case.

It was made by Topcon, a name we had never heard of, but it was definitely affordable.

We began our trek back from the PX to the transit area after a busy day of not fighting the NVA, what a treat- just the two jerks up on Freedom Hill and we definitely got the best of them. We got back to the transit area and spent the night BSing with other guys we recognized from our days of training in California prior to heading off to Okinawa.

It was a short night, we were all exhausted and we wanted to take full advantage of being able to sleep the night through without having to stand watch or anything, it was a real treat. During the night, I was thinking about the men we had left up on the ridge and was wondering how they were. There was always a reason to feel guilty and now I felt guilty for not being with them.

326

We got up early and had some chow, still trying to soak this new life in of actually being able to sit down at a table to eat and to have a real cup of coffee, it all seemed too good to be true. We knew we had to officially check out and have our gear inspected, and after chow, we cleaned up and headed down to get that done. We thought we would be early but by the time we got there, there were already long lines of men trying to get home the same as us. We simply moved along slowly in the lines, dragging our sea bags and other gear along with us. We got up to the Marine who was checking people out and I went first, Tom being right behind me.

He did a quick inspection of my sea bag and all that it had in it was my stateside uniforms and other Marine regulation gear. Then he got to the other captured items that I wanted to bring home and he said they could definitely not go, but Tom and I knew better. I said to hang on, that I had all the signed paperwork from our officers in S2 indicating that these items were ok for me to bring home. The clerk looked at me and said that those documents didn't mean shit to anyone in Da Nang and they would still need to confiscate all of my stuff.

I was really pissed, but not as mad as Tom who leaned forward to me and said that he had an M-26 frag in his pocket and we could take care of this asshole right here and now. I stepped back and asked him to look outside at the jet liners on the runway and said that in a few hours we were going to be getting on one of those to get out of this hell hole, and none of this stuff was enough to stop me from going home. Still not happy, Tom started mouthing off to the clerk and we got a sergeant involved as well but to no prevail, all my war
trophies were to stay behind and I'm sure that one of those pukes packaged them up and sent them on to their home address as their war trophies- good luck, you need to live with what you did or didn't do.

327

Tom checked out quickly and we went outside to wait for our flight. There was a large transit building at the edge of the airstrip and we sat there on the benches, bullshitting and looking around for others we might recognize. Some time had passed and they said for us to load onto a certain plane that would be bringing us to Okinawa.

This is where the first level of anxiety began. There were always rumors of men sitting on a plane, getting ready to go home and they got shot right through the window, so obviously no one wanted to sit anywhere near a window. Tom and I were determined to sit together and I remembered
arguing over who would get the window, I don't know what I said or did, but Tom took that seat and I grabbed the much safer aisle seat.

Everyone sat nervously in their seats, waiting for the plane to begin to move. This was not a military transport, it was a regular TWA jet liner with a normal crew, very strange for all of us who had been away for a while. Eventually the plane began to move, headed out to the beginning of the takeoff runway, and sat there. We were all sweating pellets and no one was saying a word, the plane was dead quiet.

Finally it started rolling forward, picking up ground speed as it went along and we could hear and feel the wheels leave the runway as the plane began to climb. It seemed like an
eternity, but I'm sure it was only 30 seconds or so when we all realized that we were out of range of any enemy ground fire. The plane was filled with screams and cheers of excitement, we had really made it, we are really getting to go home. The flight to Okinawa is a blur, other than the takeoff, I can't remember much of anything.

Upon arriving in Camp Hanson, Okinawa, we were transported to a transit area and settled into our temporary barracks. As luck would have it, they came around with night watch assignments and both Tom and I were on the list. My shift was early in the morning and his was from midnight to 4 A.M.

We threw our gear near some bunks and headed for the showers, still trying to get the layers of dirt off of us and it was obvious it was going to take numerous showers. We got dressed for the first time in somewhat cleaner jungle fatigues and headed out to see what this base had to offer. We had never been here before, that is unless you count the day we got to Okinawa on our way over.

We knew we needed to be back for a formation in a little bit but we could at least find where the NCO club was, which would come in handy later. We got back in time for the formation, which was basically a time for them to lay out our schedule for the next day and a half. For the most part we would be getting physicals, any medical treatment necessary, dental work if needed, and instructions on all the pills we all needed to take for the next 30 days, mostly malaria related.

They also made mention that we were now out of a war zone and we were all required to salute again. We were all dragging our feet on this and sometimes it was fun. Many of the officers you encountered had never been to Vietnam but they knew what the rules were. Although they were somewhat peeved when you didn't snap a salute, they were also a bit intimidated with who we were and what most of us had been through. Occasionally they would jump on our case and when that happened, we would act innocent and told them we were working on getting back to normal but weren't there yet.

When we went in for our briefing on medications we saw Sgt Connelly there, which surprised Smitty, Tuckett and me. His actions up on Mutter's Ridge were not well received and we all thought that he kept volunteering 2nd Platoon to continue to go down the hill, we were also convinced that his actions got a lot of good men wounded and some killed. When we went to leave that building with our own inventory of medical
supplies, he came up to us to say hi. You don't have to salute a sergeant, but in this case we didn't show him any respect either, in our eyes he didn't deserve it. We all merely glanced at him and walked by his out stretched hand, I hope he got the point.

Sometime that afternoon, I got a haircut in a village barber shop just outside the main gate and it was my first real hair cut in well over a year, it felt good trying to get cleaned up again. During chow, Tom said that he had met up with someone he knew from the States and he wanted to sneak out on liberty
with him, but with his pending security watch, he couldn't do it, that was unless I traded with him. I had no specific plans so I said sure.

We got cleaned up again, still looking kind of grungy according to stateside standards, but still an improvement and we headed out to the NCO club. The place was hopping, they had a live band there and I immediately recognized numerous faces from my unit. This was the 60s don't forget, and there was still a lot of racial tension, depending on where you were. Here at the club, there were a lot of men on their way over and they couldn't appreciate the camaraderie we all had in combat. Here at the club however, it was the white guys sit over there and we'll sit over here, there was way too much pressure all around.

A bunch of us from Alpha Company sat together and what a weird feeling. Our spirits were quite mellow, we were trying to have fun, but none of us were laughing a whole lot. A sergeant came over and joined us, and I recognized him immediately. He was with us during staging in California and the NTA training in Okinawa on our way over, but for some reason I don't think he was a grunt, but I definitely remembered him. He said hi to those of us he knew and we discussed how we knew each other.

This was our DEROS day, which meant that everyone who had gone through staging together in California should be on Okinawa this day on their way home, that is if they made it that far. He went on to say that he had gone over to the command office to try to get some feel for how many actually made it back. His news made us all stop.

According to the records at the office, less than 20% of the original organization had survived the 13 month tour. That's not to say they all died, we knew better than that, but for
whatever reason, they wouldn't be joining us at the club that night. I think that each of us in our own minds knew it was bad, but never to that extent. We sat there drinking for a while without a whole lot being said, those numbers really made me feel awkward sitting there, not sure why I was allowed to survive and to go home.

At one point the band started playing "If You're Going to San Francisco" and the entire room went hush. There were some stateside boys who were talking but they were quickly told to shut up. Everyone there on their way home listened to each and every sweet word, now knowing that we would be back there soon.

First night of being in a safe place, on Okinawa on our way home mid October 1968.
Tomie on the left Janicki on the right
(Young innocence is gone)

The drinks at the club were extremely cheap and there were numerous glasses in front of each of us, it was going to be a long night for some. Tom had stood my afternoon watch and eventually joined us at the club. He didn't stay long and left relatively early to go join his friend for a night on the town, can't blame him- I had wished I had that option. Our table got caught up in the bar game "let's try one of everything the bartender can make," what a mistake. I do remember some of the night and I actually remember leaving to get to the barracks to stand Tom's midnight watch, I was a mess.

I checked in at the guard station and told them I was there to stand watch for Tom England. They checked the roster saw the Tom had stood my watch earlier and wrote my name in next to his.

I vaguely remember making one, possibly two, walks around the 3 barracks and through the center squad bays of each. I was completely wasted and all I wanted to do was lie down and go to sleep. In an attempt to stay awake and to sober up as much as possible, I went back to my barracks, stripped down and went into the shower.

I turned 4 shower heads in the same direction and set the water to medium warm. I sat there on the shower floor with my head tilted back, resting on the wall and let the water just pour down on me as I sat there for quite a while. Eventually I dried off, but the comfort of my bunk was too enticing, and some time later I chose to lay down, what a mistake. A few hours
later, Tom was shaking me awake and he wasn't very happy
with me being in the rack.

Sometime after I had gotten in my bunk, some trouble started behind one of the barracks, some racial trouble inspired by alcohol, it was not uncommon in those days. There was a fight on Tom's watch, that's what Tom was mad about. No one got hurt badly and no real pressure was placed on Tom or me, we were still scheduled to go home in a matter of hours.

We had a delicious breakfast at the mess hall and went back to the barracks to change into our summer dress uniforms; you couldn't fly home in fatigues. It was nice to get dressed up and I know we all felt proud of the rows of ribbons we had on our chest that we earned in the past 13 months. We grabbed our sea bags, went outside and climbed on the buses that were waiting. I can't remember the ride to the air strip or how long it took, but I do remember what was going on inside me just prior to getting on the plane.

We arrived at the air strip and piled our sea bags off to the side, and they were eventually loaded into the civilian transport plane that would be coming in a few minutes. After a brief wait, we saw a plane pulling up a short distance from where we stood and slowly we saw some activity by the exit ramps. We were instructed to follow the path out to the plane and wait for someone to tell us to get on board. We were walking out the path slowly and there were Marines walking on the other side who had come off the plane on their way to Vietnam. I clearly remembered the day many months ago that it was me walking on the other side and how mad I was that none of the returning Marines had wished us good luck or given a thumbs up.

Now it was my turn to be walking out towards the plane going home and I knew what was going on in their heads, but I didn't do anything. I could not look up to any of their faces, I couldn't give them any encouragement, none at all. For where they were going, they would need a miracle to return, a mere thumbs up or verbal good luck wouldn't do them any good at all, now I understood.

The Trip Home - Not what I expected

For some reason, Tom and I didn't sit next to each other on the long flight back to El Toro. From what I remember, it was a quiet flight with very little conversation, again everyone trying to figure out what they were going to do when they got home and not sure exactly what they were going home to.

After an extremely long flight, we landed at El Toro Marine Air Base, just south of Los Angeles. We filed off in relative silence and I can remember when I actually got to the bottom of the ladder, I kneeled down and kissed the tarmac, I was really home.

We were ushered into a receiving facility and were told that all of our gear needed to be examined carefully because of the known contraband that was being smuggled home. To make matters worse, we needed to strip down to our underwear to prove that we were not hiding something under our clothing. Here we'd been home for only a few minutes and already you got an uneasy feeling, hopefully this would be the end of this kind of crap. Eventually Tom and I made our way outside with our sea bags, looking for the transport buses that would bring us to the airport. Within a matter of minutes, one pulled up and the driver had a great attitude. He had returned a number of months ago and knew exactly how we felt, and promised to get us to the airport as quickly as possible.

I had tickets for TWA from LA to New York's JFK airport and Tom had a flight that would eventually get him to Atlanta, where I was sure his father would be waiting. Over the last few days we discussed our promise to split our 30-day leave as we did on our way to Vietnam. For the first phase, I joined Tom and his family in the mountains of North Carolina for my last two weeks of leave. This time, Tom would be coming to Connecticut and he had never been anywhere in the northeast. The driver dropped me off in front of the TWA terminal and I told Tom that I looked forward to seeing him in a few weeks.

Down in the distance I could see a large group of hippies standing out in front of the doors. I really didn't know what to expect. I slung my sea bag over my shoulder and walked down the sidewalk to the main terminal doors and walked through the outer doors taking in the yells of "baby killer," "mother killer," "murderer," and varied pieces of debris.

I had made it this far and I turned to go through the second set of doors but was greeted first by a longhaired male who was very mad at me. He was yelling everything that I had heard outside and more but he got physical. Before I could do anything, he came up to me quickly and punched me in the head, knocking me down. He quickly ran outside to rejoin his buddies and a female employee of TWA quickly tried to help me up, apologizing for what the jerk had just done. She helped me find out what gate my flight was coming into and also helped me check in.

After depositing my sea bag at the check-in counter, I made my way to an upper area lounge for a drink. I looked around and it looked peaceful enough, no hippies at least, and I took a seat at the bar. I ordered a drink I had while in Okinawa called a Singapore Sling, which was quite tasty.

Right after I had ordered it, a man a few stools down to my left leaned forward and told the bartender that the drink was on him and then looked at me and said, "Welcome home." What wonderful words to hear, you have no idea what those two words meant to me already on my return. Before I could feel too good about that, a man two or three stools down to my right leaned forward and yelled at the guy who bought me the drink and said, "What the hell are you buying him a drink for, don't you know where he's coming from?" and the saga continued.

Somewhere in the days prior to me actually starting to come home, I had somehow gotten in touch with my brother-in-law, Ted. If things were to work properly, he was going to meet me at the TWA terminal at JFK.

I finally made it to the plane with no more incidents and found it mostly empty. I took a seat and one of the stewardesses said that I could basically sit anywhere I wanted except for first class. I got a nice window seat and sat back as we took off for the East Coast. Some time after takeoff, she came back to see what I wanted to eat. She was in no rush, again the plane was almost empty and she didn't have too much to do.

She asked if I was on my home from Vietnam and I told her that I was and had only landed a few hours earlier. With that, she offered me the menu choices from first class and I had a wonderful steak dinner with all the trimmings. After dinner, I started dozing off and slept most of the rest of the way back east.

The flight got to New York on time and it took me a short while to make my way to the baggage claim area. I was standing there for a bit when I noticed Ted walking towards me. Ted had been in the Air Force but never served any duty overseas, and he always had a million questions about the Marines. We grabbed my sea bag and headed outside to where he had parked his small sports car.

There was barely room for him and me and the bag, but we made it work. We had no sooner gotten into the car and began to pull away from the curb and he turned to me and said,

"Well, how did it go?" That statement definitely caught me off-guard, almost as if I had gone away for some kind of test or something and he was asking on how I felt I did. Ted had told my sister Judy that he was going to the school library to do some studying, which was his cover for coming to pick me up; Ted was using his G.I. Bill smartly and had been attending Bridgeport University at night. So Judy was at home with no idea that I was only minutes away, I always thought he did a great job pulling that off. We got to their house in West Haven and he went in first as I slithered onto the front porch trying not to make any noise. Judy was in the kitchen in the back of the house, the long living room separating the kitchen from the porch where I was.

Ted went in and started telling her that while he was in the library studying, he saw someone he thought he knew and eventually struck up a conversation. One thing led to another and this person wanted to follow Ted home so they could see Judy again. Judy was mumbling something as she and Ted came out of the kitchen, heading for the porch. When they were about halfway through the living room, I stepped in the doorway. I thought she was going to have a heart attack right there on the spot, she was absolutely speechless, which was very unusual for her.

It was a wonderful treat, getting to surprise her like that. She had supported me all through Vietnam. She was a supervisor in the phone company and she had all the females in her office adopt men in 2nd Platoon to ensure everyone would get something at mail call. Our mom had died when I was 10 and Judy took over as my surrogate mother and for years, and never let go of that. Of everyone, she was the most difficult to say goodbye to when I was leaving Connecticut on my way to Vietnam. I can remember sitting in a café at JFK that morning and how tough it was for her to see me go.

For many months while in Vietnam, I was obsessed with buying a new car with my year's savings. My brother Bill had a Mercury Cougar just before I left and it was a beauty, so I focused my searches on a Cougar of my own. They had facilities in Da Nang and other big base camps where you could work with factory reps and order a car at some great prices. Never having the luxury of being in a big camp like that to go through the process, I thought I was out of luck.

My sister knew of my search and offered to work with the Mercury dealer in New Haven who was willing to still give me a good deal. I wrote and described to her exactly what I wanted right down to the color of the exterior and interior, which she shared with the dealer. Eventually the order was placed and with me coming home in mid-October, I would be getting their showroom model, the new models would be just coming out.

Although Judy had no idea the exact day I would be coming home, they had a good guess on a reasonable time period. She had worked it out that the car would be there early just in case I got home sooner than expected, but as usual I was late if anything. A few days after getting home, we took a ride to the dealer who was located on Whalley Avenue in New Haven.

There in the showroom was my car with a big bow on top and quite a few people milling around to see it all. It was really cool, the car had already been registered and it was ready to go. While I was signing the financial paperwork someone moved the car outside.

When done inside, I walked out and the owner of the Mercury dealership personally handed me my keys. I got in and sat there for a few minutes, just soaking it all in, and then started the engine. The car had a big 390 HP engine in it with dual exhaust and it sounded great.

Within minutes, I was on my way and not really sure where I was going. I chose to take a ride out through Branford, eventually getting on Rt 146 which brings you along the shoreline to Guilford. From there, I got on Rt 1 and followed it out to Old Saybrook. I was in no rush, I just wanted to really enjoy my first few hours in this car and the scenery on this route is beautiful.

The first two weeks of being home, I was trying to track people down which was difficult because so many of them were also in the service and away at their current duty station. I found out that my friend Johnny was out of the Army and home, he had been in Vietnam for some of the time I was there and near where I was. I tried to find him a couple of
times as did he but we never did. I gave him a call at his dad's house and we started to get together most every day and night, we had a ball. New Haven had some great clubs, especially one called the Mad Russian, which was in the basement of a building on Crown Street.

They had live bands who were playing all the top tunes and it was our favorite hang out. I had gone out and purchased some trendy cloths so other than my haircut, it wasn't too obvious that I was in the military.

The hair difference was bad enough; everyone back then had much longer hair so you stood out like a sore thumb. On occasion, someone would ask if I was in the military and I would always say yes, regardless of what I knew was coming. They never let me down, they would begin giving me a ration of shit about what I did or didn't do and eventually I would choose to leave rather than to fight back.

My sister had a big welcome home party for me at her house and it was great to see everyone. Family and friends were there and I had a ball, in reality I had only been home a
number of hours from being pulled off of Mutter's Ridge,
where I didn't know if I would ever make it. Even then it was hard to put that in perspective, you tried to have fun for the moment, but the gremlins were already beginning to take shape.

It was great to be home, but at the same time strange. Few friends were around, so there was little to do socially and it seemed as if I was looking at the world through different eyes. All of the old image-related pressures and what your friends thought of you were gone, at least for me they were. Just a matter of hours and days earlier, I was locked in a fight for existence that none of them could even come close to understanding. With that came a total appreciation for the peace and quiet of being home- compared to where I had come from, this was tranquility base.

I spent a lot of time just riding around in my car going through varied parts of Branford, the town I grew up in. It was as if I was riding in a haze with no definite destination in mind, just driving and driving and driving.

While driving around, I decided to visit the Emersons hoping to find Mr. Emerson home. Billy and numerous other friends from Branford had joined the Air Force and I was assuming that Billy was away. Mr. Emerson was home and we sat in the kitchen and had a wonderful visit. He was not judgmental as many others had been, he just wanted to know how I was, hoping that I was ok. I said that for the most part I was ok but also said that I was somewhat numb with being home, he said that he understood that feeling completely.

Much to my surprise, Billy was home and after a bit he came back to the house- what came next I was in no way prepared for. Billy came in, like I said, one of my closest childhood friends, and immediately started to ask horrendous questions like how many children or mothers did I kill, how did it feel to be a murderer? My head was spinning and unfortunately he was not kidding, I had no idea where he was coming from.

Mr. Emerson was furious at Billy's comments and he walked with me down the hall towards the back bedroom. He said that he apologized for what Billy was saying, but for now he needed to ask me to leave, which I did. I'm very confident that Billy got his ass kicked all over Branford after I left. This was one of many more personal attacks I was to receive in the near future and over many, many years. Incidents like these added up all too quickly and you got to the point where you were cautious around everyone, not knowing what to expect from them regardless of how close you were or weren't.

I left there numb, any self esteem that I had was quickly trashed, unfortunately this was a feeling that was to come all too often and it was never easy to deal with. I drove to a Branford pub called The Phoenix. Mr. Ardilino, the owner, was a WWII vet who always had an open heart for vets, and I was hoping that included Vietnam vets- it did.

I went in and sat there with a drink, not saying much. He knew me from my Branford days, one of my good friends, Chris Averill, went out with one of his daughters. He said that he hadn't seen me for quite some time and I began to give him an update. I don't remember leaving there that night, all I know that he made me feel at home, at least I found one place where I could feel good.

One day I was visiting with my friend Ricky's parents and they both asked if I had been by to see my father yet, which I hadn't. After some coaxing, they convinced me that after I left their house, I would go over to at least say hi and that I was home safely.

I drove over there and both Gladys and Hank were home, for some reason I can't remember seeing Joanne but I'm sure she was there. My dad didn't know what to say. It was obvious that he was thrilled that I had made it home in one piece and it was also obvious that he was very proud of me.

I had caught them in the early evening and their drinking had just begun. When I recognized behavior that I didn't like, I quickly dismissed myself.

My father took issue to this and I said that when I lived there, I had to put up with shit like that but now I had the ability to leave whenever I wanted and I was choosing to leave now. He quieted down and I left, not expecting to go back for quite some time.

The first two weeks slipped by quickly. Soon Tom would be coming and we had made plans for me to pick him up at JFK. This was going to be very interesting, this would be Tom's first trip north in his entire life. He had grown up in a beautiful Appalachian town just outside of Ashville, North Carolina called Burnsville, and it was a far cry from the rest of the world. Down there, the houses were miles apart and everything went at a very slow pace- nothing like the harried pace of the Northeast.

I drove down to JFK and waited for Tom's flight to come in. Eventually he came out and it caught me by surprise when I saw him in civilian clothes, it had been a long time since we both wore that garb. We grabbed his sea bag, headed out to my new car and out to the highway for the ride back to my
sister's house. He loved the car and couldn't wait for a chance to drive it, and he started telling me about his two weeks at home, which were wonderful. Everyone in his family said to say hello, which meant a lot to me, they were a wonderful family to have in my life.

I didn't think anything of it as I drove back to Connecticut, but Tom was freaking out with all the traffic and the crazy drivers. I have to admit, we did have our share of crazy drivers screaming by on our right and our left, almost making us feel at times that we weren't moving at all and I was doing the speed limit. Within an hour or so, we made it back to West Haven and we deposited his gear at my sister's house before going out.

I wanted to show him where I grew up and more importantly, that the North was not all concrete and sky scrapers. One day we even took a ride up through northern Connecticut through the farm country which he really enjoyed. I must say, he really loved the shoreline and the beautiful islands off of the Branford coast.

I took him to see as many of my friends as possible, knowing that none of them could really appreciate the relationship that we had. Tom had joined the Marines on the buddy system with his best friend from Burnsville. Immediately after boot camp, they were separated and that is when we met. We had gone through boot camp together but in different companies, other than that we spent our entire 4 years together. The only other difference was when we were in Vietnam. At that time we were also together, but in different companies. So in a wonderful twist of fate, it would seem that we joined the Marines on the buddy system and he truly was my best friend.

For anyone that grew up in the New Haven area, there was a very special place to go, especially when you were old enough to drive. In West Haven there was a very large amusement park called Savin Rock that was built along the West Haven coastline. As young teenagers, we would go there on a weekend and have a blast going on the numerous rides and Peter Frank's Fun House, it was a wonderful place to escape.
At the far end of the Rock, there was a drive in restaurant called Jimmy's that had both a sit-down dining area as well as a walk-up snack bar.

They were famous for their great seafood like fried clams and lobster rolls, and especially for their hot dogs and french fries. We would always manage to get down to Jimmy's for a great snack before heading back to Branford.

My sister's house in West Haven was less than a mile from the Rock, and one night, I took Tomie to Jimmy's for some great food. We got in line and waited our turn to order, I think I ordered a hot dog or two and some onion rings and a soda.

Tomie was trying to take his time and the guy behind the counter was getting extremely impatient, never mind the numerous people waiting in line behind him. He finally got his order in and walked with me down to the register where our food was already waiting. The clerk grabbed Tomie's money with one hand and pushed his food across the counter quickly, as was normal at this place they always had a hustle going on. We walked back to my car quietly and sat inside, eating our snack. Tom was obviously shaken by the rude Yankee approach to eating, this was a far cry from how it worked in his mountain town of Burnsville, where everything moved at a much slower pace.

New Duty Assignment

By the time our two weeks together was up, I know he couldn't wait to get out of Connecticut and to head down to Camp LeJuene in North Carolina, where he would feel much more at home. Without much fanfare, we left Connecticut, had a wonderful drive to Camp LeJuene, and found our way to the reception building. We presented our travel orders and without much work, they assigned both of us to 3rd Battalion 9th Marines, another infantry unit, but at least now we were stateside. From the main reception building we needed to go over to 3/9's headquarters and check in there.

We both stood there at the counter as they read our orders and it was obvious they were trying to figure out what to do with us. One of them asked if either of us had a military driver's license, which both of us did, and with that Tom got assigned to be the Colonel's driver. They then asked if I had a security clearance, which I did from my work in Charleston, and with that I was assigned an office job at the battalion headquarters in their Secret and Confidential control office. While I was standing there, one of the clerks was looking at my records and said, "Oh yeah, we have something here for you." he handed me my Purple Heart- no ceremony, no nothing- boy how things had changed.

This was fine with both Tom and me, and basically they were both great assignments. Tom just hung around all day, waiting for when the Colonel needed to go somewhere and off they would go. I worked in the S&C office, reporting to a Sgt Hamilton, who was a great guy. Our basic responsibilities were to receive new documents of a sensitive nature and file them away in huge safes. At times, members of the unit would stop by our office and request a document, which they would need to sign for with a guarantee of a return.

One night, Tom and I went to one of the base movie theaters for some down time. We were just walking down the street back from the movie, having a peaceful conversation and it was a nice warm evening.

At the same time, we both stopped and looked far off into the distance to see machine gun tracers skipping off in the sky, just like we had both seen much too much of during our 13 months in Vietnam. We both had the same immediate reaction, which was to question if we were really home or not- it really put a damper on our mood for the rest of the night.
We got back to our barracks and sat on our bunks, chewing tobacco and talking about the experience that had just taken place.

Somewhere in this talk, one of us asked what we would do if we got new orders for Vietnam. These were horrible thoughts and we were not joking at all. We both knew, regardless of what they could possibly tell us, that we would definitely be assigned to another infantry unit just like the ones we just left. The thought of this was terrifying to both of us. We both said that we would each do whatever it took to not go back, if it took taking a pistol and shooting a toe or two off, that's what we would do. We both knew that our mental state would not support another tour in that hellhole.

One day, Tom and I were up at an area across from the main Post Exchange where they had facilities for washing your car. We were giving my car the once over, making it look nice for the weekend, when a car went by and for some reason both Tom and I were looking at who was driving. We were both certain it was Gunnery Sgt Smith, who we worked with in Charleston, actually he was the one that was most determined to find both Tom and me military careers that would keep us from going to Vietnam.

We jumped in my car and followed after him, eventually catching him before he went off the base. We had a nice chat and he was ecstatic that we had both made it home in one piece. It was seldom when you found someone you had served with previously, and this was a real treat and Tom and I were both thrilled we had seen him.

Our duty assignments in Camp LeJuene were great, but there were serious racial tensions building that made every day extremely uneasy. There were many nights when some white Marines were out on base liberty, basically going over to an enlisted club or an NCO club for a few drinks. Much too often, these men were run down on their way back to their barracks and severely beaten, and there were a few that actually died.

For Tom and me, the battalion headquarters was in walking distance of our barracks and we would walk back and forth to work. On more than one occasion, we were shot at on our way back to our barracks. It was always in the early evening hours, just as it was beginning to get dark and the shots always came from the same direction.

One day I was sitting on my foot locker in my barracks, listening to some record albums I had while I was polishing my brass and dress shoes. It was common for some of the Marines who lived on the second floor of our barracks to cut through our squad bay on their way to the main hallway. On this day, two or three black Marines were cutting through to the hallway and just after they walked by me, they dropped some trash on our floor and kept walking.

I spoke up and asked them to respect our area and to take their trash with them. With that, they turned around and began walking slowly towards me, giving me a ration of shit all the time and I was really yelling at myself for opening my mouth. They were a short distance from me, telling me how they were going to kick my white ass, when I heard a familiar voice from behind me say, "What do you niggers want?"

With great surprise, they looked up to see my friend Mac, who was actually about an inch shorter than me but was a hefty weight lifter who no one to mess with- oh yeah, he was also black. Mac was a great guy and had introduced me to the gym and how to work out with free weights, he's also one of the guys that I would do anything for.

The three black guys were really taken back with Mac's comments and where trying to bro him to understand where they were coming from. Mac basically said that they should turn around, pick up their trash, get out, and never cut through our squad bay again. Without much hesitation, they did exactly what he said and I never saw them again.

Another day, Sgt Ham and I were in our office when this Captain came up to our hatch with numerous boxes. He said that he wanted us to lock these away but to not look at them, which was extremely unusual- we were normally required to review all documents being filed. Sgt Ham said ok and he and I put the boxes in one of the many safes behind us. We sat down and I said, "Ham, you know what's in those boxes don't you?"

There had been rumors for months of early out orders, mostly for Vietnam returnees, allowing them to leave the Marines anywhere from 3 to 6 months earlier than their normal termination date. I shared my thoughts with Ham who couldn't disagree but also said we needed to honor the Captain's request and to not look at them at all. This worked for a few days, but I finally said to him that I was going to look whether he liked it or not and he didn't stop me. I went through the documents and sure enough, they were early out orders. I checked to see if my name and Tom's were listed and they were, and I left it at that. I didn't tell anyone other than Ham, but it was good to know.

All this came to a head quickly. Our unit was scheduled to go on a Med Cruise, replacing a unit that was already over there. Many of us who had documents in those boxes were scheduled to be released from the Marines before our unit's return date from the cruise. The officers needed to contact everyone that was receiving early out orders and ask them if they would extend to stay with the unit for the cruise. Tom and I chatted about this and quickly came to the decision that we were going to get out early. With our luck, we would extend and then a few days later do something to get a senior NCO or an officer mad and off to Vietnam we would go. We were not going to take any chance.

Although Sgt Ham had early out orders, he chose to stay, he really wanted to make a career of the Marines and the cruise would be extremely easy duty for anyone in our office. A short while after that, Tom and I were transferred to another outfit, also in Camp LeJuene, again another infantry unit. Although we were both assigned to infantry squads, we were company drivers as well. Again this really worked in our favor. Anytime the unit would go out on an exercise, Tom and I would need to drive one of the numerous jeeps or other vehicles. So while everyone else was humping with their packs and infantry gear, Tom and I were driving equipment back and forth, what a deal.

Eventually the time came when we got transfer orders again, this time to Quantico, Virginia for short timer's mess duty. Again Tom and I climbed into my car with our sea bags in tow and off we went to Quantico. Upon check-in, Tom and I were both designated as chief messmen in charge of good-sized crews. There were at least two mess halls in Quantico, Tom was working out of one and I the other down by the air strip.

351

We had a great time in Quantico, usually skipping away each weekend to his home in Burnsville, which was a very long drive from Virginia, but we did it anyway. These days in the mountains with Tom and his family were wonderful. Over the past 3 plus years Tom's family and I had gotten to know each other very well and I felt like a part of their family.

Back in Quantico, promotions were being handed out and Tom and I both became Sergeants during one of the ceremonies. Also at this time, we needed to meet with a career counselor for our eventual "shipping over lecture" where they ask you if you want to stay in the Marines. I was working with a Sergeant preparing for an eventual sit down with the unit's commanding officer, a Captain. I had a great record, one that I was proud of and I told the Sergeant that I
was really split on what to do. I really enjoyed the Marines but all the racial tension made day-to-day life miserable for everyone, he definitely understood.

The day finally came when I was to meet with the Captain and I got dressed in the uniform of the day, which were khakis with a nice display of ribbons on my left chest and new Sergeant stripes on my shoulders. My career advisor came in with me and stood at parade rest by the Captain's door, and I stood at parade rest in front of the Captain. He had my military records in front of him, which he seemed to be going through with great detail.

Eventually he looked up at me and said, "Sergeant Janicki, I can tell from reading through your records that you are a real shit bird." I almost fell over, I had no idea what to say or if I was allowed to say anything at all. He went on and on with how the Marines need good men, I was completely at a loss. Obviously I exited quickly and as soon as we got outside, my advisor came up to me with an apology. He said he had no idea of why the Captain said what he did and he himself was as confused as I was. I told him right then and there that with jerks like that Captain around, I had no desire to stay in.

As bad as the review went it at least forced me to make a decision that had been troubling me. Part of wanting to stay in was to stay within the safety of the military and not having to face the nasty American society. I was discharged in October of 1969 and after dropping my friend Lenny Tuckett off in New York city I headed home to Connecticut. Things had really changed and everyone had a grudge against all of us that wore a uniform.

If someone knew that you were either in the service or had been they made it a point to call you out on the many atrocities everyone knew we had committed. At first I took every advantage of stating my pride in my service but after being brow beaten time after time I decided to keep my mouth shut but I have to tell you it really hurt to listen to them. Even on the employment side we all learned that you didn't mention your military service on a job application. I did at first but never got a job and then one day I left that information out and got hired adding insult to injury.

There were thousands of emotions going on inside me with no one to talk to and I wasn't sure if I wanted to talk to anyone anyway.

The rest of my story will focus, in more detail, on my life after being discharged and returning to society. Many of us that served in Vietnam feel that life after the military was more difficult and emotional than our time in Vietnam. It took me many years to put the first chapter to words and I hope to get started on the final chapter soon.

The following poem written by a very special Vietnam Veteran friend who puts into words how many of us that served in Vietnam feel about our service there. I received permission from Sky to add this to the end of my story.

Soldier
By
George L. Skypeck

I was that which others did not want to be.

I went where others feared to go, and did what others failed to do.

I asked nothing from those who gave nothing, and reluctantly accepted the thought of eternal loneliness ... should I fail.

I have seen the face of terror; felt the stinging cold of fear; and enjoyed the sweet taste of a moment's love.

I have cried, pained, and hoped ... but most of all, I have lived times others would say were bestforgotten.

At least someday I will be able to say that I was proud of what I was ... a soldier.

Semper Fi! to all my fellow Vietnam Veterans, I hope your lives have been happy and full.

Leech.